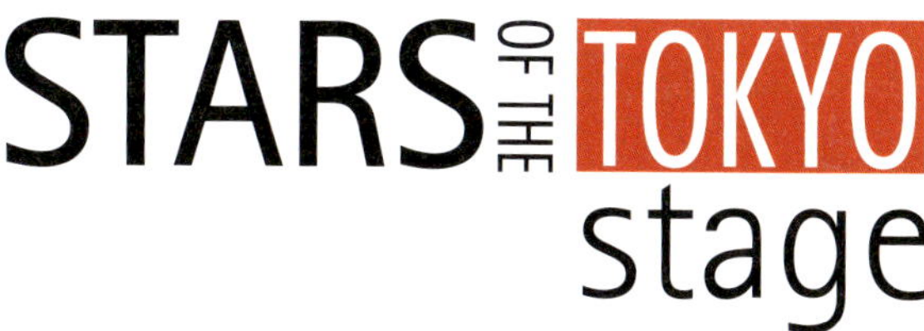

STARS OF THE TOKYO stage

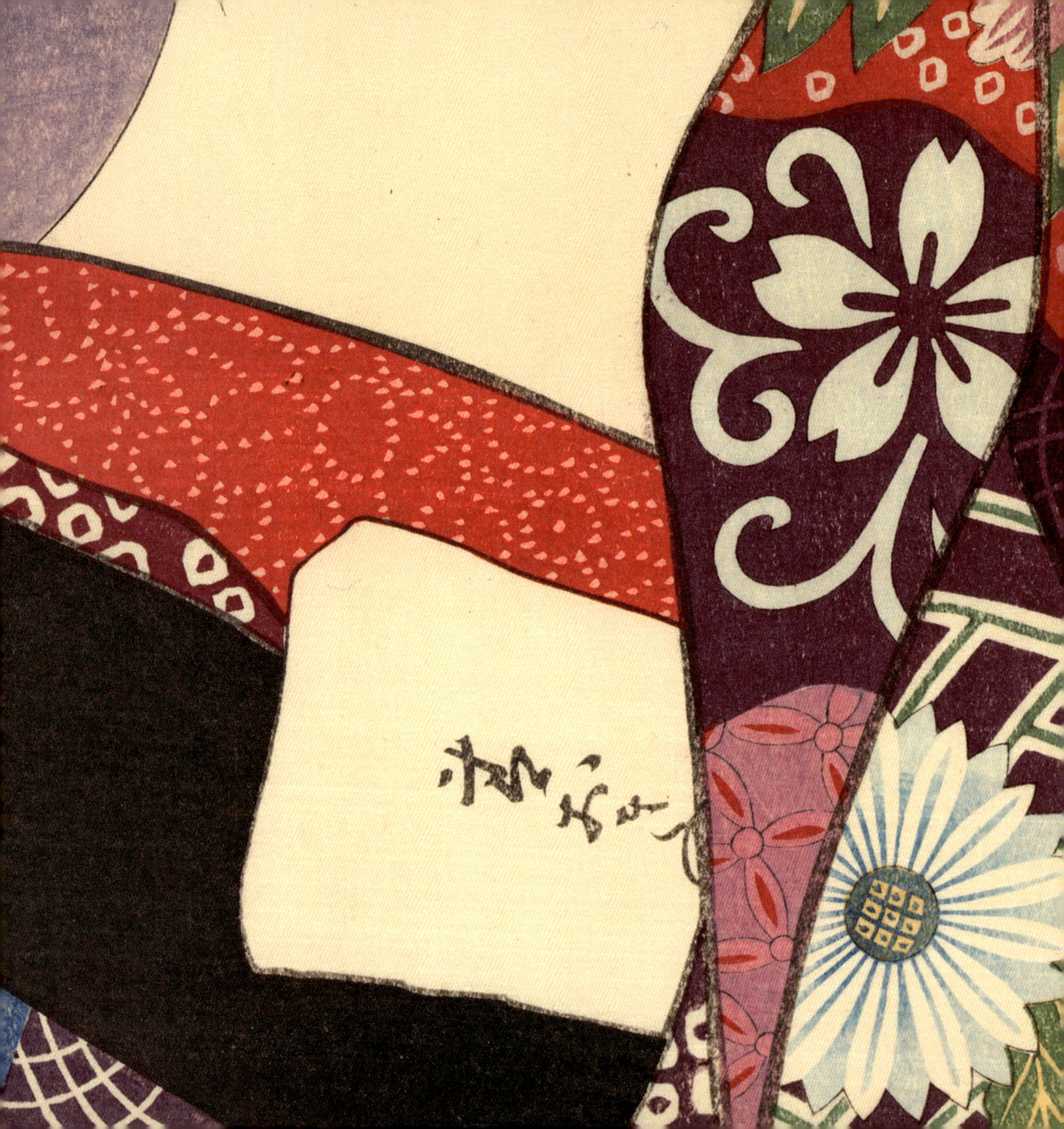

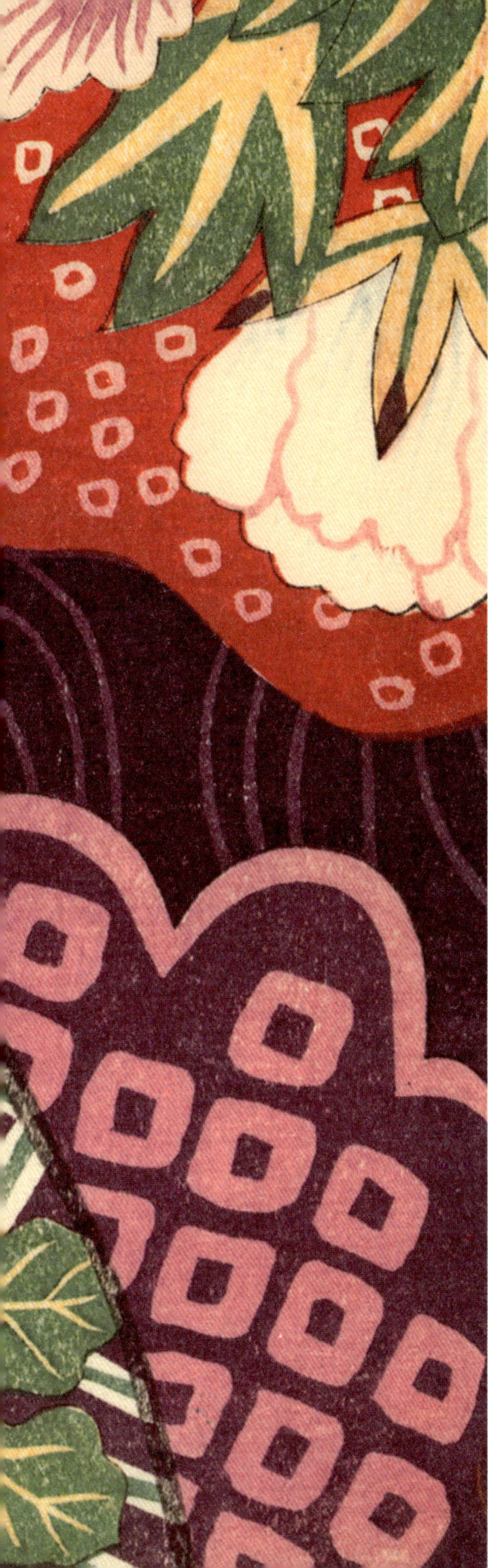

Natori Shunsen's kabuki actor prints

STARS OF THE TOKYO stage

Lucie Folan

Chiaki Ajioka
Melanie Eastburn
C Andrew Gerstle
Robyn Maxwell
Amy Reigle Newland

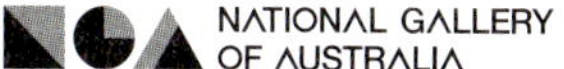

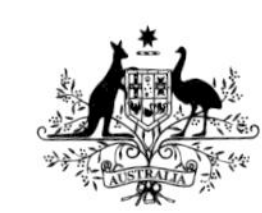 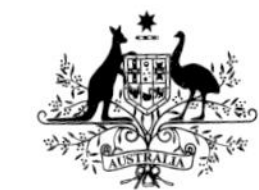

Australian Government

National Collecting Institutions
Touring & Outreach Program

Australian Government

Visions of Australia

This exhibition is supported by the National Collecting
Institutions Touring and Outreach Program, an Australian
Government program aiming to improve access to the
national collections for all Australians; and Visions of Australia,
an Australian Government Program supporting touring
exhibitions by providing funding assistance for the development
and touring of cultural material across Australia.

CONTENTS

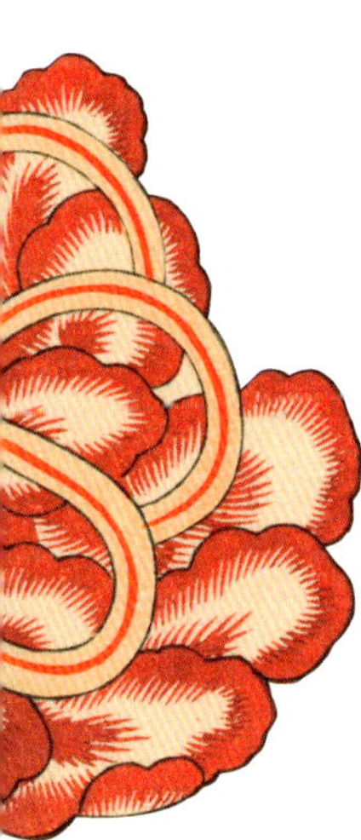

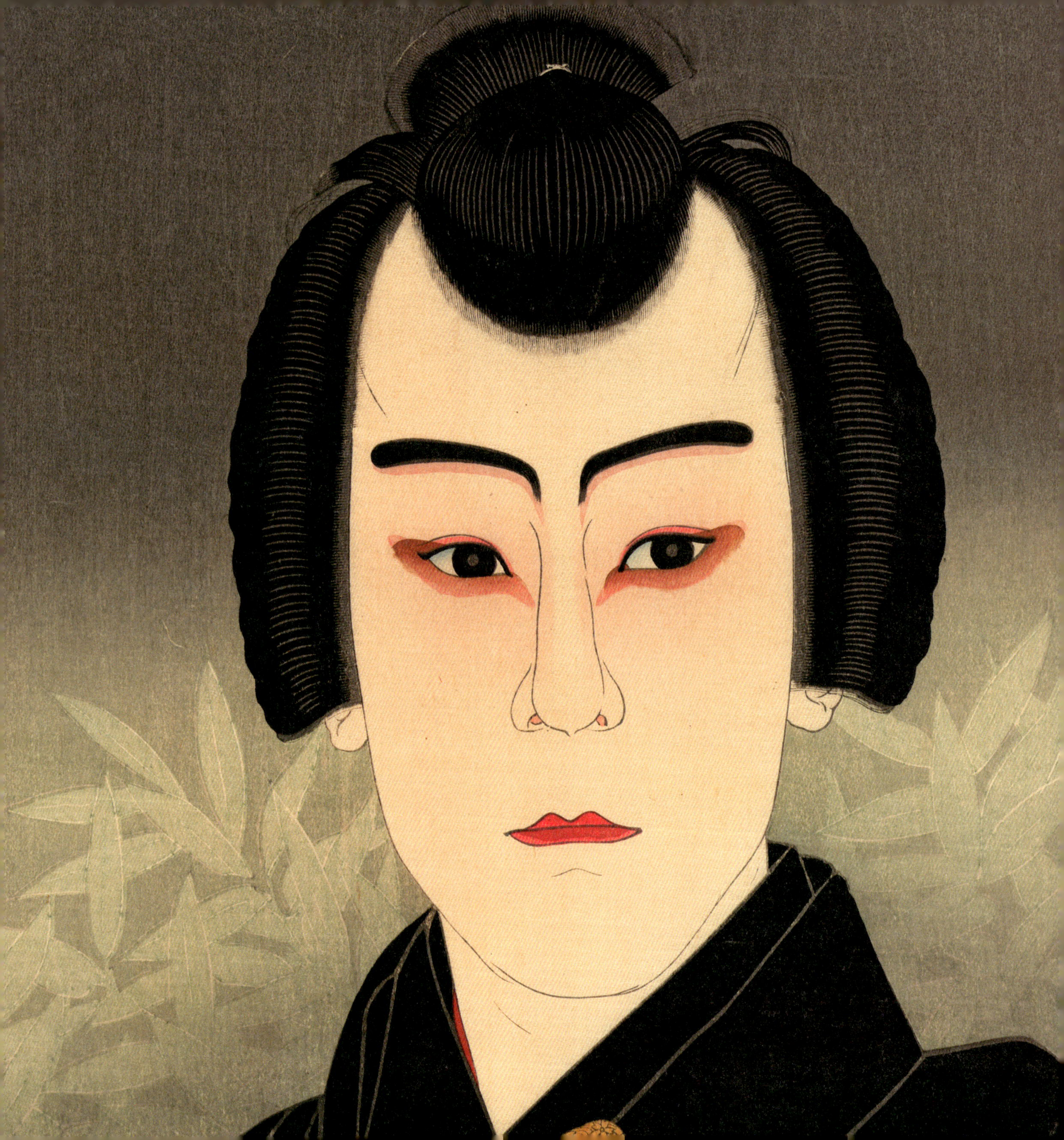

DIRECTOR'S PREFACE

While there has long been international appreciation of Japanese woodblock prints from the Edo period (1615–1868), the early-twentieth century portraits of Natori Shunsen are not widely known. It gives me enormous pleasure that the National Gallery of Australia's publication and exhibition, *Stars of the Tokyo stage: Natori Shunsen's kabuki actor prints,* will introduce this significant Japanese modern artist to a broad audience.

Shunsen was one of the artists grappling with modernisation and national identity in the 1920s and 30s, when movements to preserve traditional Japanese art coexisted with those dedicated to introducing modern Western practices and ideas. Many artists sought to synthesise these seemingly opposed approaches. Shunsen's kabuki actors prints are consummate examples of the *shin-hanga* (new print) movement, established to preserve and reinvigorate traditional printmaking, but also reflect modern Western influences. Kabuki theatre was changing in the 1920s as well, in response to competition from other forms of entertainment and modern pursuits. The popular theatre produced new dramas, some of which incorporated Western theatre techniques, and restaged classics with even greater emphasis on visual spectacle, elaborate sets and extravagant costumes.

Taking as its starting point the celebrated *Collection of creative portraits by Shunsen,* the artist's deluxe series of actor portraits of the 1920s, *Stars of the Tokyo stage* brings together bold prints and fabulous costumes to explore kabuki theatre and the artistic and social milieu of early-twentieth century Japan. I am particularly grateful for the contributions of three internationally recognised Japanese art experts: Professor C Andrew Gerstle, Amy Reigle Newland and Dr Chiaki Ajioka. The Gallery's Asian Art staff—senior curator Robyn Maxwell and curators Melanie Eastburn and Lucie Folan, assisted by Olivia Meehan—have ensured that the publication and exhibition is a visual feast.

I am especially proud that the *Stars of the Tokyo stage* exhibition and the catalogue of works in this publication are drawn entirely from the National Gallery of Australia collection. Since an initial gift of 31 Shunsen prints in 1998, the Gallery has worked hard to acquire the remaining five works in the *Collection of creative portraits by Shunsen,* as well as a number of prints from the supplement to the series. I wish to express my gratitude to the Shōchiku Theatre Company (Shōchiku Kabushiki Kaisha) and Shōchiku Costume Company (Shōchiku Ishō Kabushiki Kaisha) for the honour of allowing the National Gallery of Australia to acquire a number of kabuki costumes in 2011, and for providing advice and assistance.

I extend my sincere appreciation to the Australian Government's National Collecting Institutions Touring and Outreach and Visions of Australia programs for generously supporting the Gallery's ambition to introduce little-known aspects of Japanese art to audiences across Australia.

Finally, I am especially grateful to Pauline and John Gandel for assisting with the recent acquisitions of works by Shunsen as well as the superb kabuki costumes. The National Gallery of Australia is indebted to the Gandels for their continuing philanthropic support.

Ron Radford AM
Director
National Gallery of Australia

(opposite) **Natori Shunsen** *Ichikawa Sumizō VI as Shirai Gonpachi in 'The floating world's pattern and matching lightning bolts'* 1926 (detail) (p 126)

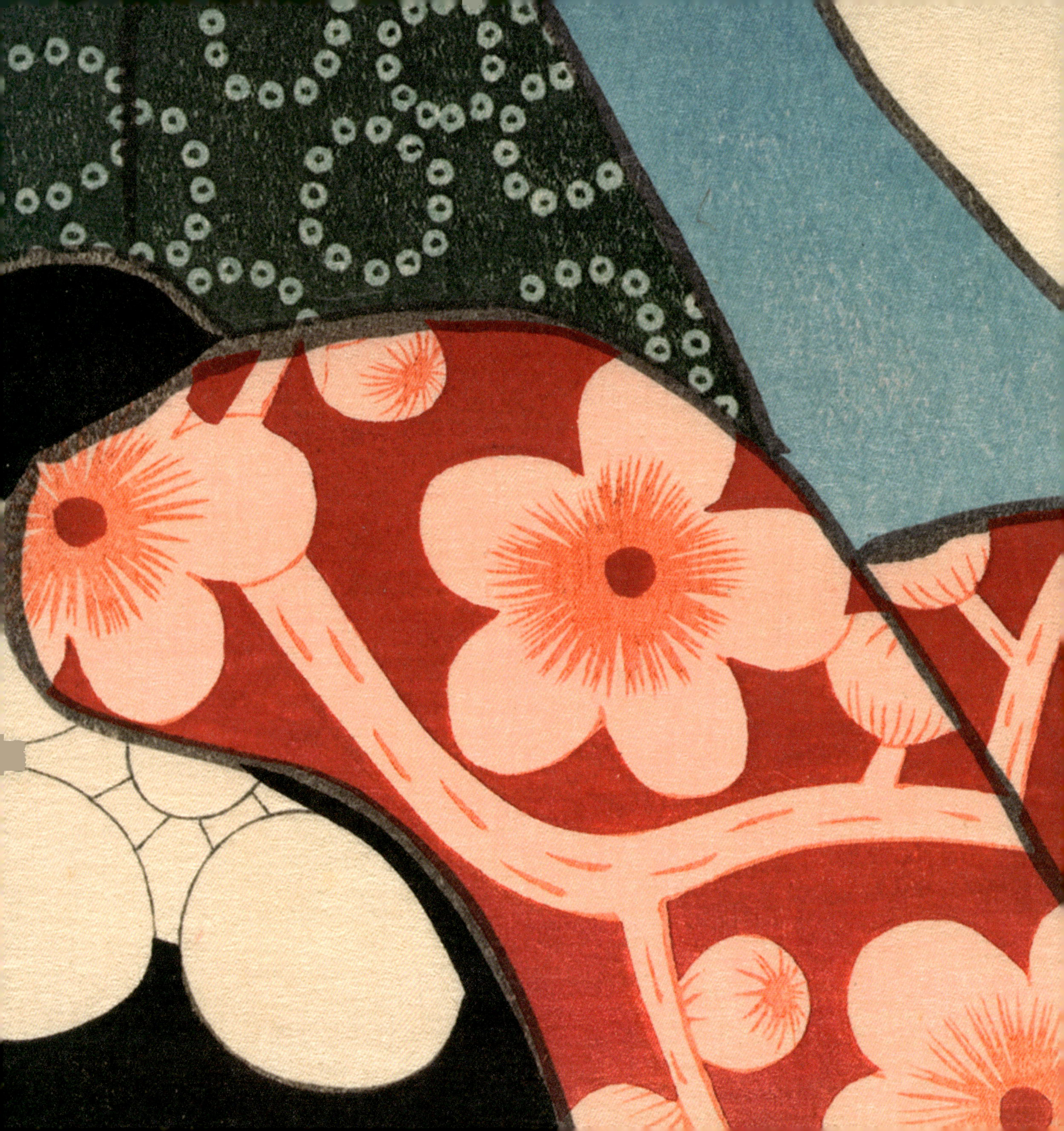

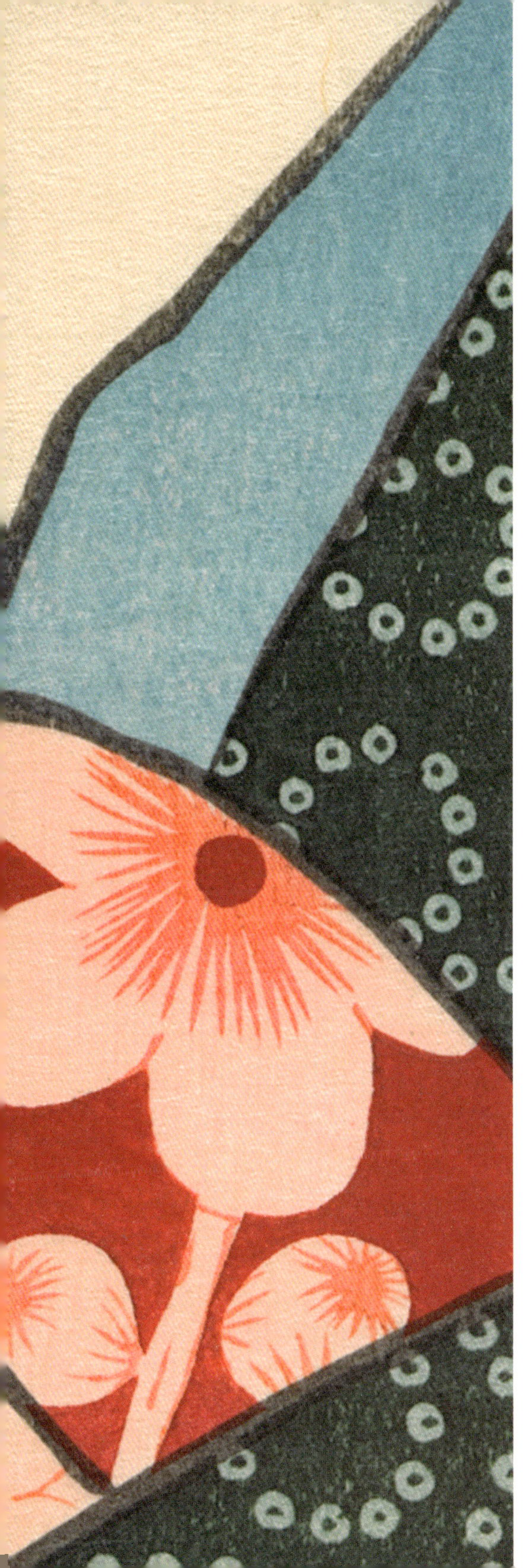

NATORI SHUNSEN:
ARTIST OF TOKYO

Lucie Folan

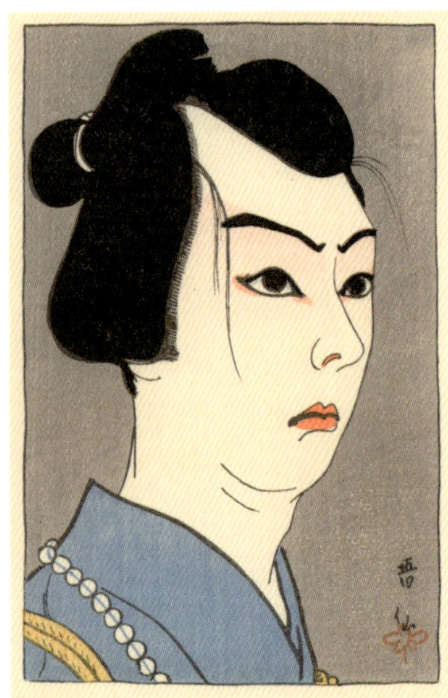

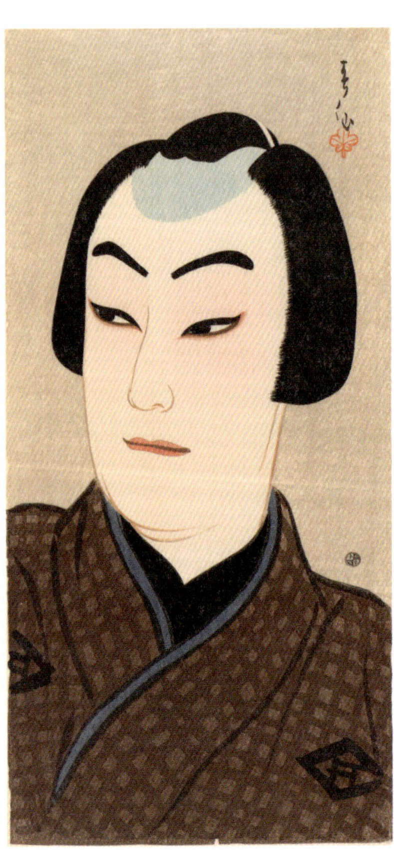

In the 1920s and 30s the Tokyo printmaker, painter and illustrator Natori Shunsen (1886–1960) produced a series of bold actor prints that have become internationally famous as outstanding examples of Japan's *shin-hanga* (new print) movement. Published by *shin-hanga* founder Watanabe Shōzaburō (1885–1962), the remarkable portraits depict prominent kabuki actors of the day in performance as legendary characters at pivotal moments. While the prints are a fascinating record of Japan's traditional kabuki theatre during the Taishō (1912–26) and early Shōwa (1926–89) periods, Shunsen's life and career also provide insights into issues facing artists during this period of rapid modernisation and social change.

Shunsen, originally named Natori Yoshinosuke, was born in a semi-rural area now part of Minami Alps city in Yamanashi prefecture, a mountainous region west of Tokyo. His father, Natori Ichijirō, was a goods and textiles trader.[1] When Shunsen was an infant, the business failed and the family moved to the bustling metropolis of Tokyo. The Natori family was part of a tide of migration associated with Japan's industrialisation: between 1890 and 1920 Tokyo's population grew from approximately one million to three million people, mainly as rural Japanese arrived in search of opportunities and employment. Shunsen attended school in Tokyo and spent the rest of his life living in various homes around the city.

Shunsen's artistic talent was encouraged from an early age. He began studying painting at the age of 11, and was a student of Kubota Beisen (1852–1906) from 1900. (Shunsen was the artist's adopted professional name, and includes the 'sen' syllable from the name Beisen). Beisen was a *Nihonga* (Japanese-style painting) artist, concerned with traditional Japanese aesthetics, subject matter and art history. Shunsen later studied with Hirafuku Hyakusui (1877–1933), who continued his strong grounding in *Nihonga* while also providing an introduction to European and American art.

From 1902 Shunsen's paintings were shown in mainstream exhibitions, including those held by the Japan Art Institute (Nihon Bijitsuin).[2] The young artist also joined a group formed in opposition to established art schools, the Voiceless Society (Museikai), which was interested in bringing naturalism and techniques of *Yōga* (Western-style painting) to traditional Japanese art.[3] In 1904 he enrolled in the Tokyo School of Fine Arts (Tokyo Bijutsu Gakkō), but soon left to earn a living. While continuing to exhibit paintings, Shunsen worked as a book and magazine illustrator and, from 1907, as a graphic artist for the *Tokyo Asahi Shinbun* daily newspaper. Shunsen became a successful commercial artist and caricaturist. Over the years he produced illustrations for important writers, including leading novelist Natsume Sōseki (1867–1916). His newspaper illustrations included images of prominent members of society, theatrical performances, vignettes of contemporary life and historical events.

In 1915 Shunsen was among the founders of Coral Society (Sangokai), a forum for exchanging ideas and exhibiting paintings. In the same year he contributed prints of kabuki actors to the magazine *New Portraits* (Shin nigao). The publication was a conscious effort by a group of artists to revitalise Japan's traditional theatre,[4] which was facing competition from modern Western entertainment such as cinema, jazz, cafés and the spectator sport of baseball. *New Portraits* included many fine prints and marked Shunsen's first serious foray into portraying the stars of the Tokyo stage.

In 1916 Shunsen's painting of the actor Nakamura Ganjirō I came to the attention of publisher Watanabe Shōzaburō. Watanabe sensed a commercial opportunity and asked Shunsen to adapt the image for print. The resulting woodblock print was published and another similar format print, of the actor Onoe Baikō VI, was released in 1917. The prints were included in exhibitions held by Watanabe in the 1920s and 30s.[5] It was in this period that Shunsen married his first wife, and began to favour drawing and printmaking over painting.

Shunsen again designed prints for Watanabe Shōzaburō in 1925. Watanabe was seeking artists to revive traditional Japanese printmaking and produce commercially viable original prints; an art movement now known as *shin-hanga*. Watanabe took over a series of Shunsen's actor prints abandoned for financial reasons by publisher Kikuchi Yoshimaru.[6] Together the designer, publisher, block-carvers and professional printers created the 36 actor prints comprising *Collection of creative portraits by Shunsen* (Sōsaku-hanga Shunsen nigao shū). A number of watercolours—preparatory images for unpublished prints—survive from the late 1940s and 50s, and it can be assumed that Shunsen prepared similar drawings and paintings for this series. The prints were sufficiently successful to warrant the production of an additional 15 prints between 1929 and 1934, a series known as the *Supplement to collection of portraits by Shunsen* (Shunsen nigao shū tsuika).

The prints are exquisite. Made for theatre aficionados, each portrait presents one or two of the stars revered by Shunsen. Details of extravagant costumes, makeup and pose convey the magical appeal of performances, while the focus on each actor's expression indicates the intensity of kabuki and the complex stories of its characters. The images display the influence of both historical Japanese actor prints and the modern international concern with realistic

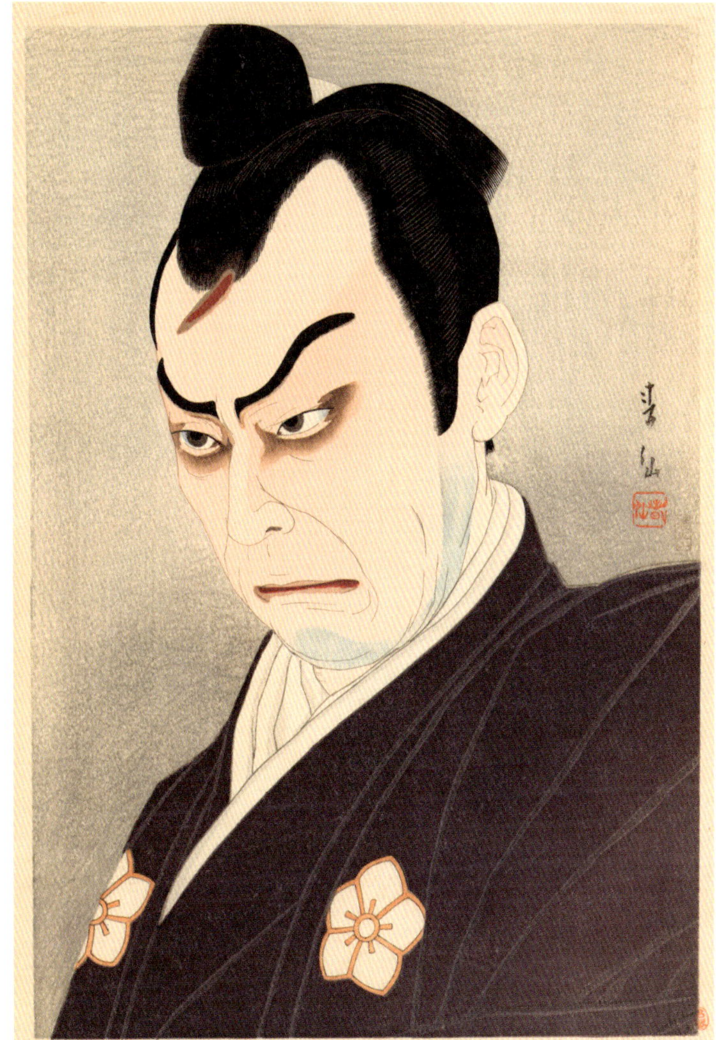

(above) **Natori Shunsen** *Nakamura Kichiemon I as Takechi Mitsuhide in 'The banner of rebellion'* 1925 (p 56)

(opposite above) **Natori Shunsen** *Ichimura Uzaemon XV as Shirai Gonpachi in 'Suzugamori'* 1915 from the magazine *New Portraits*
woodblock print; ink and colour on paper, 18.4 x 12.1 cm
Lavenberg Collection of Japanese Prints; IHL Cat #490

(opposite below) **Natori Shunsen** *Nakamura Ganjirō I as Kamiya Jihei in 'The love suicides at Amijima'* 1916
woodblock print; ink and colour on paper, 51.5 x 24.8 cm
Freer Gallery of Art and Arthur M Sackler Gallery, Smithsonian Institution, Robert O Muller Collection

(right) **Natori Shunsen** *Ichimura Uzaemon XVI as Minamoto no Yoshitsune in 'Yoshitsune and the thousand cherry trees'* 1949
watercolour on paper, 38.1 x 25.4 cm
National Gallery of Australia, Canberra,
Pauline and John Gandel Fund, 2011

(far right) **Natori Shunsen** *Ichikawa Jukai III as Yasuke in 'Yoshitsune and the thousand cherry trees'* 1949
watercolour on paper, 38.1 x 26.0 cm
National Gallery of Australia, Canberra,
Pauline and John Gandel Fund, 2011

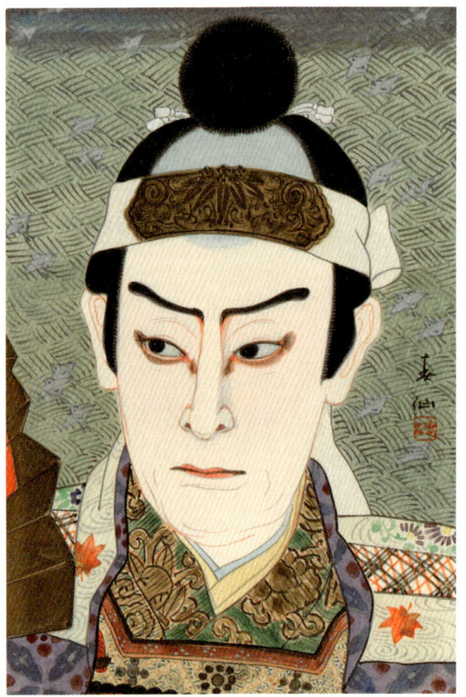

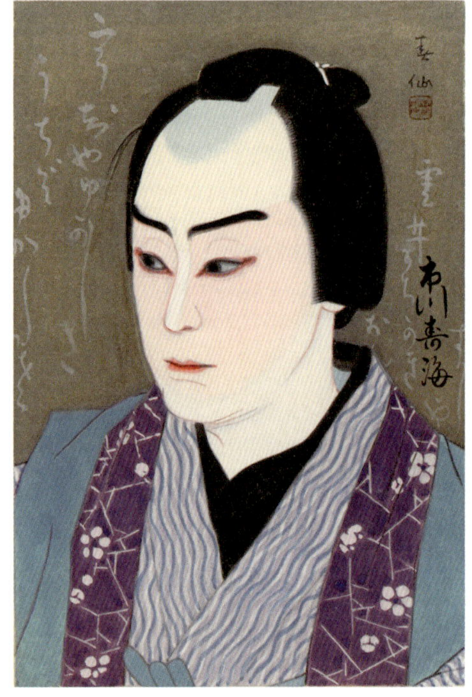

representation. Viewed as a whole, the two series provide a visual who's who of Tokyo actors and a catalogue of their best-loved roles. While all but one of the original 36 prints depict kabuki actors, Shunsen also reflected the fashions of the period by including portraits of modern theatre progressive Sawada Shōjirō and the movie star Ōkōchi Denjirō.

In a deliberate strategy to create prints that were sought after for their high-quality, the series was crafted from expensive materials—fine paper, inks and dyes, and often embellished with embossing or sparkling mica pigment. Enthusiastic kabuki fans formed a receptive market for the luxury prints, which were sent to subscribers approximately once a month between 1925 and 1929. This coincided with a period of renewed interest in kabuki. By 1923 Japan's major kabuki producer, Shōchiku,

had gained control of theatres in Kyoto, Osaka and Tokyo. With significant resources, Shōchiku was able to create and actively promote its productions and stars, helping to foster a resurgence in the popularity of kabuki.[7]

Shin-hanga and Shunsen's actor portraits also proved attractive to foreign collectors and audiences, at a time of fashionable international interest in Japan. Private and institutional foreign collectors acquired Shunsen's prints, either from Japan or through sale exhibitions such as those held at Toledo Museum of Art in Ohio, USA, in 1930 and 1936.[8] The artist was featured in the *American magazine of art* in 1930, and his work was displayed in an exhibition in Warsaw, Poland, in 1933.

In 1931 Shunsen's wife died. He remarried in 1934 and his second wife Shigeko gave birth to a daughter, Yoshiko, in 1936. Throughout the 1930s Shunsen was the epitome of a successful modern commercial artist; his images of contemporary culture circulated widely via newspapers, books and prints and became well known across Japan.[9] In addition, Shunsen exhibited his prints and drawings at the exhibitions of major art associations and at small shows in Tokyo, including those held at department stores. One of Shunsen's most notable works from this period is a brilliant diptych portrait of kabuki megastar Matsumoto Kōshirō VII in his signature role as Benkei in *The subscription list* (see page 130). Shunsen was an active participant in art movements and organisations of the period, joining various book illustration and art societies, including the Japanese Theatrical Painters' Association (Nihon Gekiga Kyōkai).[10] He also established a fine arts group in his hometown.

During the Second World War (1939–45) and American occupation of Japan (1945–52), kabuki performances and printmaking were heavily restricted. In the 1950s Shunsen produced his final actor portraits with Watanabe, *New version of portraits of actors in plays* (Shinban butai no sugata-e). Despite the graphic appeal of the series, Japanese printmaking had declined and the prints were not made with the quality materials and technical precision of Shunsen's earlier work.

In a scenario worthy of a kabuki play, Shunsen's only daughter died from pneumonia, a tragedy from which Shunsen and Shigeko never recovered. In 1960 they committed suicide by consuming poison together at the family grave at the Kōtoku Temple in Aoyama, Tokyo. Shunsen's actor portraits stand as the artist's most important artistic achievement, emblematic of his great interest in retaining and adapting Japanese traditions for a modern world.

Notes

1. Kushigata Shunsen Museum of Art, *Natori Shunsen: collection of Kushigata Shunsen Museum of Art*, Kushigata Museum of Art, Kushigata, 2002. Where not otherwise acknowledged, information presented in this essay is drawn from this publication.

2. Helen Merritt, *Guide to modern Japanese woodblock prints: 1900–1975*, University of Hawaii Press, Honolulu, 1992, p 108.

3. Jackie Menzies (ed), *Modern boy, modern girl: modernity in Japanese art 1910–1935*, Art Gallery of New South Wales, Sydney, 1998, p 160.

4. Amy Reigle Newland (ed), *Printed to perfection: twentieth century Japanese prints from the Robert O Mueller collection*, Hotei Publishing, Amsterdam, in association with Arthur M Sackler Gallery, Smithsonian Institution, Washington DC, 2004, p 27.

5. Watanabe Shōzaburō, *Catalogue of woodcut colour prints of S Watanabe*, S Watanabe, Tokyo, 1936.

6. Merritt, p 217.

7. Samuel L Leiter, *A kabuki reader: history and performance*, M E Sharpe, New York, 2002, p 354.

8. Dorothy Blair, *Modern Japanese prints: printed from a photographic reproduction of two exhibition catalogues of modern Japanese prints published by the Toledo Museum of Art in 1930 and 1936*, Toledo Museum of Art, Toledo, 1997.

9. For examples of Shunsen's drawings, paintings and book illustrations see Kushigata Shunsen Museum of Art, *Natori Shunsen: collection of Kushigata Shunsen Museum of Art*, Kushigata Museum of Art, Kushigata, 2002.

10. Merritt, p 108.

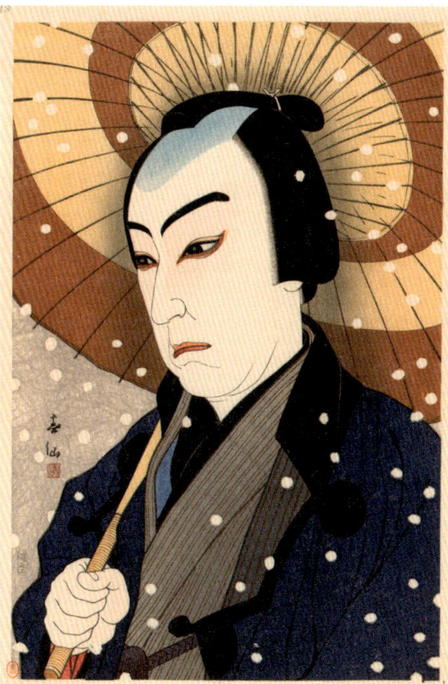

(above) **Natori Shunsen** *Sawamura Sōjūrō VII as Narihira Reizaburō in 'A flower in a snowstorm: Oshizu and Reiza'* 1927 (p 110)

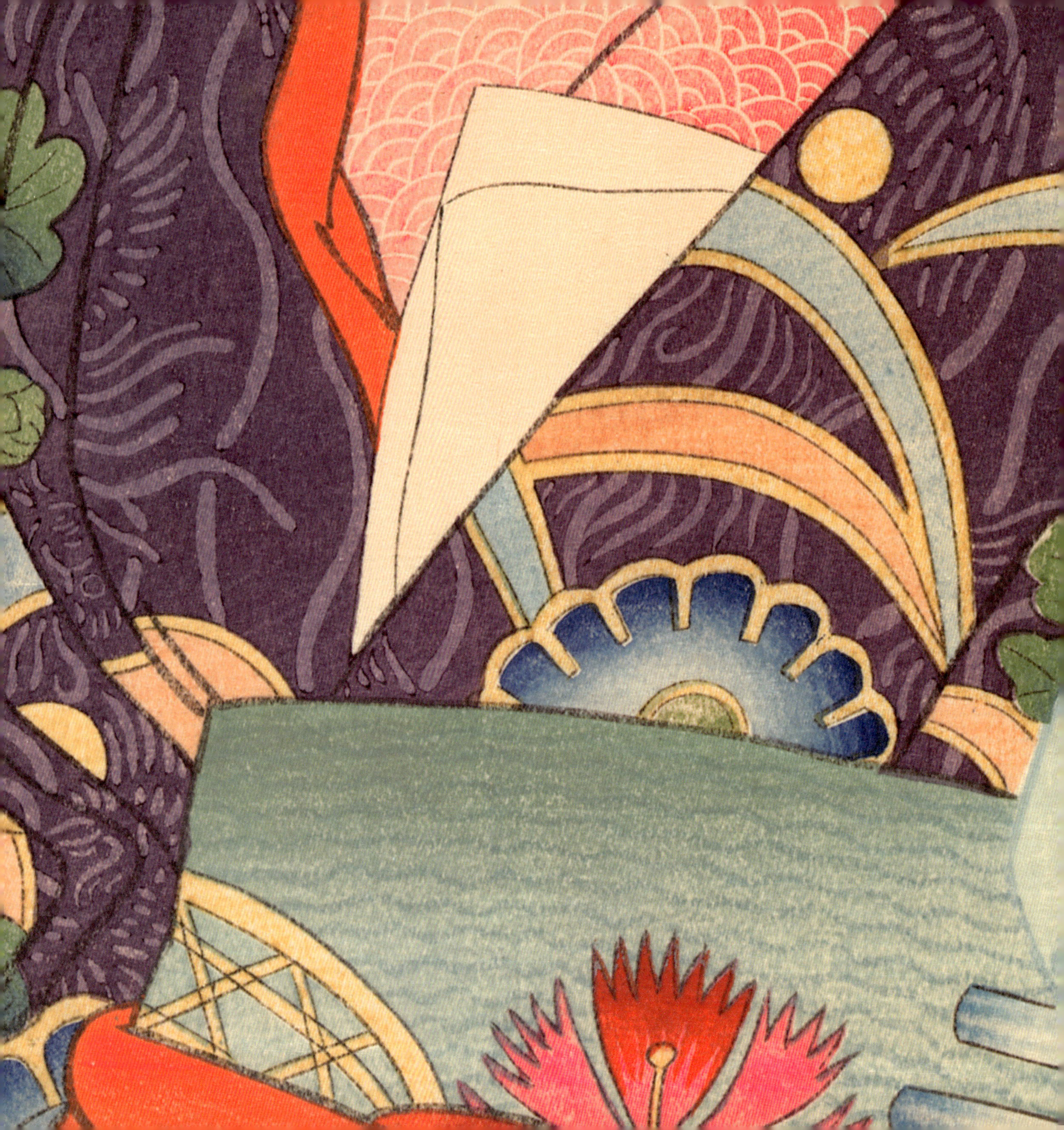

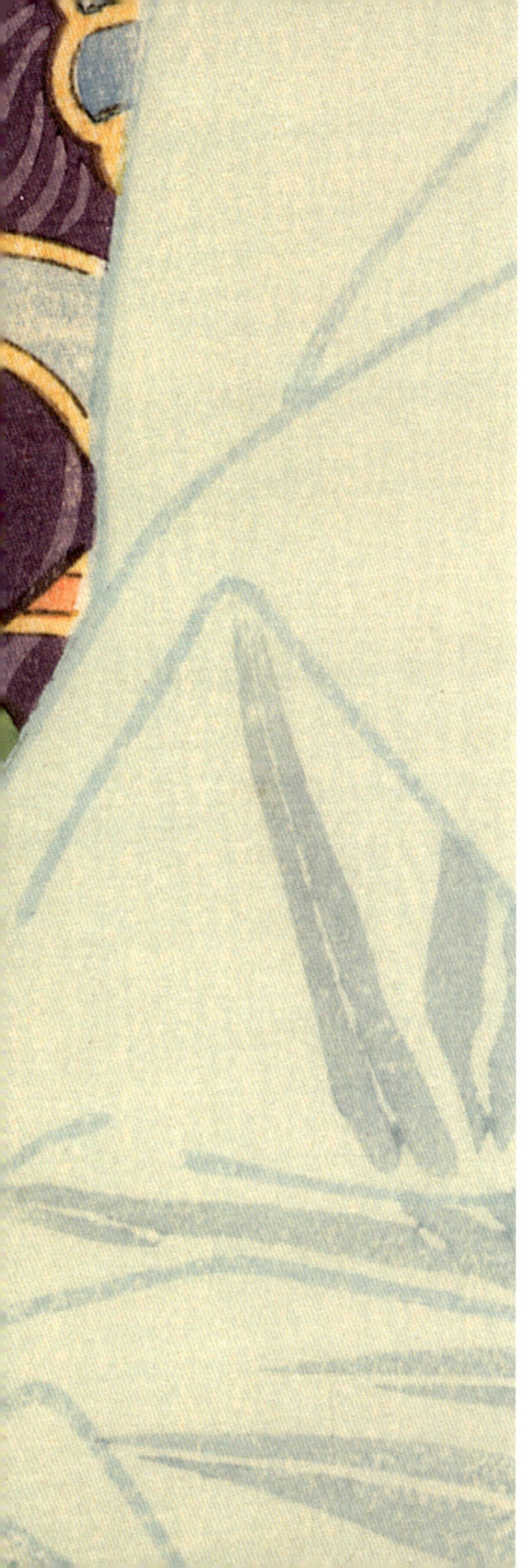

CULT OF THE ACTOR

C Andrew Gerstle

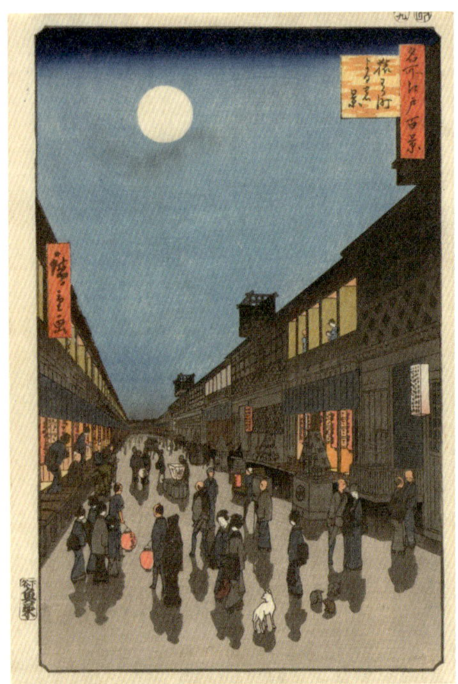

Kabuki is today written with Chinese characters that mean 'skills in song and dance'. However the term originates in the verb *kabuku*, meaning 'to be crooked, bent, odd, to do as one pleases'. From its beginnings kabuki had an air of outrageousness, with cross-dressing, sexual innuendo, bravado and exaggerated histrionics. It was popular urban theatre, licensed and restricted by the government but off-limits for the samurai class. Theatres were considered to be dens of iniquity, like the urban pleasure quarters, yet were allowed as outlets for the universal desire for passion and fantasy. The heroes and heroines were often criminals and prostitutes since, until the late-nineteenth century, kabuki actors were on the pale of society, beneath the official four-class system of samurai—farmer—artisan—merchant. The irony is that these outlaw-like figures came to be popular superheroes—sexual and cultural icons.

A further irony is that although kabuki began with women dancers around 1600, today's kabuki actors are all male. Women were banned from the public stage in 1629 because of public disorder due to actresses' links with prostitution. Thereafter, kabuki actors developed effective ways to present both male and female gender on the stage. The fantastic and sophisticated art of the *onnagata* female-role specialists developed out of necessity, since men had to perform women's roles.

Kabuki has been at the centre of Japanese life for centuries, with many commercial theatres in the major cities and extensive networks of travelling, semi-professional and amateur troupes throughout the country. It has also been popular for both men and women to learn kabuki dance and music as hobbies. As in most societies, Japanese actors were originally held in low repute by the authorities. This led to the predominance of professional, guild-like families from early on. Sons carried on the tradition ideally, but adoption was common. An important consequence is that actors have usually trained from an early age and literally grown up in the theatrical milieu.

From its origins out of dance, kabuki has kept the actor's body as the focus. Audiences, even today, are concerned less with the play and its storyline and more with their favourite actors and how they perform particular roles. The focus is on the sensual body, voice, movement and limbs;

(above) **Utagawa Hiroshige** (1797–1858) *Evening view of Saruwaka Street* 1856–58
woodblock print; ink and colour on paper, 35.6 x 24.4 cm
National Gallery of Australia, Canberra, gift of Orde Poynton Esq, AO, CMG, 2000

(right) **Utagawa Hiroshige III** (1842–94) *Street scene outside the Shintomi Theatre* 1882
woodblock print; ink and colour on paper, 36.4 x 72.5 cm
National Gallery of Australia, Canberra, purchased 2010

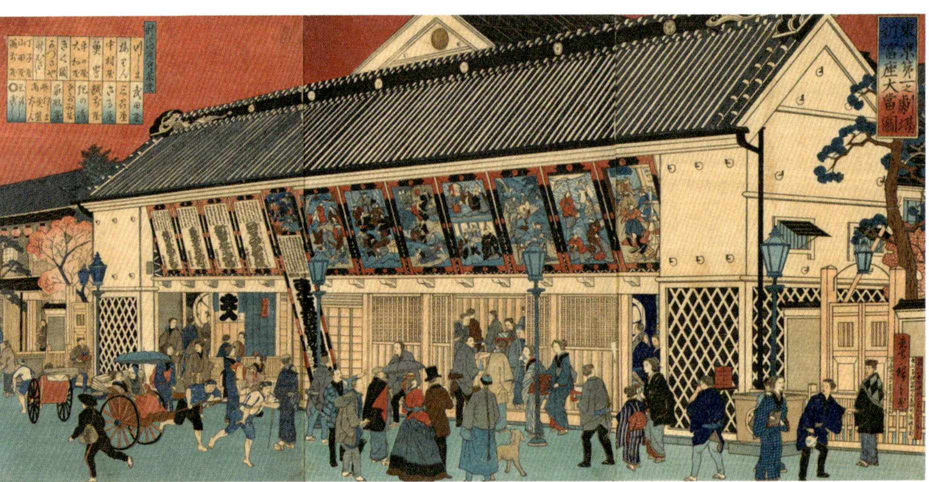

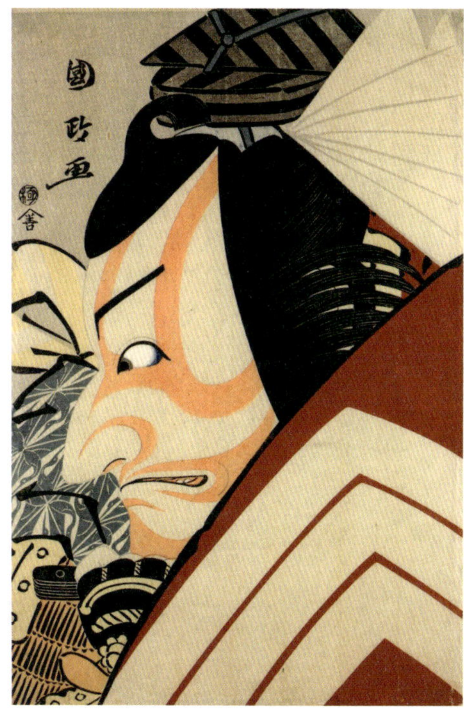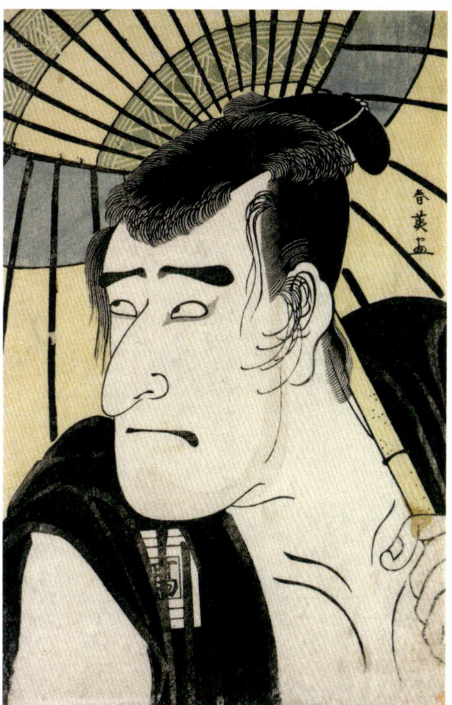

eroticism and passion are essential to an actor's success. This obsession with the actor's physical body led to a kind of 'cult of the actor' that regarded the text of the play as the performance itself, which dissipates at the close of the curtain. Kabuki theatres did not permit the publication of plays, a potentially substantial source of revenue, until the late-nineteenth century. This was not unique to kabuki and has parallels with Shakespeare's plays, which were seen as the sole property of the theatres themselves and not published until after the playwright's death. Japan's *bunraku* puppet theatre stands in stark contrast, since *bunraku* plays were published in full authorised editions from the first day of the performance.

Kabuki's lack of published play-texts did not mean that kabuki discouraged all publication. Actor critique books (*yakusha hyōbanki*) on the major kabuki productions in Kyoto, Osaka and Tokyo (Edo) were published once or twice a year between 1687 and the 1880s, giving us the fullest account of performances and critiques in the history of world drama. Further, there is a steady stream of books on kabuki theatre and a long tradition of graphic representations of actors that begins at the end of the seventeenth century and flourishes from the 1760s, with the development of commercial colour-printing. From this time, actor prints move towards more realistic (*nigao-e*) actor portraits and representations of stage action. Two magnificent examples of this trend are the Katsukawa Shun'ei 1794 print of Ichikawa Komazō III as the robber Sadakurō from *The treasury of the loyal retainers*, and the 1796 print by Utagawa Kunimasa of Ichikawa Danjūrō V in *Just a minute!*. The actor portraits by Natori Shunsen were an early-twentieth century revival of this obsession among fans for actor portraits.

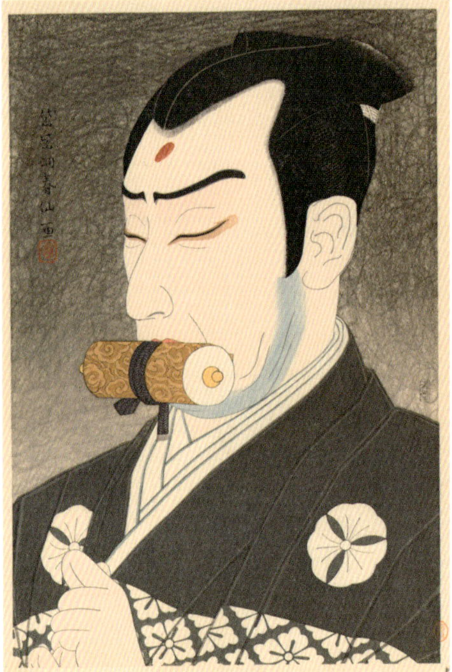

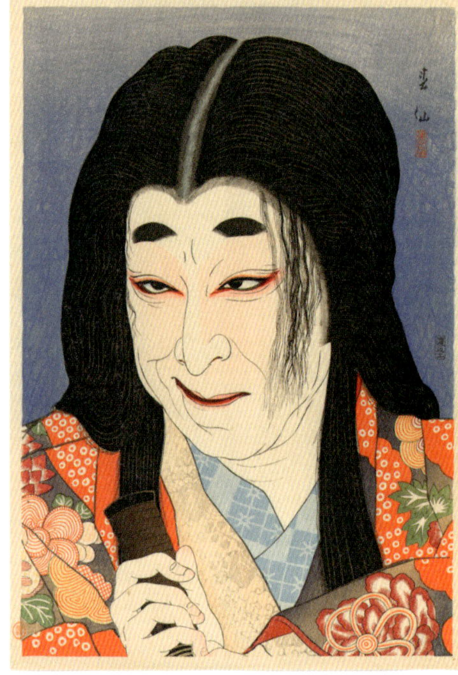

The Meiji Restoration of 1868 fostered changes in kabuki as high government officials exerted pressure to make the theatrical form a more respectable art that could showcase Japanese culture to the world. Reformers suggested radical changes—getting rid of the *onnagata*, music and extravagant histrionics, and making the actors subservient to the playwright rather than the reverse. But although kabuki has made many adjustments throughout its history to maintain audiences, it has remained actor-centred to this day.

Kabuki survived government pressures and flourished again in the early-twentieth century, with performances of both classics and newly written plays. Natori Shunsen's prints from about 1916 to the 1920s capture an array of superstars from what is considered a modern golden age of kabuki. His portraits are virtually all of actors in traditional roles that have distinctive *mie* (dramatic poses) at crucial moments of action or introspection. The aim of both Shunsen's art and the *mie* is to capture the intensity of the actor's performance, the essence of the feeling expressed. Shunsen's success would have been impossible without a deep knowledge of kabuki performance.

How would kabuki fans of the time have looked at a Shunsen actor portrait? A good example is *Jitsukawa Enjaku II as Danshichi Kurōbei in 'Summer festival: mirror of Osaka'*. The character is a young man from Osaka. He has just been released from prison, but is basically a good person. His father-in-law, however, is a despicable old man who, at the climax of the play, goads Danshichi so far that in the end Danshichi kills him. The audience knows all this and more: Shunsen must convey the complexities of the ruggedly handsome but ill-fated figure from just one moment of the play.

Another useful illustration is the portrait *Ichikawa Kigan V as Otomi in 'Sympathetic chatter*

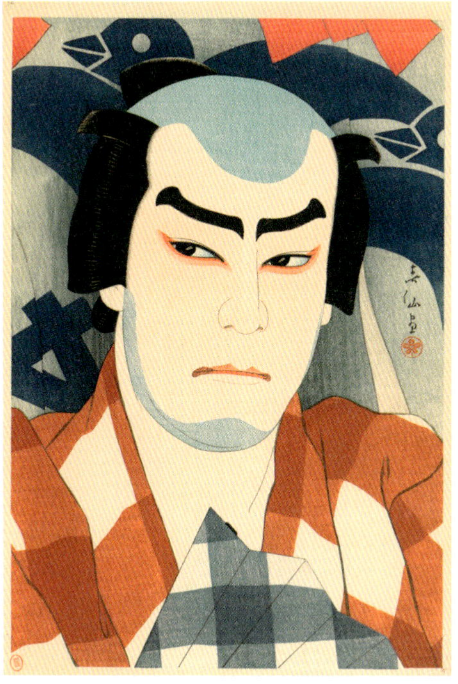

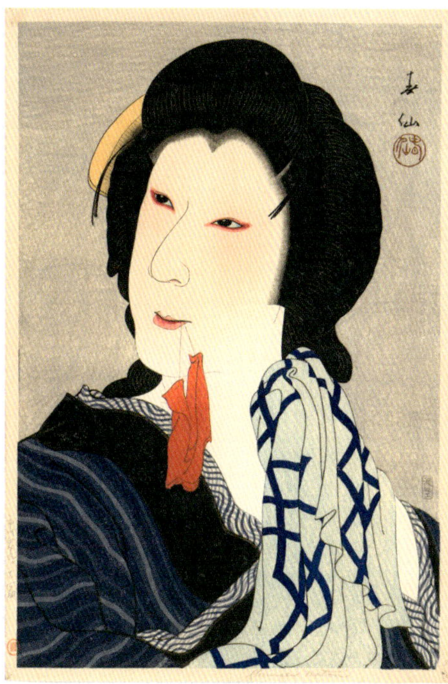

and the scandalous haircomb'. The portrayal of *onnagata* is not easy since the man must appear attractive as a woman on the stage. Does the artist make the actor into a woman, or does he try to capture the erotic cross-dressing element of the role? Otomi is a fascinating character: a woman who, with her lover Yosaburō, tries to commit a love suicide by drowning. Both are saved. He falls on hard times and gets his face all cut up, while she is rescued to become the mistress of a wealthy man. They meet years later when he comes to extort money from the house where she lives. The actor and the artist must capture this woman, attractive and sexy, a woman with a past who unexpectedly meets her old flame.

The *aragoto* or rough, exaggerated style of Edo (Tokyo) kabuki is well represented in the role of Benkei from *The subscription list* which Shunsen depicts being played by Matsumoto Kōshirō VII (see page 130). This is the ultimate bravado role where the samurai Benkei disguises himself as a mountain ascetic on a pilgrimage to raise funds for a temple, but is really trying to escape with his master Yoshitsune. In order to pass the border gate Benkei has to fake reading from a temple donor list to prove that he is a priest. The actor and artist must portray this bravado, as well as the intense feelings that lie behind his surface composure. Like the character itself, the makeup, costume and dramatic pose are more exaggerated than in the other two prints. Shunsen's portrait conveys that moment of pause within a flow of powerful movement and gesture.

Shunsen's actor portraits offer a magnificent window into the stars of the kabuki stage in early-twentieth century Japan—a period of innovation and revival in both theatre and printmaking, art forms that share a long history of popular appeal.

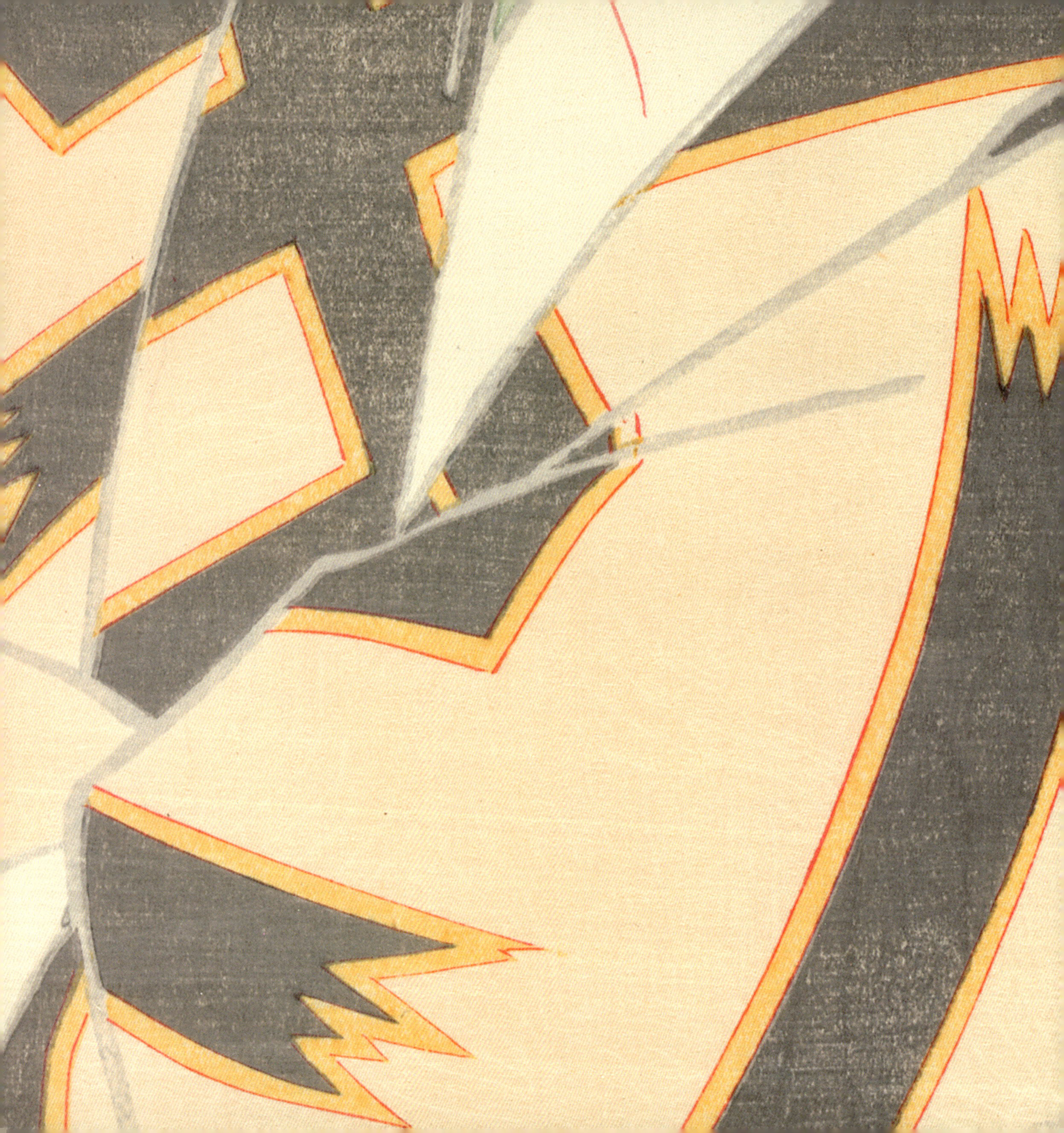

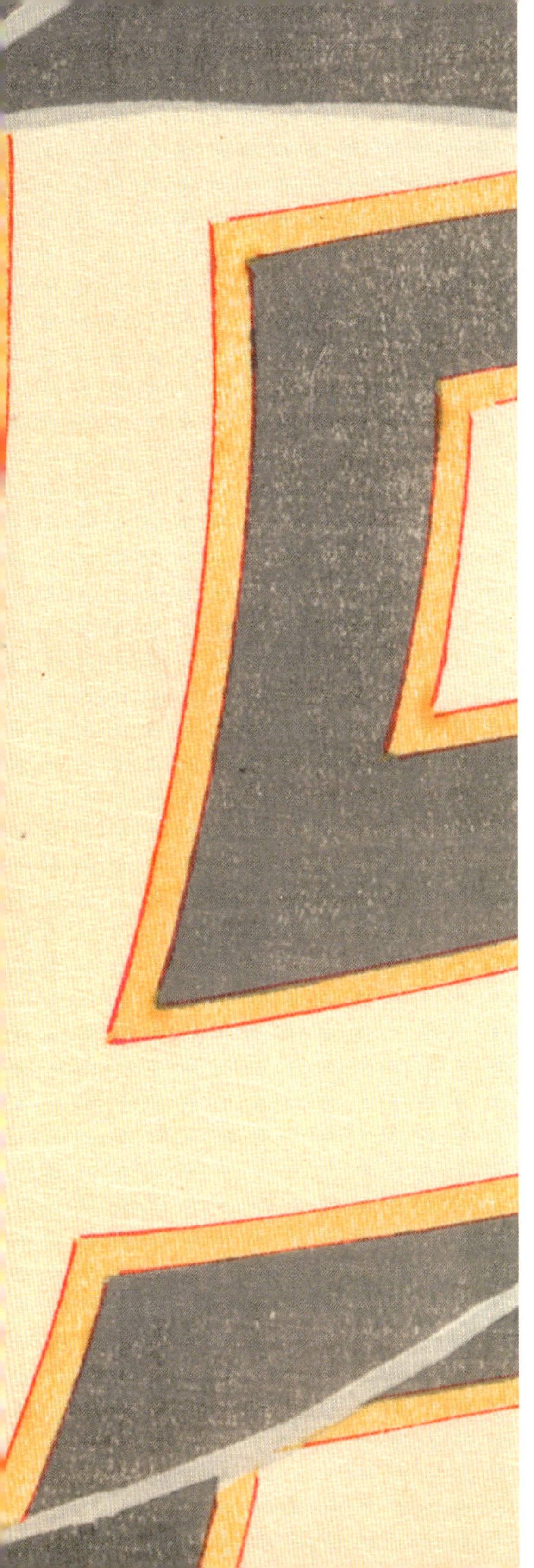

MODERN TOKYO:
THE 1920s AND 30s

Chiaki Ajioka

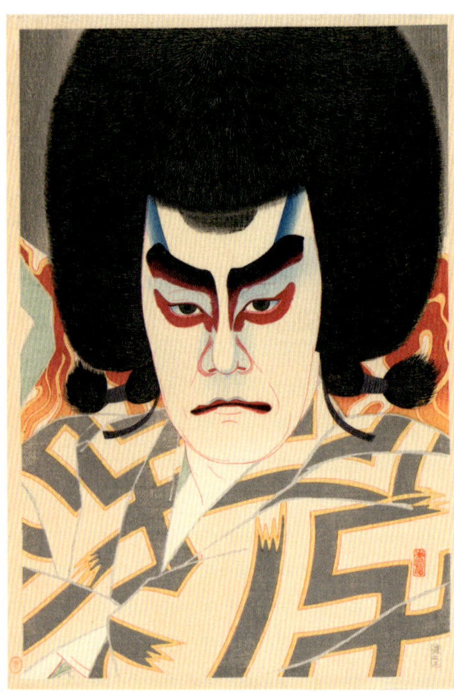

It was in the 1920s and 30s when the foundations were laid for many of the social and cultural characteristics of today's Tokyo. This dynamic period, during which Natori Shunsen produced his dramatic prints, was a pivotal time for the establishment of Japanese modernism. The new urban environment, faster pace of life and new kinds of family and workplace relationships demanded fresh cultural expressions. This was reflected in the arts, including traditional dance and theatre.

During the preceding Meiji period (1868–1912) Japan's utmost priority had been to avoid colonisation by Western powers, which was achieved largely by dismantling feudal systems and replacing them with modern institutions based on Western models. Modernisation was pushed forward under slogans such as 'Enrich the Nation, Strengthen the Military' and 'Japanese Spirit, Western Learning', the latter promoting adoption of Western knowledge without compromising Japan's 'national character'. Conventional Confucian ethics were preserved in order to demand individual loyalty to family and, in turn, to the divine Emperor, the ultimate patriarch of the country. This ideology was shared by all social strata and underpinned government strategies that often required sacrifices from the people.

The grip of this ideology on the people was loosening by the time Japan triumphed in the Russo-Japanese War (1904–05), showing that it had become a nation to be reckoned with on the world stage. The First World War boosted Japan's economy and by the end of the 1910s the urban centres of Tokyo and Osaka had become the embodiment of Japan's progress. In this new society industries were driven by private corporations with headquarters in major cities, each administering its own salaried office workers.[1] The 'salaryman' became not only ubiquitous in the cityscape but also the key constituent of a new social group—the anonymous consumers of mass-produced goods and mass-entertainment. Salarymen were also the protagonists for a fundamental change in society: good education, rather than family status, became the key to good employment, which was seen as ensuring security and success in life.

Young Japanese intellectuals, who had grown up in the era following the Russo-Japanese War, took Japan's new international standing for granted and rebelled against the family-based ideology. The most influential formal advocate of this new consciousness was the literary magazine *White Birch* (Shirakaba), started in 1910 by a group of young writers from privileged families. Educated at the Peer's School (Gakushūin) in Tokyo, a uniquely liberal institution at the time, and armed with advanced linguistic skills, they drew inspiration from Western thought and promoted humanism and individual freedom from patriarchal values.[2] The group's chief advocate, Mushanokōji Saneatsu (1885–1976), declared: 'we have become the children of humankind before we are the children of a particular society'.[3] The magazine exercised a profound influence over Japan's young intelligentsia, even though the privilege underlying the authors' cosmopolitanism and optimism was not shared by many of its readers.

In an attempt to broker a response to modernity in traditional dance and theatre, the young kabuki actor Ichikawa Sadanji II (1880–1940) made a study trip to Europe in 1906. In 1909 he and playwright-director Osanai Kaoru (1881–1928) jointly established the Free Theatre, which initially performed modern Western plays in translation. Osanai in turn went to Europe in 1912–13, joining composer Yamada Kōsaku (1886–1965). Together with other young Japanese artists they absorbed new forms of

Western art, music and theatre. In 1924 Osanai Kaoru and Hijikata Yoshi (1898–1959) established the avant-garde Tsukiji Little Theatre (Tsukiji Shōgekijō). The theatre staged challenging works, such as the Expressionist play *From morn to midnight* by George Kaiser, and provided a space for collaborations between performers, photographers and designers.[4]

At the other end of the spectrum to the avant-garde Tsukiji Little Theatre was Takarazuka, an all-female troupe and theatre founded in 1914 by a railway company to attract users to its new line between Osaka and the suburb of Takarazuka.[5] True to the founder's motto, 'pure, proper and beautiful', Takarazuka was based on a rigidly run school system that taught girls to sing, dance and act. The theatre earnt a reputation for healthy, family entertainment. In the 1920s Takarazuka began performing European-style revues that integrated Western approaches to storytelling, choreography, costume and music, without overstepping conventional Japanese moral codes. Takarazuka eventually opened a permanent theatre in Tokyo in 1934.

Modernity was also manifested in the visual arts. *Nihonga* (Japanese-style painting) artists began experimenting with new subjects and techniques. Some chose to depict the hardships of workers or the human face of a geisha, while others adopted chiaroscuro and linear perspective in their work. In craft, there was a shift in focus from skills to the expression of ideas. This approach emerged initially from outside the existing craft industry but was soon adopted by the younger generation of traditional makers.

On 1 September 1923 the Great Kantō earthquake caused catastrophic damage throughout Tokyo. The destruction of the old environment, however, became a catalyst for accelerated growth of the new city. With an acute shortage of housing,

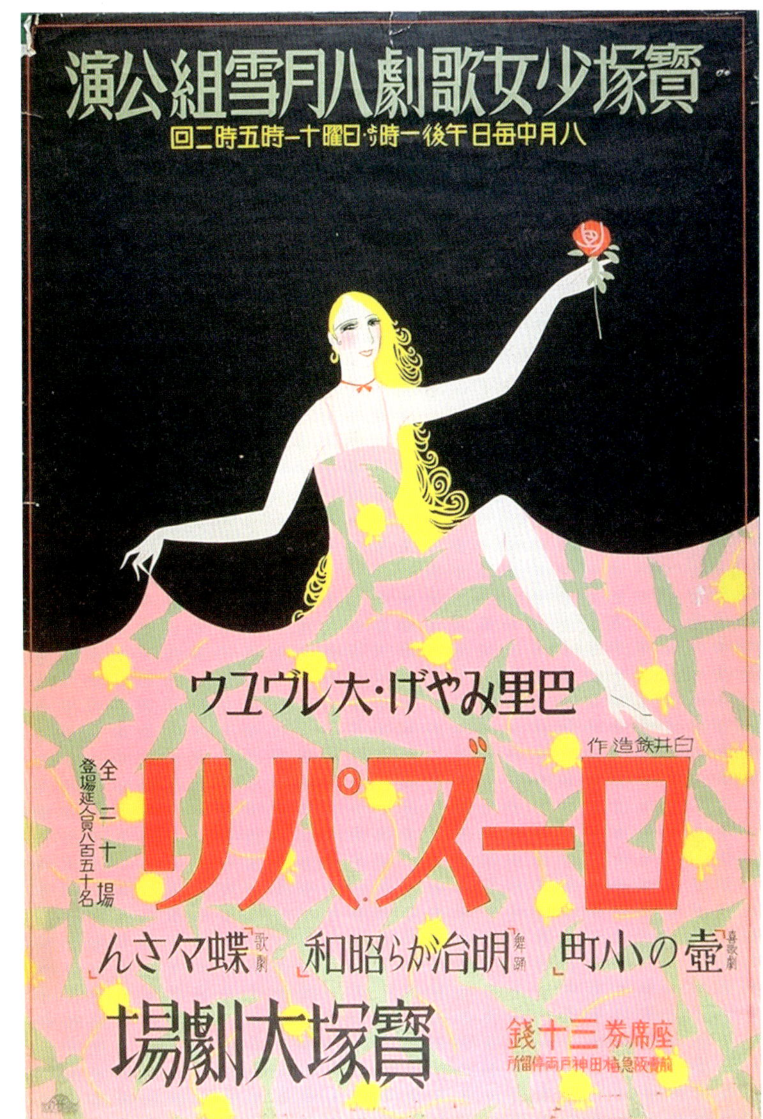

Poster for Takarazuka production *Rose Paris* (Rōzu Pari)
Performed August 1931
Courtesy of Ikeda Bunko, Osaka

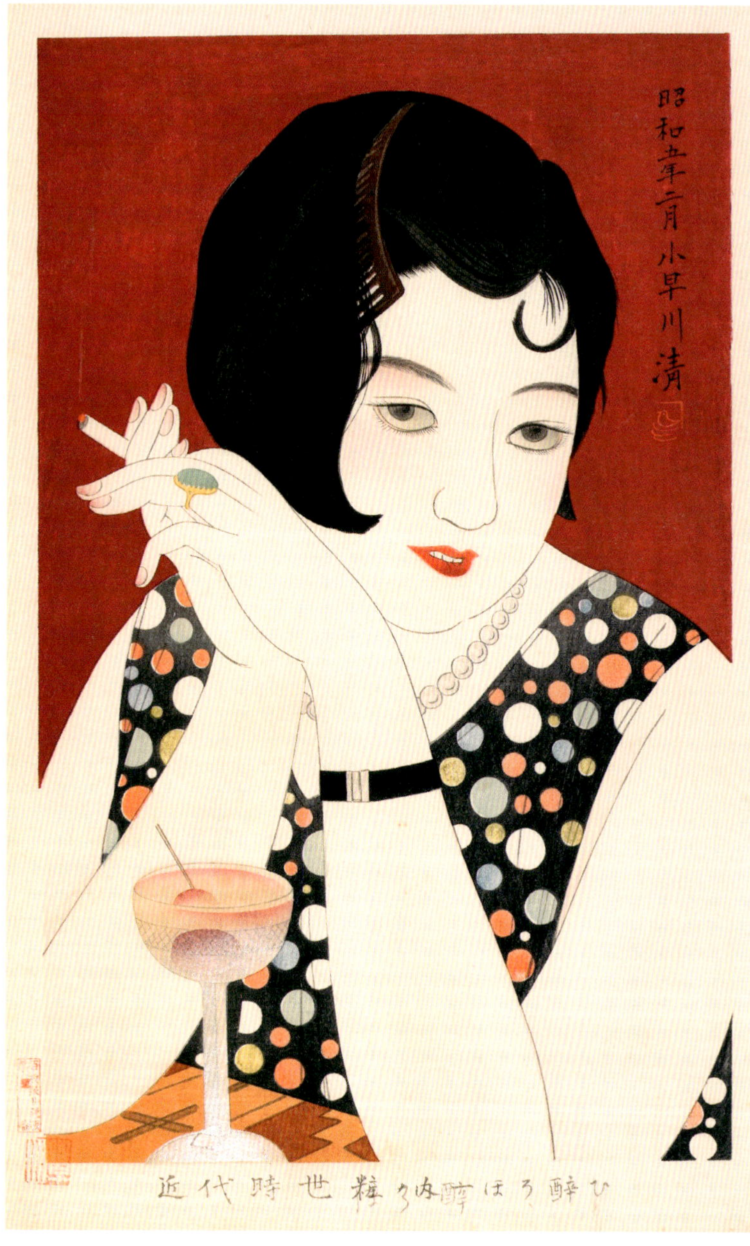

Kobayakawa Kiyoshi (1819–1948) *Tipsy* 1930
woodblock print; ink and colour on paper, 43.8 x 27 cm
Honolulu Academy of Arts, gift of Philip H Roach Jr, 2001

the government founded a building society, Dōjunkai, to construct earthquake-and-fire-proof apartment buildings across Tokyo. The new multistorey concrete blocks became symbols of the modern lifestyle; their residents were major consumers of Western-inspired, mass-produced household items.

The department store, where these modern goods could be purchased, became the provider of culture in the form of commodities. A seminal example is Mitsukoshi Department Store.[6] Originally established as a kimono store, like most other modern Japanese department stores, Mitsukoshi had its origins in the seventeenth century. In the twentieth century it set out to become Japan's Harrods by expanding its products and services to attract a wide range of clientele. For wealthy patrons, Mitsukoshi's lifestyle magazine provided information on new fashion and products while in-house galleries and halls staged art exhibitions, concerts and performances. For ordinary workers and their families, the store became a major holiday destination—to enjoy window shopping, the restaurant and various free attractions, including a rooftop playground, lifts and escalators.

The 'modern boys' and 'modern girls' who roamed the streets of Ginza, Tokyo's trendy shopping district, and frequented its cafés and cinemas, were the target market for a new mass-circulation magazine, *New Youths* (Shinseinen), published between 1920 and 1950. Unlike *White Birch*, which was aimed at a small elite audience, *New Youths*'s circulation was in the tens of thousands. Best known for detective stories, both in translation (Arthur Conan Doyle, Agatha Christie, Maurice Leblanc, among others) and by Japanese writers, *New Youths* also featured comments and cartoons on international affairs. However, the magazine that captured the most readers and best epitomised the popular culture of the era was *King* (Kingu).

The first issue of *King* was published in 1925 and sold 740 000 copies.[7] It was packed with fiction, non-fiction and humour as well as practical tips, with an authoritarian undertone of conventional ethics—such as diligence, filial duty and self-sacrifice. A typical issue might include the success story of a European migrant to America, alongside a maxim by a Japanese politician or artist, a 'Mills & Boon' style romance and a report on the latest scientific discoveries. Offering something for everyone, its readership extended from upper-class households in the city to villagers in the countryside.[8] Designed to 'entertain and inform' rather than encourage the reader to think and question, *King* was a far cry from the idealism of the likes of *White Birch*.

In the 1920s and 30s, the fruits of Japan's progress became available to Tokyo's middle class. However, material progress was accompanied by inevitable social issues. When Japan introduced universal suffrage (for men only) in 1925, it was packaged with the Security Maintenance Law. While the former was a step towards modern democracy, the latter granted authorities greater powers to crack down on the socialist, communist and labour movements that had become prominent in the 1920s. In 1931 Japan invaded China. As the nation's commitment to the war deepened, the harsh application of the Security Maintenance Law crushed proletarian movements of all forms and prepared the Japanese people for all-out war. This had many implications for popular culture and the arts. The avant-garde Tsukiji Little Theatre, for example, dissolved after many of its left-wing members were arrested in 1940. And in 1943 *King* was forced to change its name from the transliteration of the 'enemy language' to that of Japan's most sacred mountain, *Fuji*. Artistic freedom and exchange with the West lay dormant until the country's reopening after the Second World War.

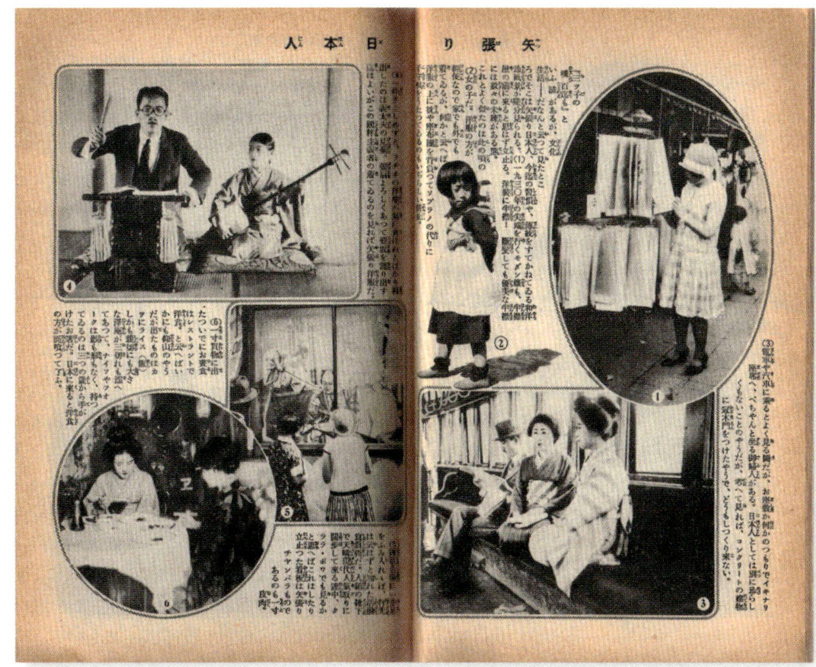

Pages from *King* (Kingu), Kodansha, August 1930
'Still Japanese'; a girl in Western clothes looking at kimono collars; women in the train sitting in a Japanese way; after a drink, a man in a Western suit performing a traditional number; women eating Western food with chopsticks.

Notes

1 For background to the popular culture of this period, see: Takemura Tamio, *Taishō Bunka* (The culture of the Taishō period), Kodansha, Tokyo, 1980; Satō Takumi, *Kingu no jidai : kokumin taishu zasshi no ko kyo sei* (The era of King: the public nature of the magazine for the masses), Iwanami Shoten, Tokyo, 2002.

2 See Sekikawa Natsuo, *Shirakaba-tachi no Taishō* (The Taishō period for the Shirakaba group), Bungei Shunjū, Tokyo, 2005, chapter 3.

3 Mushanokōji Saneatsu, *Shirakaba,* Sept 1911, p 162.

4 *Dance in Japanese modern art*, Tochigi Prefectural Museum of Fine Arts, Tochigi, 2003.

5 *Yume-o egaite hanayakani: Takarazuka Kageki 80-nen-shi* (Picturing dreams, spectacularly: 80 years of Takarazuka Revue), Takarazuka Kagekidan, Takarazuka, 1994.

6 See Henshū Iinkai, *Kabushiki Kaisha Mitsukoshi 85-nen no kiroku* (Records of the 85 years of Mitsukoshi Co), Mitsukoshi Co, Tokyo, 1990.

7 From Noma Seiji, *Watashi no hansei* (My life until now), Dai Nihon Yūbenkai Kōdansha, Tokyo, 1939, posted by the Electronic Literature Editorial Room, Japan Pen Club, viewed 14 December 2011, http://www.japanpen.or.jp/e-bungeikan/guest/publication/nomaseiji.html.

8 Takemura, p 137.

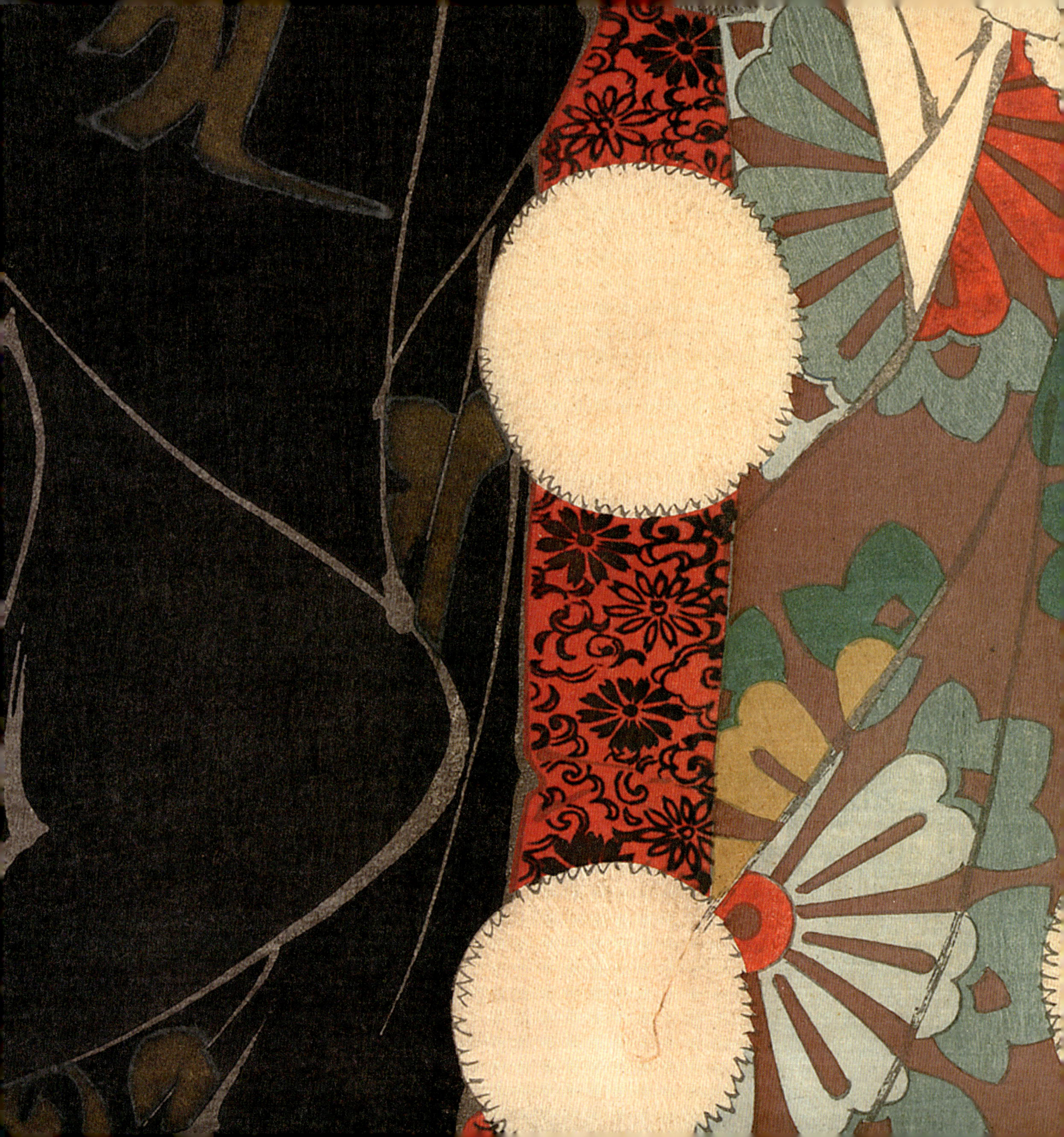

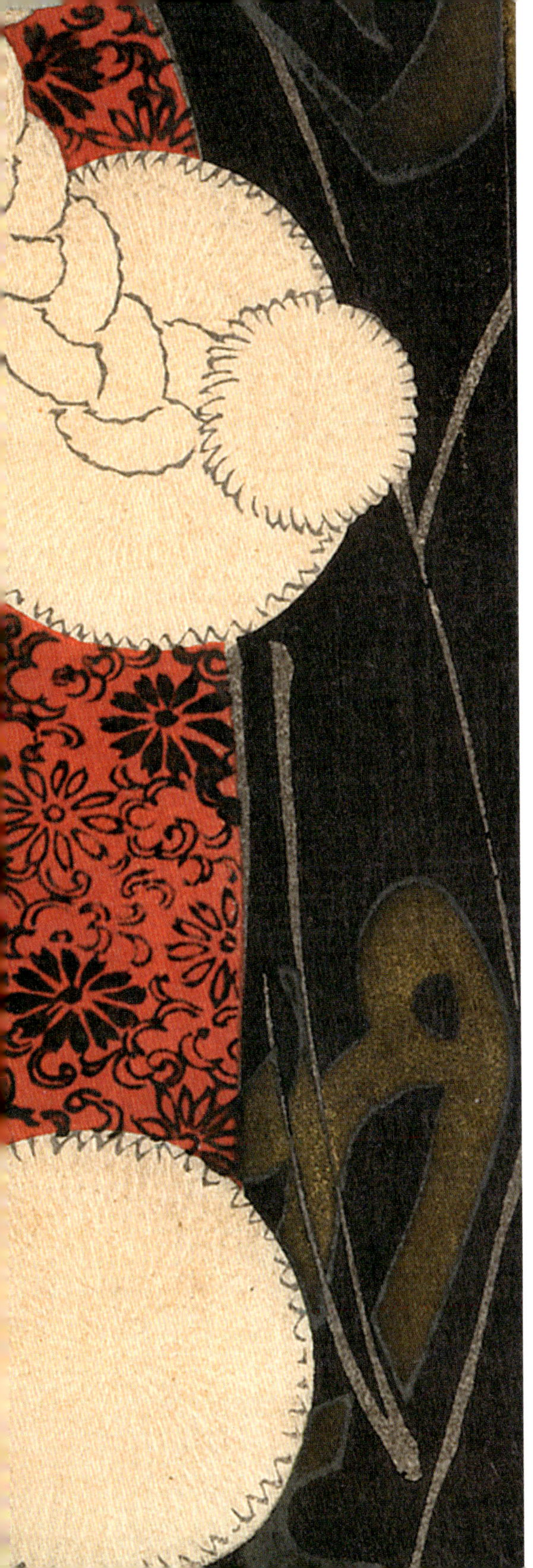

IN THE ACTOR'S IMAGE: KABUKI PRINTS IN A TIME OF CHANGE

Amy Reigle Newland

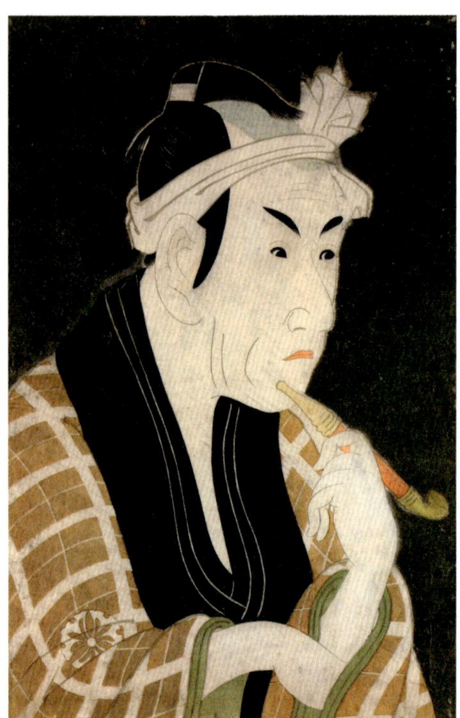

(above) **Tōshūsai Sharaku** (active c 1794–95) *Matsumoto Kōshirō IV as Sakaya Gorōbei* 1794
woodblock print; ink and colour on paper, 36.4 x 24.0 cm
British Museum, London. © Trustees of the British Museum

(right) **Toyohara Kunichika** (1835–1900) *Nakamura Shikan IV as Taira no Kanemitsu* 1873
woodblock print; ink and colour on paper, 36.0 x 71.6 cm
National Gallery of Australia, Canberra, gift of Orde Poynton Esq, AO, CMG, 1999

The era corresponding to Natori Shunsen's childhood and formative artistic training—the decades from the 1880s to the 1920s—represents a rich period in the history of Japanese woodblock prints. It marks a transitional phase from the older tradition of woodblock prints, known as *ukiyo-e* or 'pictures of the floating world', to newer approaches by artists working both in conventional and modern modes of expression. Each response was shaped by the shifting political, economic and cultural milieu of Japan at this time.

Ukiyo-e grew out of the popular culture of the Edo period (1615–1868). It emerged as a distinct genre by the early-eighteenth century and comprised both printed matter, in the form of independent sheet prints and illustrated books, and paintings. The first printed examples were monochromatic, leading to hand-coloured images and then to printing with a limited number of colours. The technology of printing culminated about 1765 with the development of the full-colour print, *nishiki-e* or 'brocade pictures'. The reference to these prints as 'brocade pictures' was a bold assertion of their parity with the beautifully coloured brocades of the then imperial capital of Kyoto. These woodblock prints were, in the main, commercial commodities. Their production and subject matter had evolved into an elaborate industry with well-oiled mechanisms of production, marketing, distribution and consumption.

The portrayal of 'likeness' pictures, or *nigao-e*, of stars of the kabuki stage was a mainstay in the *ukiyo-e* repertoire from its early history. In the first half of the nineteenth century the genre was dominated by the Utagawa school, with Utagawa Kunisada (1786–1865) as its main proponent. During Shunsen's childhood, kabuki stars provided the subject matter for *ukiyo-e* actor specialists such as Tsukioka Yoshitoshi (1839–92) and Kunisada's student Toyohara Kunichika (1835–1900). The artistic legacy of the *ukiyo-e* kabuki actor print, in particular print designers of the late-eighteenth and early-nineteenth centuries such as Tōshūsai Sharaku (active around 1794–95), would later inform the art of Shunsen and other *shin-hanga* (new prints) artists working in the genre.

In the mid-nineteenth century, with the opening of Japan to outside trade after almost 250 years

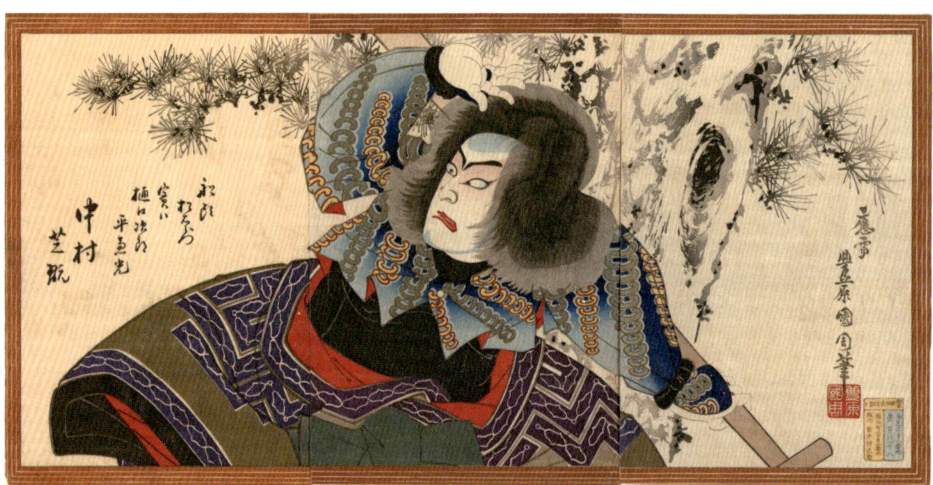

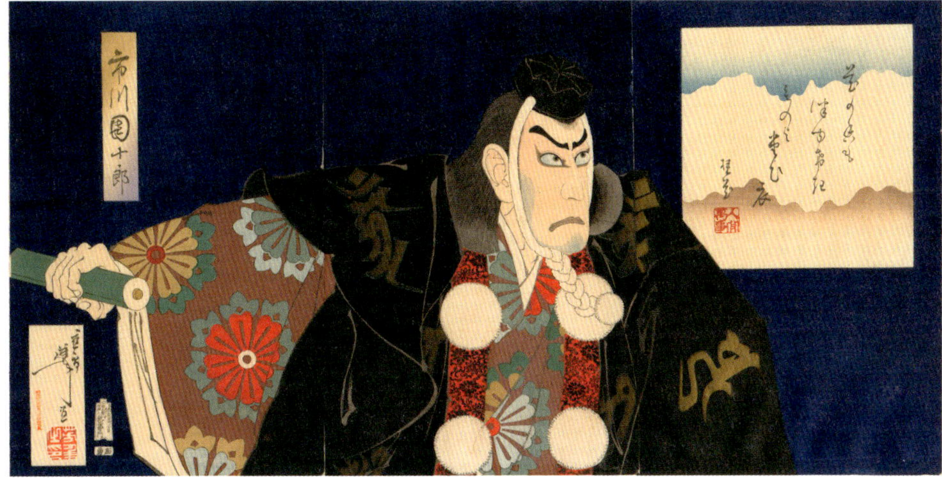

Tsukioka Yoshitoshi (1839–92) *Ichikawa Danjūrō IX as Musashibō Benkei in 'The subscription list'* 1890
woodblock print; ink and colour on paper, 36.6 x 74.1 cm
National Gallery of Australia, Canberra, purchased 1995

of relative isolation, the woodblock print industry faced increasing competition from newly imported reprographic media such as lithography, photo-mechanical processes and photography. Japan's growing urbanisation and modernisation was accompanied by artistic exchanges with the West in terms of subject matter as well as theoretical and technological approaches. In the late-nineteenth century, Edo-period prints were much sought in the West, while in Japan photography was becoming popular and demand for woodblock-printed kabuki images dwindled dramatically.

By the turn of the century—a crucial phase in the history of the woodblock print—a number of print publishers had ceased operation or turned their attention to other fields. The role of the full-colour print thus entered a twilight phase, with a final gasp seen in propaganda triptychs depicting the Russo-Japanese War of 1904–05. Woodblock printed imagery was, however, enlisted in the delicate compositions for the frontispieces (*kuchi-e*) of literary journals and emerging journals such as *Art World* (Bijutsu sekai) and *Theatre Illustrated* (Engei gahō), the latter published from 1907 to 1943. Astute

publishers also saw the public appeal of Edo-period *ukiyo-e* masters and exploited this new niche market by releasing reproductions of the works of artists such as Utagawa Hiroshige (1797–1858) and Suzuki Harunobu (1725–70). One such publisher was Watanabe Shōzaburō (1885–1962), who had established his own business in Tokyo in 1906 and embarked on a handful of high-quality reproductions of Edo-period *ukiyo-e* prints in 1915, 'to give the Japanese public an opportunity to appreciate the pleasures of the genre by assembling a group of masterpieces from the very limited stocks that are still available in this country'.[1]

Artists producing prints within a traditional mode of woodblock production were not necessarily trained as apprentices in the studio of an acknowledged master at this time, as they had been earlier. Like Shunsen, a growing number had received instruction in other fields of artistic endeavour, namely painting, in art schools such as the Tokyo School of Fine Arts (Tokyo Bijutsu Gakkō, established 1887). These artists began to look at newer approaches in an attempt to embrace tradition while at the same time surpassing it. In the case of kabuki

(clockwise from top left) **Natori Shunsen** *Onoe Baikō VI as Ibara in the play Hitotsuya* 1915 from the magazine *New Portraits*
woodblock print; ink and colour on paper, 18.1 x 11.4 cm
Lavenberg Collection of Japanese Prints; IHL Cat #468

Matsuda Seifū (1880–1978) *Kataoka Nizaemon XI as Hachirōbei* 1915 from the magazine *New Portraits*
woodblock print; ink and colour on paper, 25.4 x 11.1 cm
Lavenberg Collection of Japanese Prints; IHL Cat #347

Yamamura Kōka (1885–1942) *Onoe Matsusuke IV as Kōmori (bat) Yasu* 1917
woodblock print; ink and colour on paper, 29.8 x 27.6 cm
Nihon no Hanga Museum, Amsterdam; Inv no PO757

Yamamura Kōka (1885–1942) *The actor Nakamura Kichiemon I* 1915 from the magazine *New Portraits*
woodblock print; ink and colour on paper, 18.6 x 11.4 cm
Lavenberg Collection of Japanese Prints; IHL Cat #244

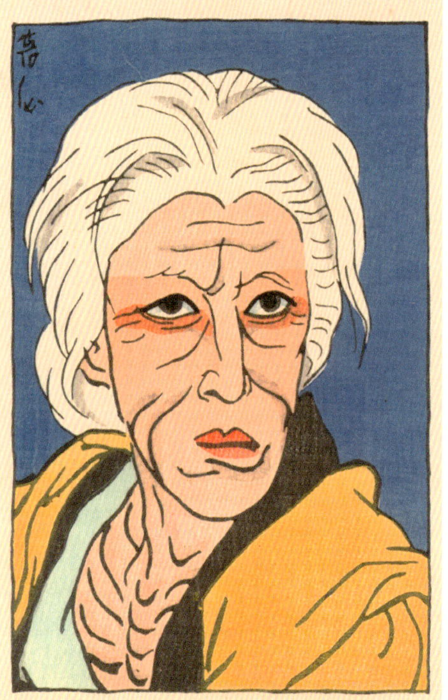
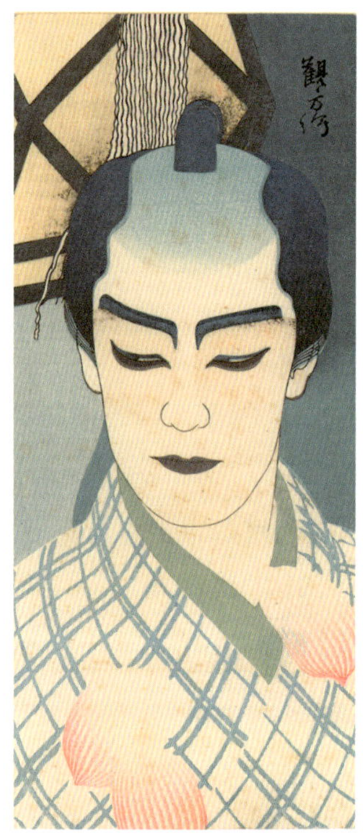
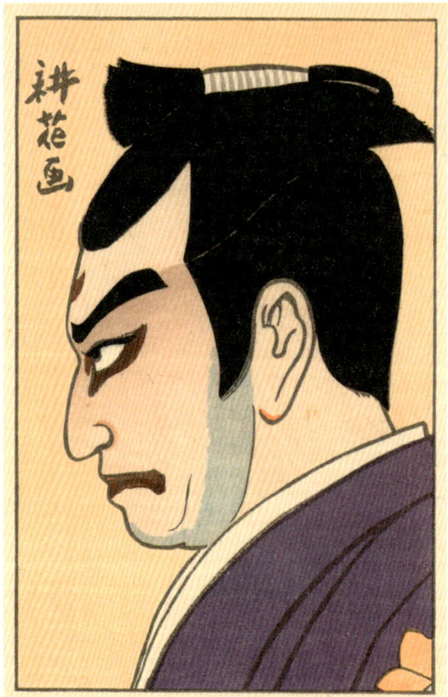
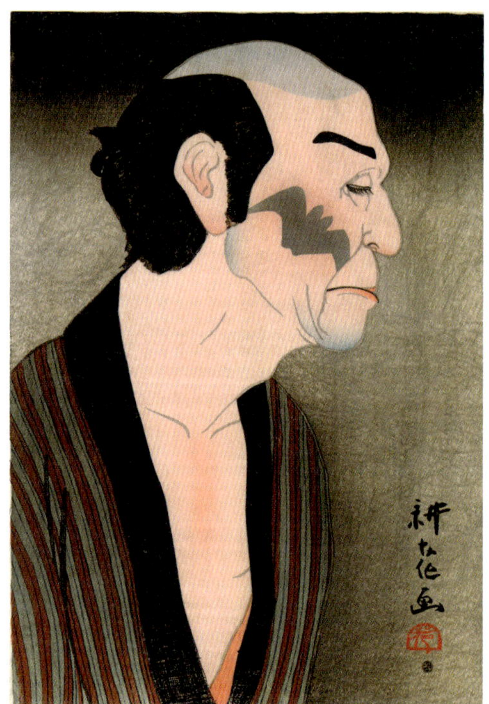

actor imagery, for example, formative attempts to imbue the genre with new life are seen in the frontispieces from *Theatre Illustrated* and in a 1911 series entitled *Stage sketches* (Sōga butai sugata-e) by two artists trained in Western-style painting, Ishii Hakutei (1882–1958) and Sakamoto Hanjirō (1882–1969). Hakutei also participated in *New Portraits* (Shin nigao), a magazine published in 1915 that included two later leaders of *shin-hanga* kabuki imagery, Shunsen and Yamamura Kōka (1885–1942).[2] The artists collaborating in *New Portraits* would most likely have been familiar with classic *ukiyo-e* kabuki imagery by artists such as Tōshūsai Sharaku.

The small format images in *New Portraits* sought to revivify the bust portrait tradition through new approaches to the portrayal of subjects and to technique, at times exhibiting a more dynamic style of carving. The image of Kōmori (Bat) Yasu by Yamamura Kōka, for example, would later be released as full-sized prints and become signature works in the *shin-hanga* repertoire. While *New Portraits* ceased after only five issues, it remains important as a bridge between earlier traditions and efforts to reinvigorate kabuki portraiture in the early-twentieth century. Indeed the preface to the third issue makes reference to the decline in the genre, and infers hope for a reversal in the trend:

> … in the past there were actor portraits (*nigao-e*) by the Torii and Utagawa schools, but the actor portrait gradually declined by the end of the Meiji era despite the craftsmen's skill in the technique of printing with the *baren* and the skill of the woodblock print master. It is indeed regrettable that other media like lithography and colour photography appear to be spreading as the proud face of our times.[3]

What is also noteworthy about the *New Portraits* project is the collaboration between artists like Shunsen, who would later become identified with the *shin-hanga* movement, and Ishii Hakutei who is often considered a theoretician of the supposedly oppositional *sōsaku-hanga* (creative print) artists.[4]

The *shin-hanga* movement is generally understood to have begun in earnest with the publication of the print *Nude woman with towel and basin* by Hashiguchi Goyō (1880–1921) in 1915. The central figure in the movement was the entrepreneurial publisher Watanabe Shōzaburō, who was driven as much by an altruistic desire to reinvigorate the tradition of woodblock printing as by a savvy understanding that beautifully designed works would appeal to a potentially lucrative foreign clientele.[5] Watanabe promoted the idea that the 'new prints' represented a mode of expression that drew upon the collaborative nature and repertoire of earlier *ukiyo-e* to showcase a modern aesthetic vocabulary. They were intended as objects worthy of artistic appreciation. He referred to prints as *shinsaku-hanga* (newly created prints), even though today these prints are commonly referred to as *shin-hanga* (new prints). Watanabe advocated the conventional collaboration long known in *ukiyo-e* between publisher, artist, printer and block-carver. These *shin-hanga* works are distinguished by the high level of printing and use of sumptuous materials.

Perhaps motivated by the early-twentieth century demand for reprints of the work of *ukiyo-e* artists and recent ventures in kabuki portraiture such as *New Portraits*, Watanabe commissioned actor prints from Yamamura Kōka and Natori Shunsen in 1916. Shunsen, in fact, became a leading figure in the genre within Watanabe's stable of artists. Following his first print in 1916, he worked regularly with the publisher from the 1920s until the early

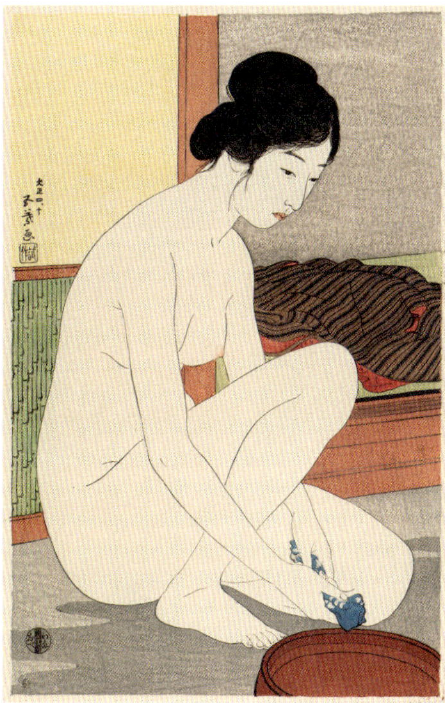

Hashiguchi Goyō (1880–1921) *Nude woman with towel and basin* 1915
woodblock print; ink and colour on paper, 41.8 x 27.7 cm
Museum of Fine Arts, Boston
Museum purchase with funds donated by Mrs Charles Gaston Smith's Group 35.1875

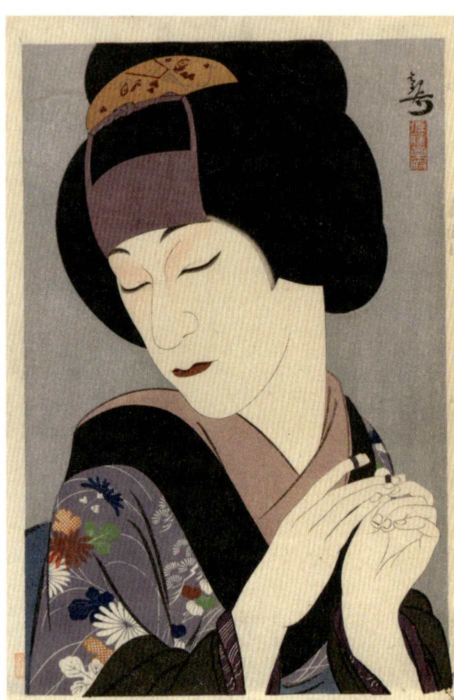

(above) **Yoshikawa Kanpō** (1894–1979) *The actor Kataoka Gadō IV as Miyuki in 'The tales of the morning glory'* 1924 woodblock print; ink and colour on paper, 42.6 x 32.8 cm National Gallery of Australia, Canberra, The Poynton Bequest, 2005

(opposite) **Natori Shunsen** *Kataoka Ichizō IV as Benkei in 'The cherry trees of the Imperial Palace'* 1927 (detail) (p 94)

1950s. Shunsen's kabuki portraits differ from most earlier actor imagery in that the association between a particular performance and the image illustrated is no longer the primary concern. Rather, the focus is the individual actor and the connoisseurial value of the portrait as a work of art. The scale of output also shifted. Unlike earlier *ukiyo-e* designers like Kunisada whose theatre prints could number into the thousands, *shin-hanga* artists had a noticeably smaller output. Shunsen, for example, produced just over 80 kabuki prints for Watanabe, and Kōka only 16, thus adding an element of exclusivity to their work.

While Watanabe is justifiably credited as the guiding figure in the history of *shin-hanga*, other publishers and artists also espoused the *shin-hanga* style. Noteworthy, for instance, is the work of Kyoto artist Yoshikawa Kanpō, who collaborated with the publisher Satō Shōtarō in 1922–24 to create some of that region's earliest *shin-hanga* kabuki imagery.

The *shin-hanga* movement crystallised in the late 1910s and into the early 1920s. Tragically, the Great Kantō earthquake of September 1923 devastated Watanabe's shop, destroyed his stock and woodblocks. After this time he abandoned his elaborate reproduction projects and focused on *shin-hanga*. He rekindled former collaborations, including with Shunsen, and forged new relationships, but *shin-hanga* was further hampered by the Second World War. Certainly with Watanabe's death in 1962, the movement came to a silent close. Today *shin-hanga* remain unparalleled, not only as an expression that coalesced tradition and modernity, but also as works of outstanding artistic and technical achievement.

Notes

1   From Watanabe's most ambitious project of reproductions, *Ukiyo-e hanga kessakushū* (A collection of *ukiyo-e* print masterpieces, 1916–20); it also states that 'most prints that could be described as masterpieces have already been exported to America and Europe'. See Abe Setsuko, 'The publisher Watanabe Shōzaburō and the *shin-hanga* movement: its beginnings until the 1930s,' in Amy Reigle Newland (ed), *The Hotei encyclopedia of Japanese woodblock prints*, Hotei Publishing, Amsterdam, 2005, p 294.

2   Other artists who contributed to *New Portraits* included Torii Kotondo (1900–76), Matsuda Seifū (1880–1978), Koito Gentarō (1887–1978), Kondō Kōichiro (1884–1962), Ogawa Hyōe, also known as Ogawa Heibei (active around 1915), Terasawa Kotarō (active around 1915) and Ishizuka Kan (active around 1915).

3   Each issue of *New Portraits* contained a woodblock print affixed to the cover, a frontispiece and 'tipped-in' woodblock prints of actors in role. Including the cover illustrations and depending on the volume, there were 13 to 20 images; issue one measures 18.5 x 12.5 cm; the remaining issues average 25.0 x 18.5 cm in size. The works were carved by Igami Bonkotsu and printed (in some cases) by Nakamura Sanjirō. See also Amy Reigle Newland (ed), *Printed to perfection: twentieth century Japanese prints from the Robert O Muller collection*, Hotei Publishing, Amsterdam, in association with Arthur M Sackler Gallery, Smithsonian Institution, Washington DC, 2004, p 27.

4   *New Portraits* challenges the notion, commonly held by scholars in the past, that clear-cut boundaries exist between *sōsaku-hanga* and *shin-hanga*, with artists of the former being involved in all aspects of the 'creative process' in making a print, while adherents of the latter were involved in a more collaborative dialogue with printer and block-carver.

5   The path towards Watanabe's realisation of his *shin-hanga* vision appeared early in the twentieth century in his experiments with Japanese artists such as the Hiroshige-inspired compositions by Takahashi Hiroaki (1871–1945) for the export market in 1906 and foreign artists including Fritz Capelari (1884–1950).

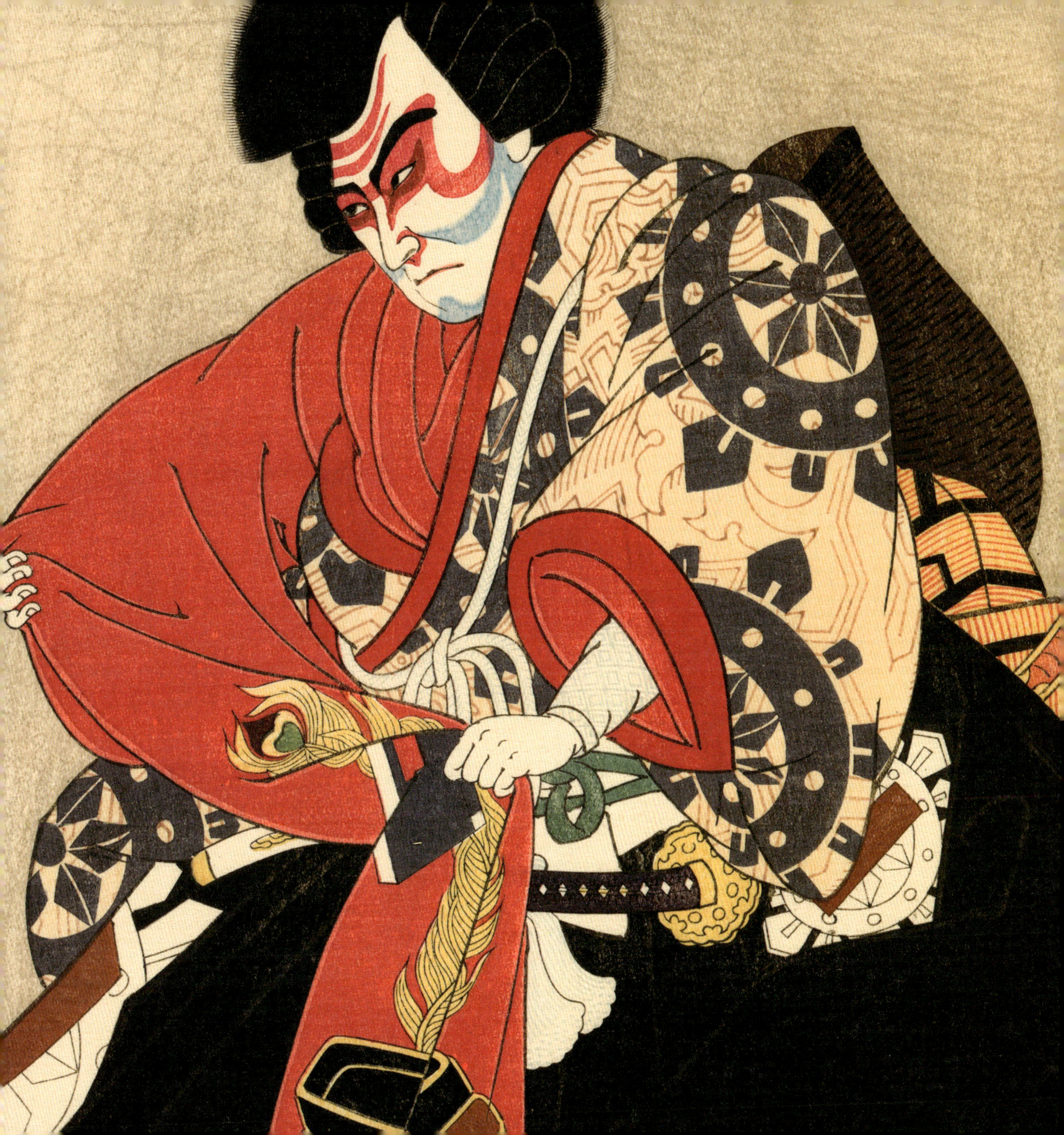

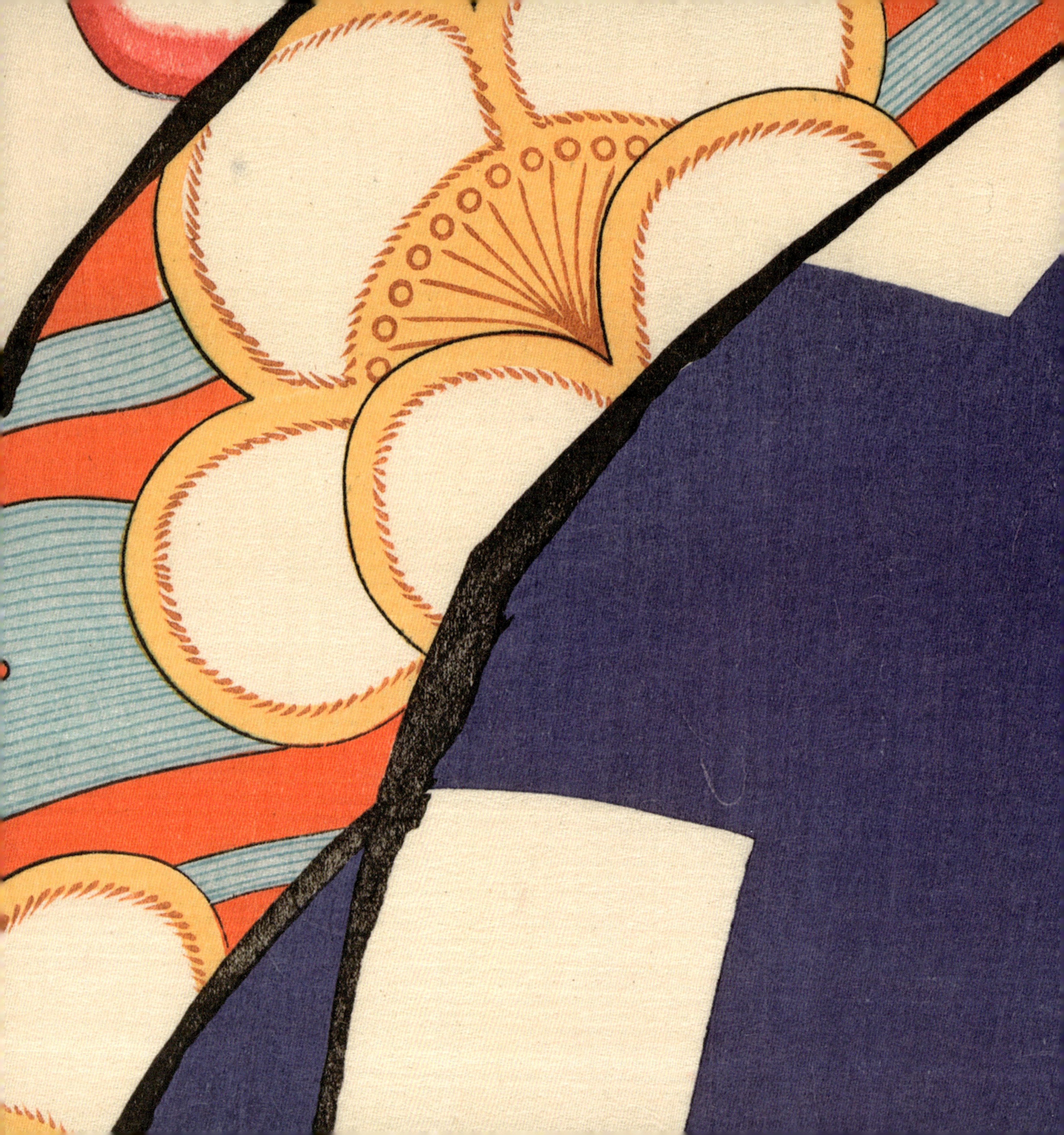

BEYOND THE STAGE

Melanie Eastburn

Kabuki was experiencing renewed vigour and reaching broad audiences, including foreigners, when the first of Natori Shunsen's *Collection of creative portraits by Shunsen* was released to subscribers in 1925. The same year, one of the very few early English-language accounts of kabuki was published in London. *Kabuki: the popular stage of Japan* was the product of 12 years of kabuki attendance and research by Zoë Kincaid (1878–1944), a Canadian journalist and kabuki enthusiast based in Tokyo. The book's acknowledgments pay tribute to some of the finest kabuki stars of the era—Nakamura Utaemon V, Onoe Baikō VI, Matsumoto Kōshirō VII, Onoe Kikugorō VI, Nakamura Kichiemon I and Nakamura Ganjirō I—each immortalised in at least one portrait by Shunsen.[1]

Kabuki actors have been regarded as superstars, adored and gossiped about, since the art form's beginnings in the seventeenth century.

The lifestyles of many eminent actors have contributed to their notoriety. Two of the great early stars were Kyoto's Sakata Tōjūrō (1647–1709) and Tokyo's Ichikawa Danjūrō (1660–1704). Tōjūrō was the pioneer of *wagoto*, a naturalistic and romantic style of acting. Aware of the value of an intriguing offstage persona, Tōjūrō is said to have worn his clothes just once and to have eaten only the best and most expensive foods. When performing in Osaka, he apparently insisted on Kyoto water and for each grain of his rice to be inspected. On stage, however, Tōjūrō often played ordinary people in performances informed by experience and insightful observation of daily life.

At much the same time Ichikawa Danjūrō initiated the contrasting *aragoto* or rough exaggerated style of acting, specialising in powerful, fantastic and often aggressive characters. The son of a samurai who relocated to Tokyo after losing his master, he was the first

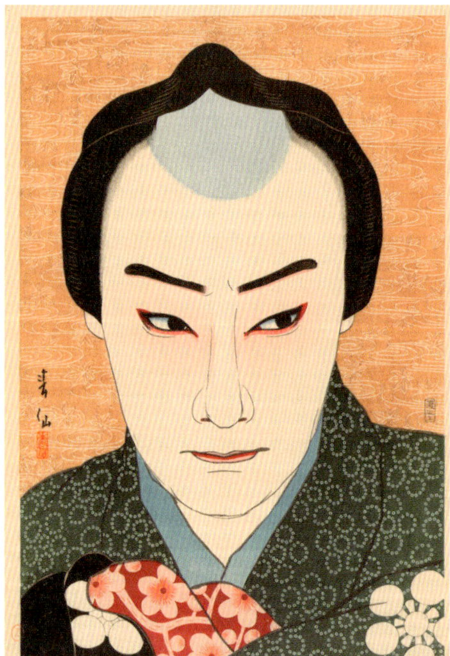

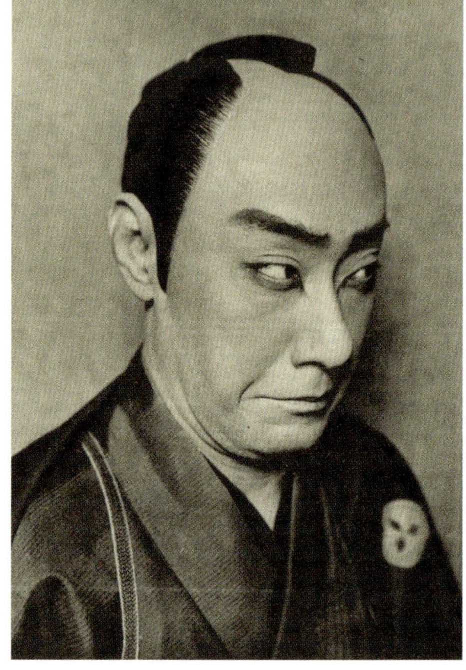

(left) **Natori Shunsen** *Nakamura Ganjirō I as Sakata Tōjūrō in 'Tōjūrō's love'* 1925 (p 72)

(right) Nakamura Ganjirō I, published in Zoë Kincaid, *Kabuki: the popular theatre of Japan*, 1925

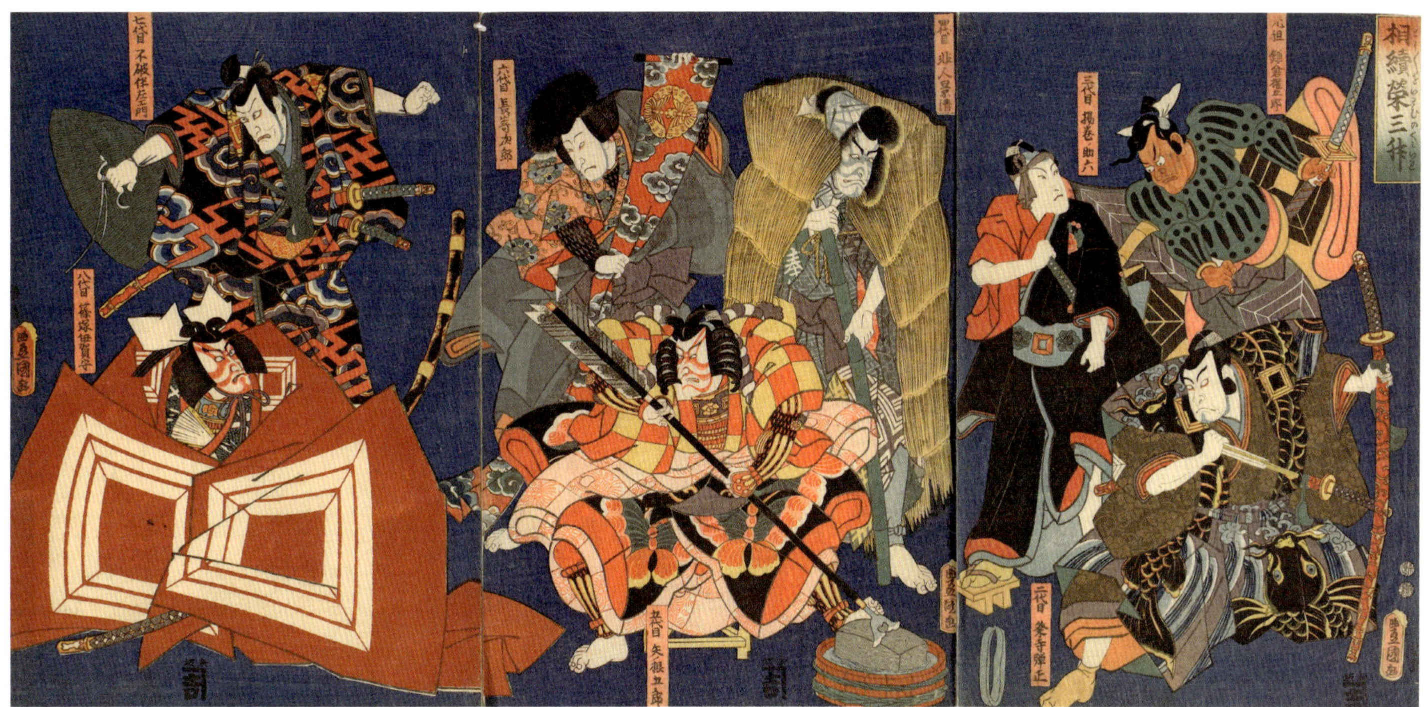

in a long and continuing hereditary line of actors to play *aragoto* roles and bear his stage name. Danjūrō made his stage debut in 1673 under the name Ichikawa Ebizō, playing a child hero to immediate acclaim. Two years later he took the name Ichikawa Danjūrō, a title he retained until he was murdered on stage at the age of 44.

It is traditional for kabuki actors to change names at certain points in their careers and to use additional titles for pursuits beyond the stage. Danjūrō used the name Mimasuya Hyōgo when writing plays and Saigyū for poetry. Danjūrō's son was also a playwright and an innovative actor who incorporated aspects of the soft *wagoto* style into *aragoto*. He took the name Ichikawa Danjūrō II (1689–1758) at 17. With no son to inherit the family name, Ichikawa Danjūrō II adopted a much-loved pupil who, at 14, became Ichikawa Danjūrō III (1721–42). Danjūrō II continued to act under another of his father's

names, Ichikawa Ebizō II. When his chosen heir died aged 21, the name was unused for over a decade until he adopted Matsumoto Kōshirō II (1712–78), an actor already in his forties when renamed Ichikawa Danjūrō IV.[2]

Danjūrō IV's son, Matsumoto Kōshirō III (1741–1806), became Ichikawa Danjūrō V at the age of 29. His ascension was accompanied by the first of what are now customary *shūmei hiro* (name-taking) ceremonies for kabuki actors. His declaration that the name Ichikawa Danjūrō was famous throughout the land, followed by a display of what had become the family's signature pose and glower with rolling eyes (*nirami no mie*), has been replicated in ceremonies taken by each recipient of the name, including the current holder Ichikawa Danjūrō XII (born 1946).[3] Utagawa Kunisada's triptych *Buckets of good wishes* shows eight generations of the Danjūrō family in character.

Utagawa Kunisada (1786–1865) *Buckets of good wishes year after year: the inherited glory of the Ichikawa clan* c 1850 woodblock print; ink and colour on paper, 35.3 x 73.5 cm Freer Gallery of Art and Arthur M Sackler Gallery, Smithsonian Institution, Washington DC, the Anne van Biema Collection

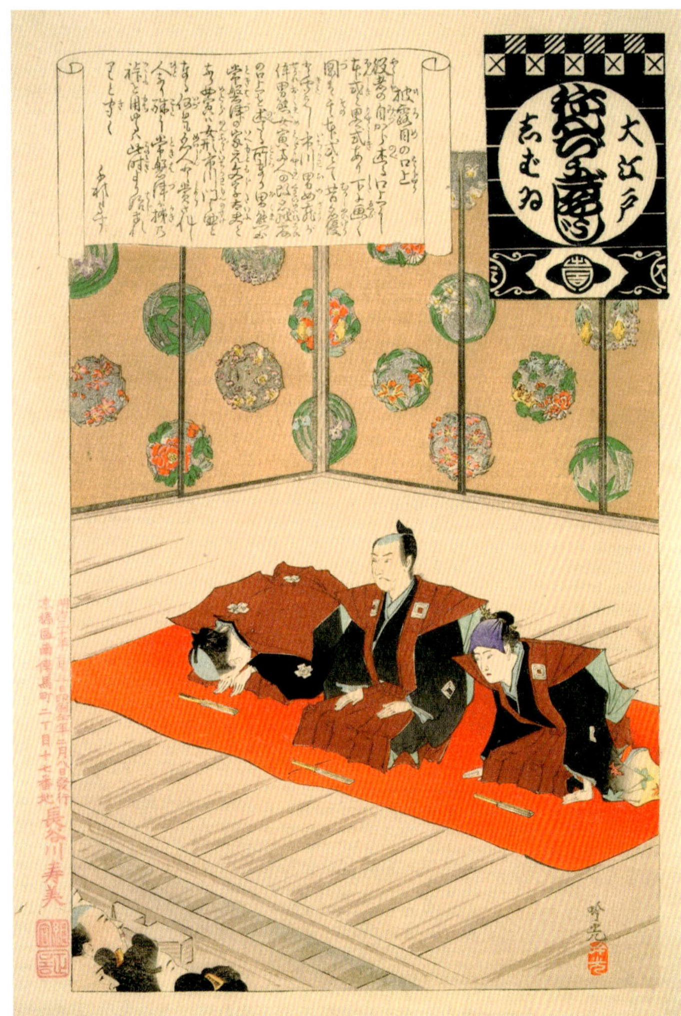

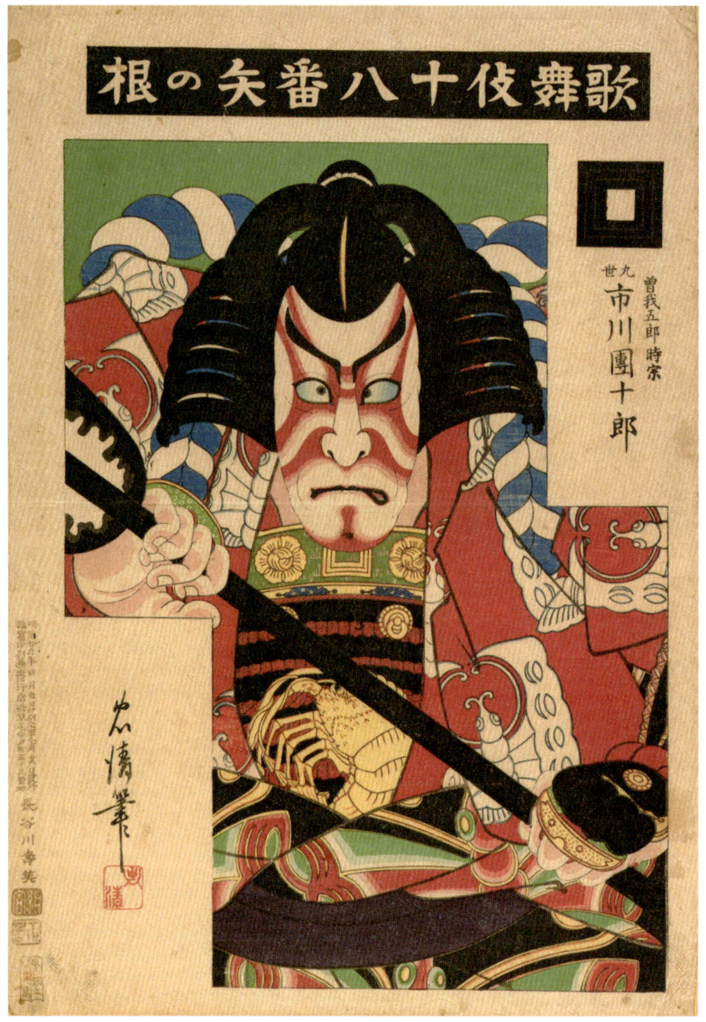

(above) **Adachi Ginko** (active 1874–97) *Annual events of the Edo Theatre* 1897
woodblock print; ink and colour on paper, 37.4 x 25.1 cm
British Museum, London © Trustees of the British Museum

(above right) **Kiyotada Torii** (1875–1941) *Ichikawa Danjūrō IX as Soga Gorō in 'The arrow sharpener'* 1896
woodblock print; ink and colour on paper, 38.0 x 26.0 cm
National Gallery of Australia, Canberra, gift of Roderick Bain, 1998

With actors and their lives as fascinating as their performances, the various ceremonies of the kabuki season are exceptionally well attended. The actors and plays for the coming season are announced and previewed during the annual *kaomise* (face showing). At ceremonies to mark an actor's promotion in status, the recipient is dressed in formal robes and kneels on stage while a senior colleague speaks for the ascending star. He, in turn, modestly assures the audience of his determination for continual improvement and requests forgiveness for mistakes.

New actor names are rarely created, with already acclaimed titles usually accompanying advances in status. The name conferred must be peer approved and there have been a number of upsets, in which an anticipated title is bestowed elsewhere. For example, as a child Matsumoto Kōshirō VII (1870–1949) was much admired by Danjūrō IX, who considered passing the Danjūrō

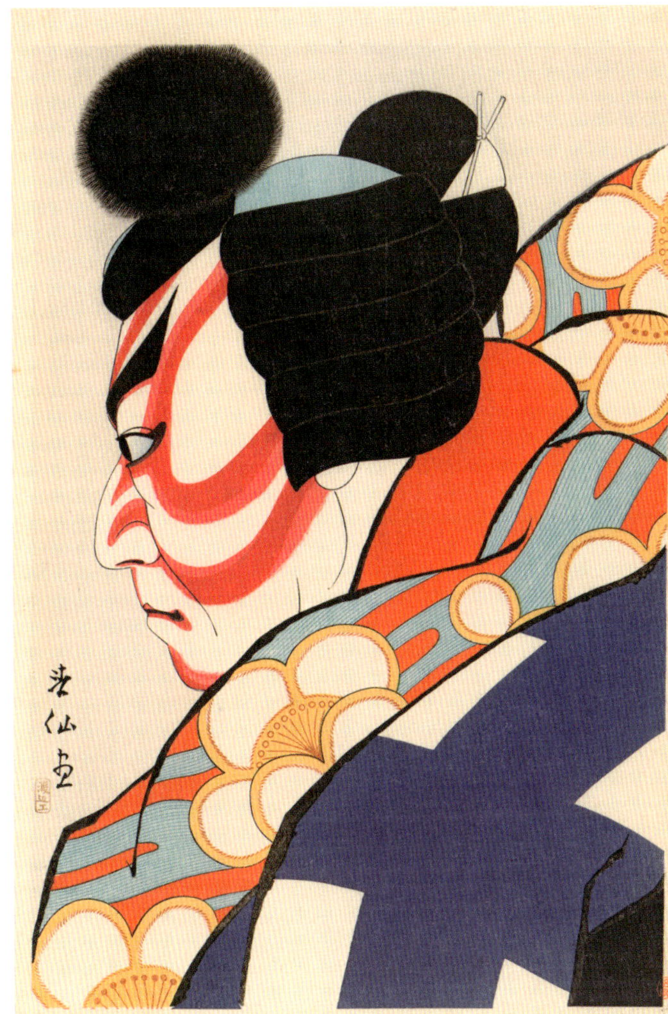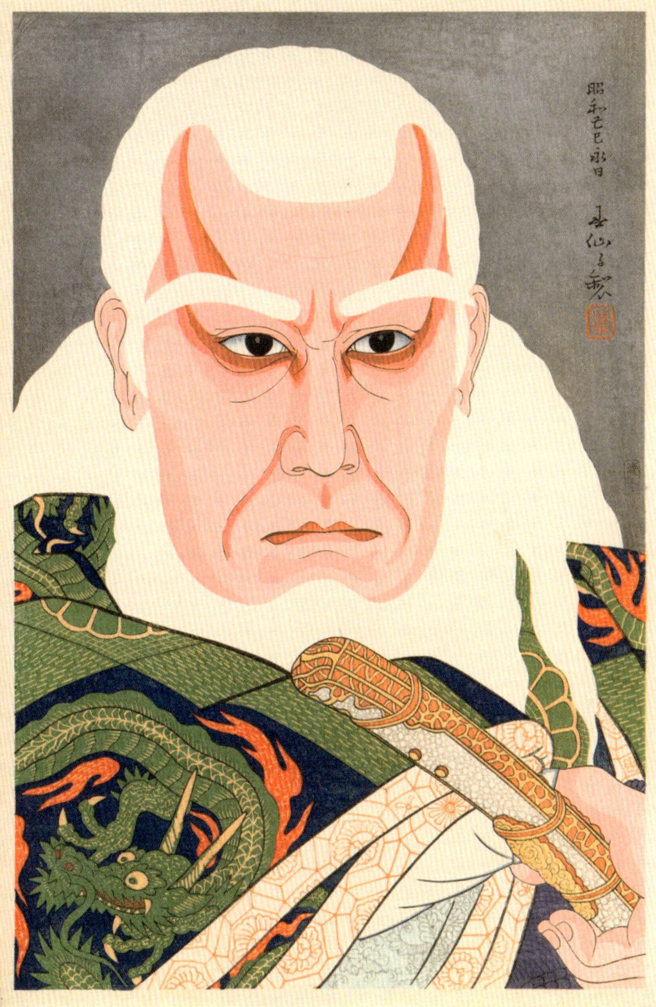

name to him. Kōshirō VII was ousted by Danjūrō IX, however, following indecorous behaviour (the nature of which was undisclosed). His exile from the Tokyo stage lasted until several years after Danjūrō IX's death in 1903. Kōshirō VII became an influential actor renowned for his ingenious use of makeup. Shunsen portrays him in three very different guises—in profile with vigorous red markings as Umeōmaru in *Sugawara's secrets of calligraphy*, as the villain Ikyū in *Sukeroku: flower of Edo* and as Benkei in *The subscription list*.

While some names have been handed down in almost unbroken succession for centuries, others have faded away or been revived after extended absences. In 2005 Nakamura Ganjirō III (born 1931) resurrected the title Sakata Tōjūrō, which had been out of use since 1774. Although not related to the legendary Sakata Tōjūrō, the current Sakata Tōjūrō IV is an official Living National Treasure known for his brilliant performances in both male and female roles.[4] His grandfather, Nakamura Ganjirō I, was devoted to

(above left) **Natori Shunsen** *Matsumoto Kōshirō VII as Umeōmaru in 'Sugawara's secrets of calligraphy'* 1926 (p 63)

(above) **Natori Shunsen** *Matsumoto Kōshirō VII as Ikyū in 'Sukeroku: flower of Edo'* 1929 (p 134)

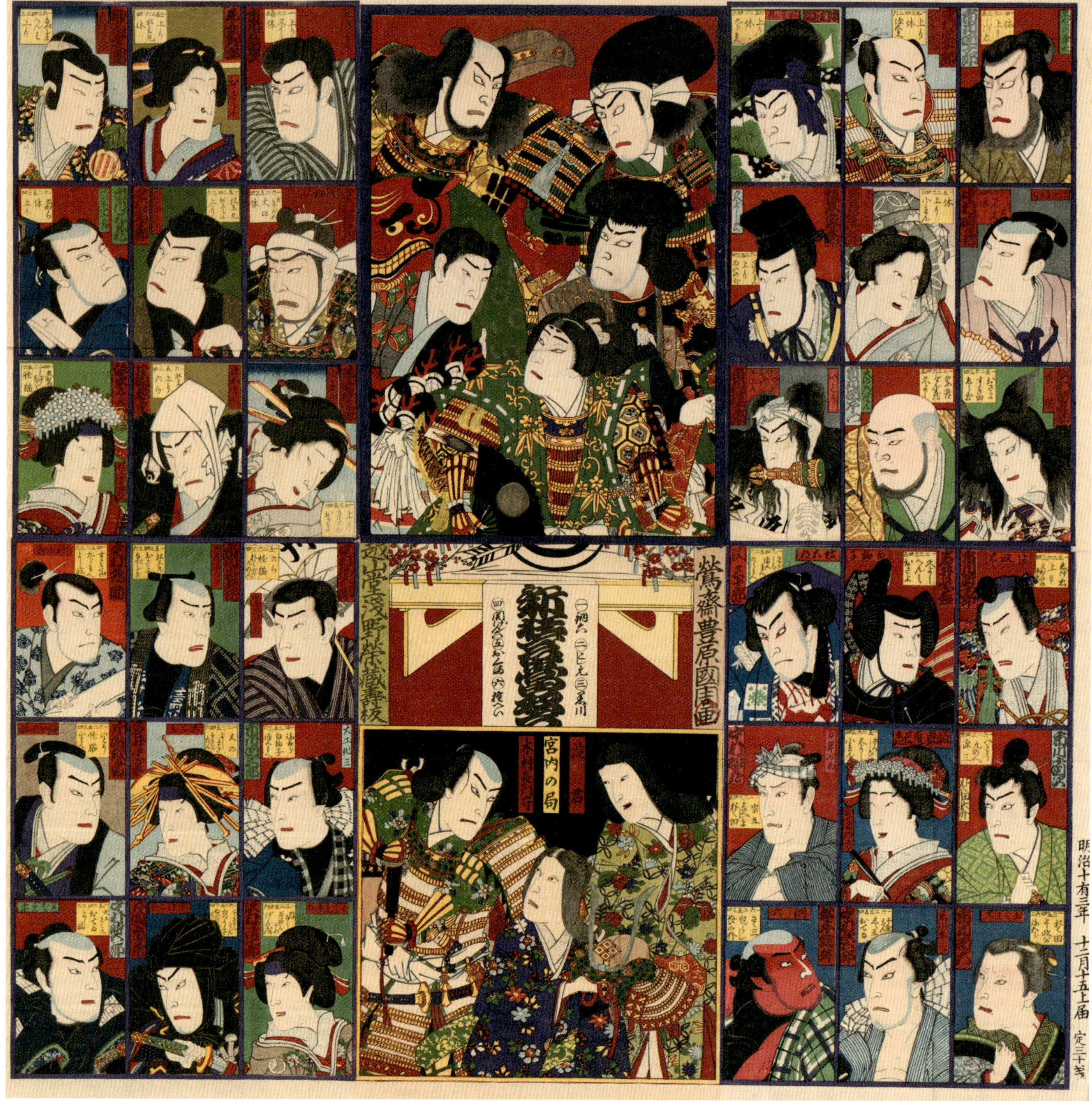

the tender *wagoto* acting style of Sakata Tōjūrō and excelled at playing the romantic hero in *Love letters from the licensed quarter*, a role launched by the first Tōjūrō. An exquisitely refined print by Shunsen shows Nakamura Ganjirō I (1860–1935) as Sakata Tōjūrō in the play *Tōjūrō's love* (see pages 36 and 72). Although Ganjirō I did not come from a kabuki family, his talent gained him a dedicated following. There was considerable rivalry between Ganjirō I and Kataoka Nizaemon XI, with Nizaemon leaving Tokyo whenever Ganjirō was in town. His son Nakamura Ganjirō II (1902–83) also graced the stage but is best known as a screen actor, starring in 49 films including as a kabuki actor in *Floating weeds* (1959).

Like the generations of actors, fans and audiences also play an essential role in kabuki drama. Writing about the bustling and noisy kabuki audiences of the early 1920s, Zoë Kincaid describes old men smoking, grandmothers drinking tea, children eating and babies being nursed while the play is discussed over sake. Of the 'preening' geisha, she wrote: 'They form an interesting element of the audience, smoking, chatting, weeping over the play, and making up with powder puff to obliterate the traces of tears'.[5] Kincaid's account also describes ardent fans, including wrestlers and firefighters, attending in groups in support of favourite actors. The first kabuki fan clubs were established in the late-seventeenth century and fortified in the eighteenth century. They have since played a significant part in supporting and promoting the actors and theatres. Osaka, Kyoto and Tokyo fans all have their own styles, with Osaka known for particularly elaborate clapping.[6]

Fans are performers too, shouting enthusiastic and sometimes jeering comments as well as calling out the *yagō* of the actors. *Yagō* denote the family or guild to which an actor belongs, and always end in *–ya*.[7] For instance Naritaya

is the *yagō* of the Ichikawa Danjūrō family, a title chosen in honour of the Narita temple where the first Ichikawa Danjūrō had his prayers for a successor answered. In the mid-eighteenth century, fan club members wore headdresses embroidered with their club's crest and black kimono with white sashes. It later became popular for fans to wear ornate garments that they change throughout the play, like the actors onstage. With club members seated in the front row, these transformations provide entertainment for the actors as well as the audience.[8]

Kabuki's allure reaches into the lives and hearts of audiences, who follow their actor heroes from infancy to death—as increasingly prestigious names are earned or scandal results in downfall. Long family lines, such as the Ichikawa Danjūrō and Kataoka Nizaemon dynasties, are kabuki royalty. The original subscribers to Shunsen's portraits were almost certainly engaged equally with the private lives of the actors as with their performances on stage.

Notes

1 Zoë Kincaid, *Kabuki: the popular stage of Japan*, Macmillan, London, 1925, p vi. The author is indebted to Kincaid's work. Where not otherwise acknowledged, information presented in this essay is drawn from *Kabuki: the popular stage of Japan*.

2 James Brandon (ed), *The Cambridge guide to Asian theatre*, Cambridge University Press, Cambridge, 1993, pp 162–3.

3 Brandon, pp 163–4.

4 C Andrew Gerstle, *Kabuki heroes on the Osaka stage 1780–1830*, The British Museum Press, London, 2005, p 13.

5 Kincaid, pp 14–15.

6 Matsudaira Susumu, 'Hiiki renchū (theatre fan clubs) in Osaka in the early nineteenth century' in Samuel L Leiter (ed), *A kabuki reader: history and performance* ME Sharpe, New York, 2002, pp 113–4.

7 Gerstle, p 19. For a vibrant description of the calling out of *yagō* see 'Kabuki', in Alex Kerr, *Lost Japan*, Lonely Planet Publications, Melbourne, 1996.

8 Matsudaira, p 115.

(opposite) **Toyohara Kunichika** (1835–1900) *Board for Sugoroku* (traditional Japanese game) featuring famous kabuki actors and roles 1880
woodblock print; ink and colour on paper, 70.0 x 69.0 cm
National Library of Australia, Canberra

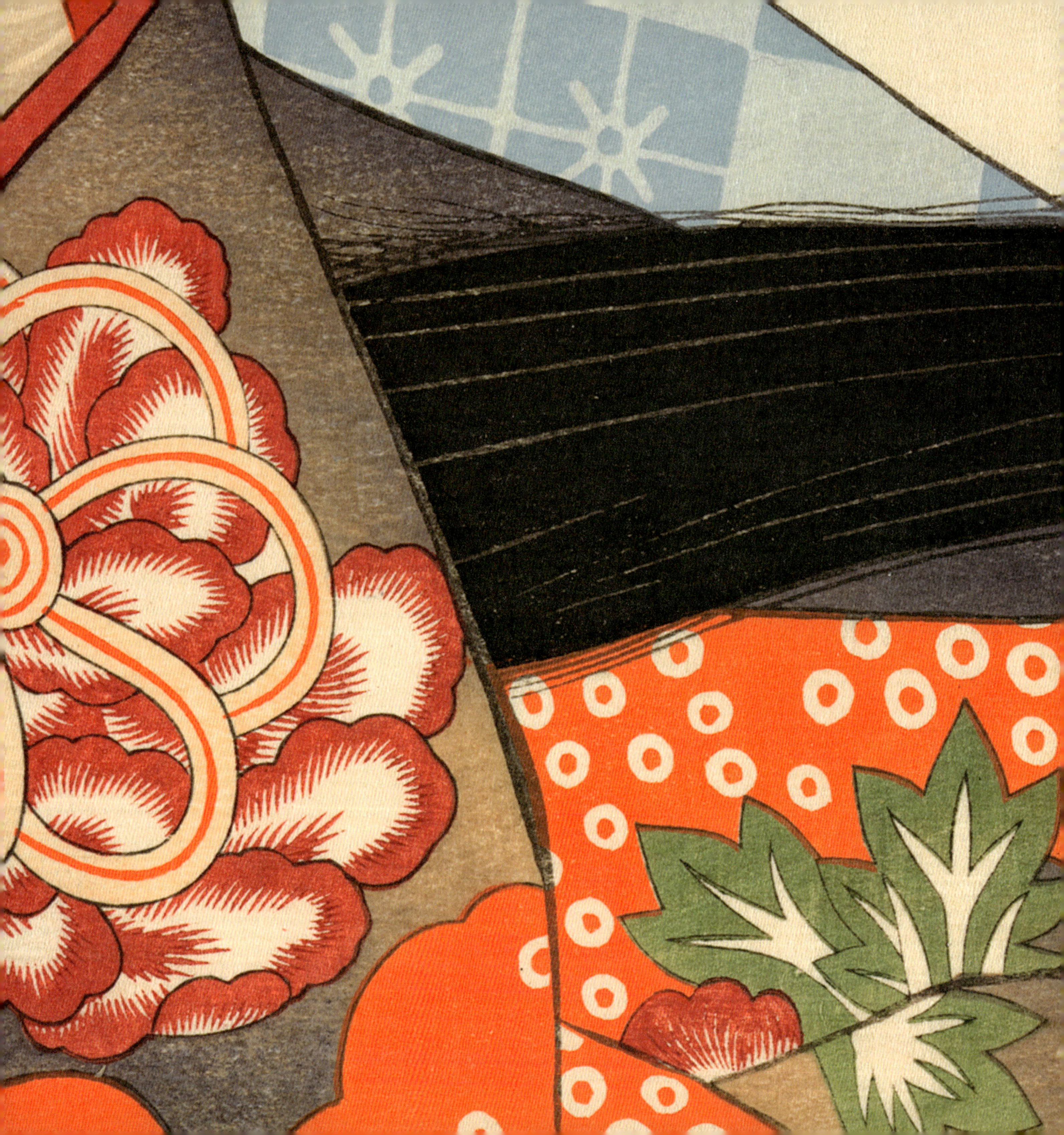

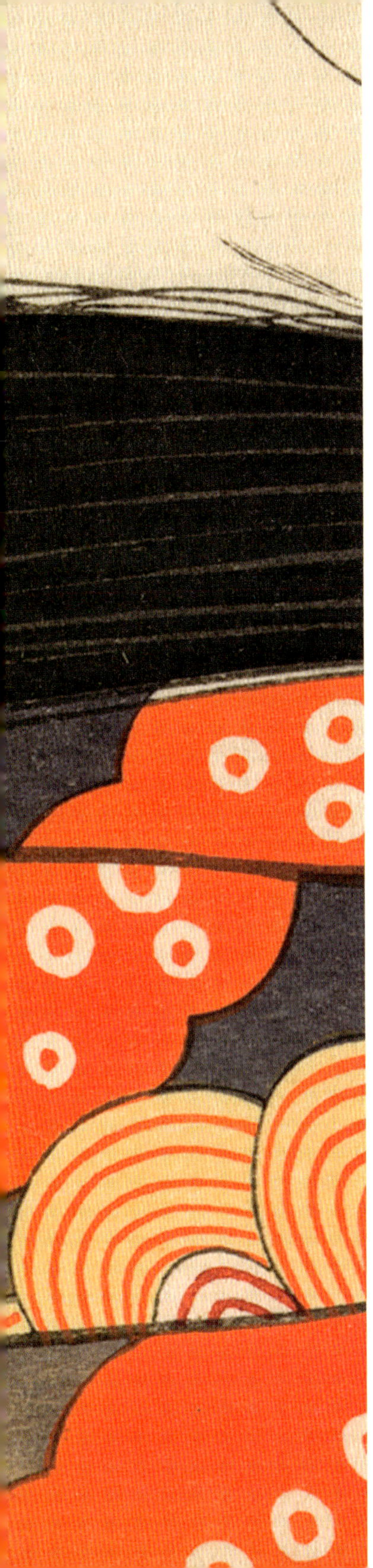

KABUKI COSTUMES: ENDURING SYMBOLS

Robyn Maxwell

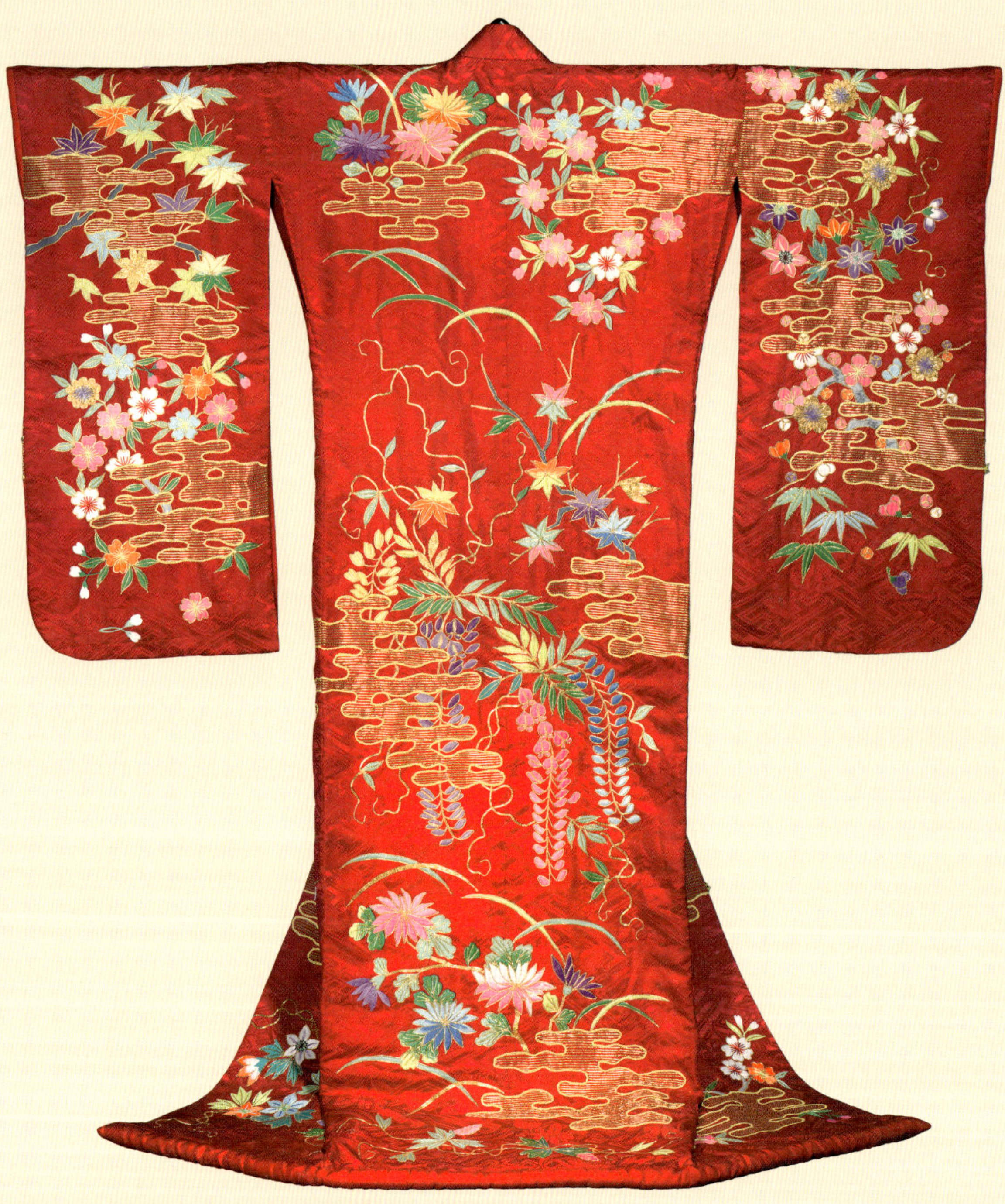

Fabulous costume and arresting makeup are essential to the glamour of kabuki. Even the most illustrious actors need the façade of fabric, grease paint and wigs to develop their characters, not least the *onnagata* (female-role actors) whose appearance is crucial in persuading audiences of their femininity. Behind the scenes are teams of wardrobe managers, costumiers and dressers who prepare and perfect the costumes and wigs for greatest impact. Shunsen's prints of the 1920s and 30s faithfully record and glorify the costume of leading actors during an era of innovation and consolidation—his eye for detail extended to the folds and fabrics of the robes and the precise execution of makeup. The postwar period has seen the transformation of kabuki from a form of popular entertainment into a codified theatre. At the same time, the costume styles illustrated by Shunsen have also been codified; twenty-first century audiences admire and anticipate essentially the same garments that thrilled audiences decades earlier.

The origins of many kabuki costumes can be traced back to the nineteenth century and the splendour and decadence of the late Edo period (1615–1868). Kabuki was an integral part of the 'floating world' of Edo (Tokyo). The close association between the theatre and the urban pleasure quarters transmitted the increasingly flamboyant dress of wealthy townspeople onto the kabuki stage. Prostitutes, courtesans and mistresses dominate the *onnagata* repertoire, providing rich material for the actors' robes. Mirroring the *bijin* beautiful women depicted in eighteenth and nineteenth-century woodcuts, *onnagata* appear on stage in a succession of glamorous kimono, the patterns, colours and sumptuousness of which often bely the characters' low rank and vulnerability in the social order, and indeed symbolically flout

the sumptuary laws that applied to dress and social rank in the Edo period. By contrast, noble characters may appear in elegant dark silk robes decorated only with their family's crest.

The flamboyant nineteenth-century *furisode* kimono, originally reserved for young maidens but also very fashionable with women of the pleasure quarters, remains a popular style in kabuki. Adept manipulation of the extraordinarily long *furisode* sleeves is a captivating element of tragic performances by great *onnagata* actors, while the heavily padded hem of the *furisode* allows the actors to glide gracefully across the stage. Shunsen captures this style of robe worn by both Bandō Shūchō III and Nakamura Shikaku II in the role of Shizuka, the hero's mistress in *Yoshitsune and the thousand cherry trees*. The full impact of an ornate *furisode* is seen in the artist's image of Nakamura Jakuemon as Yaoya (see page 122).

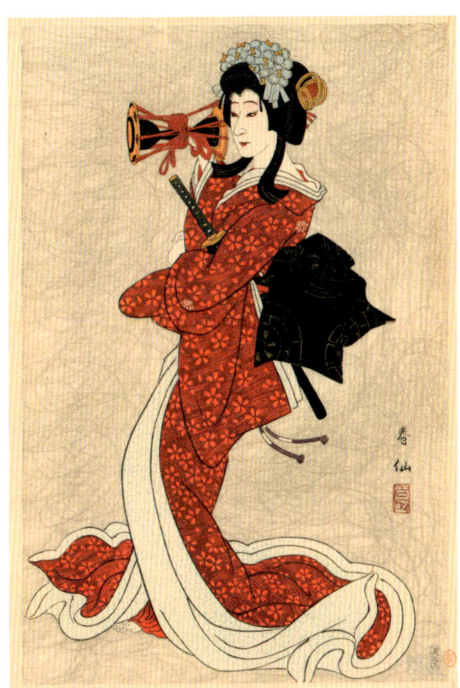

(opposite) **Shōchiku Costume Company** *Kabuki robe for Princess Yaegaki in 'Japan's twenty-four paragons of filial piety'* c 2000
silk damask, gold thread; embroidery, laid couching, 213.0 x 169.0 cm
National Gallery of Australia, Canberra, Pauline and John Gandel Fund, 2011

(left) **Natori Shunsen** *Bandō Shūchō III as Shizuka Gozen in 'Yoshitsune and the thousand cherry trees'* 1925 (p 76)

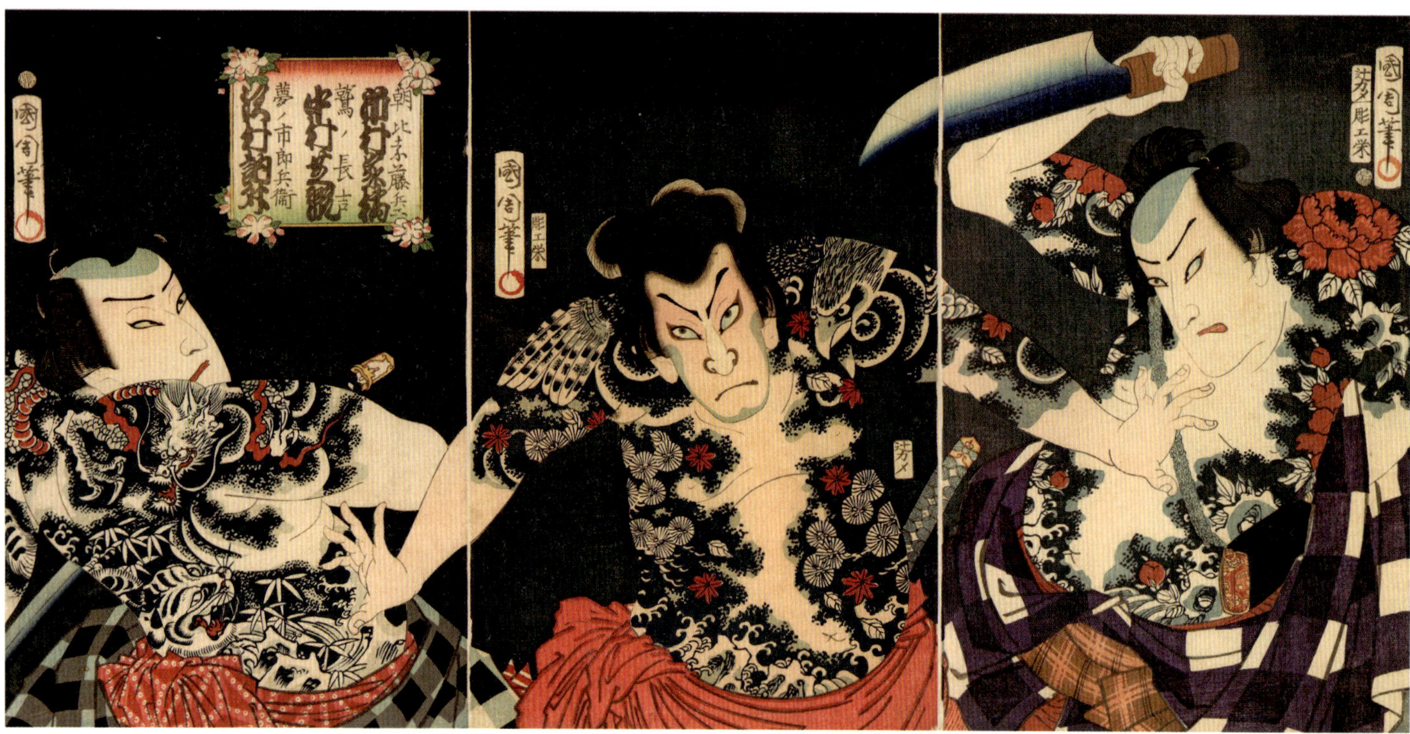

(above) **Toyohara Kunichika** (1835–1900) *Kabuki actors Ichimura Kakitsu IV as Asahina Tōbei, Nakamura Shikan IV as Washi no Chōkichi and Sawamura Tosshō II as Yume no Ichirobei IV* 1868
woodblock print; ink and colour on paper, 37.0 x75.0 cm
Art Gallery of South Australia, Adelaide, South Australian Government Grant, 2008

(opposite) **Shōchiku Costume Company** *Kabuki robe for Tadanobu Rihei in 'The glorious picture book of Aoto's exploits'* c 2000
silk; appliqué, rice-paste resist, hand painting, 168.0 x 151.0 cm
National Gallery of Australia, Canberra, Pauline and John Gandel Fund, 2011

Robes are often layered, as costume changes usually take place in full view of the audience. Stage dressers or minor actors may creep up behind the star as he holds a dramatic *mie* ('still') at a crucial moment in a powerful scene, and remove the outer garment to reveal a new and often more eye-catching robe. For some 'red princess' *akahime* roles, however, the costume comprises two almost identical red damask garments. Both are richly embroidered in silk and gold threads with plant motifs—wisteria, plum blossom, chrysanthemums, clematis, blades of grass, maple leaves or bamboo shoots—in a design held together by a golden grid-like pattern of stylised mist or winding streams. The inner robe is left plain where an elaborate obi sash would be worn, while the *uchikake* outer robe that covers both robe and obi is embellished with opulent embroidery. (Actors often retain obi from their costumes, especially fragments of old sashes, as talismanic mementos.)

Brilliant robes are not restricted to female roles in kabuki: ankle-length kimonos with short sleeves are also worn by low-ranked urban 'street knight' characters. In the tragicomedy *The glorious picture book of Aoto's exploits*, five criminals go down to the river at cherry blossom time, where they tell their life tales in colourful kimono and *geta* sandals, armed with parasols emblazoned with the character 'bandit'. In late Edo-period prints, the elaborate figurative tattoos sported by many actors are prominently displayed in portrayals of this scene. However, by the late-nineteenth century, with Meiji-era (1868–1912) modernisation well underway, tattoos were formally banned and body art had largely disappeared from the urban social scene.

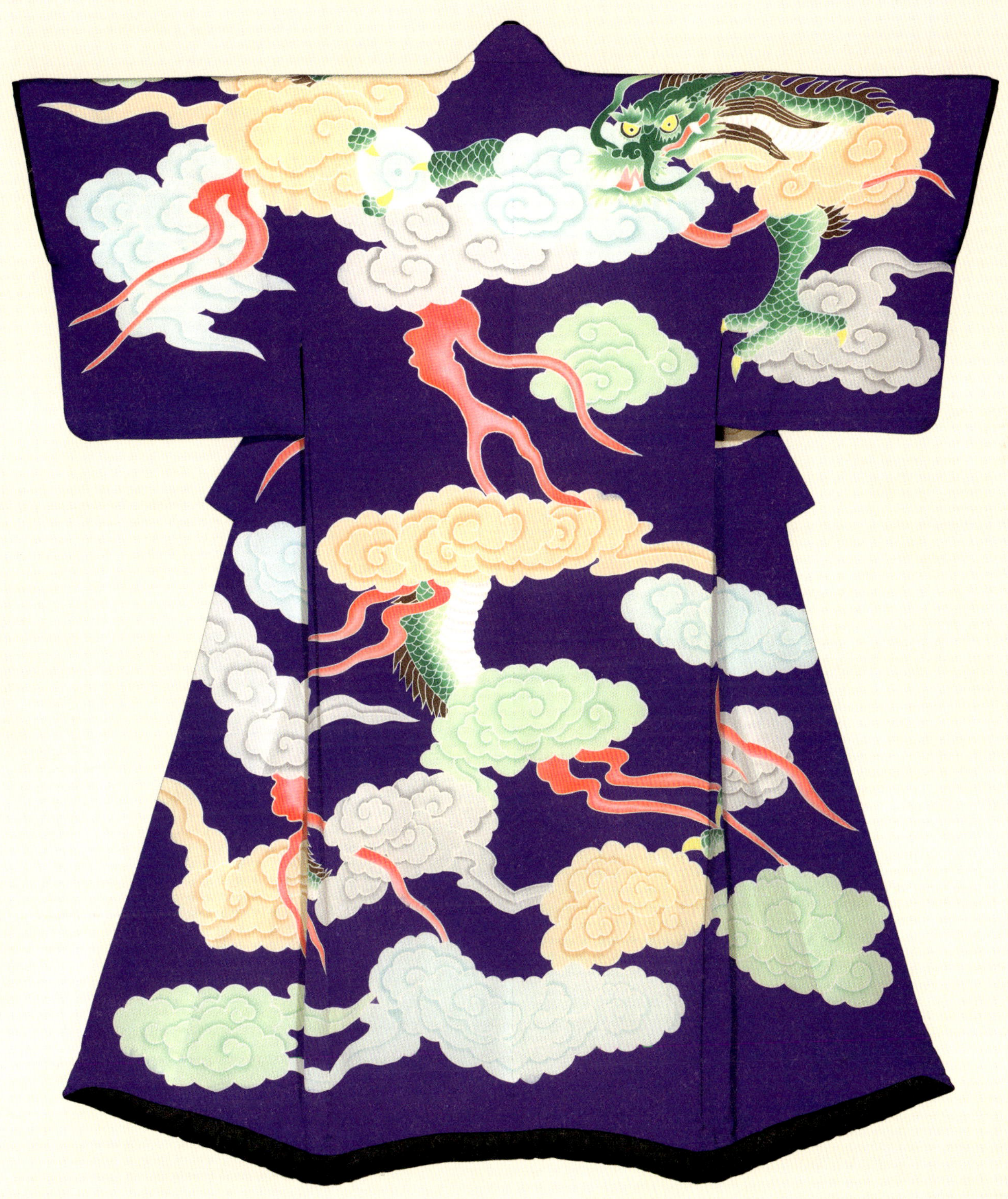

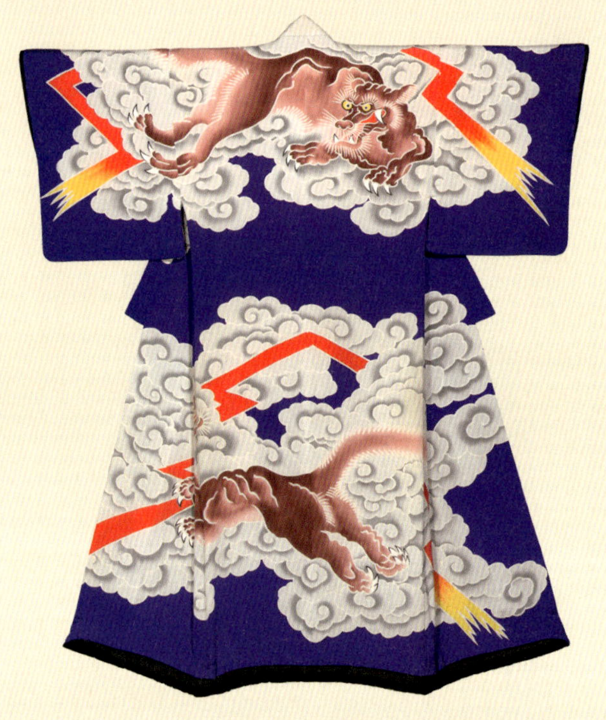

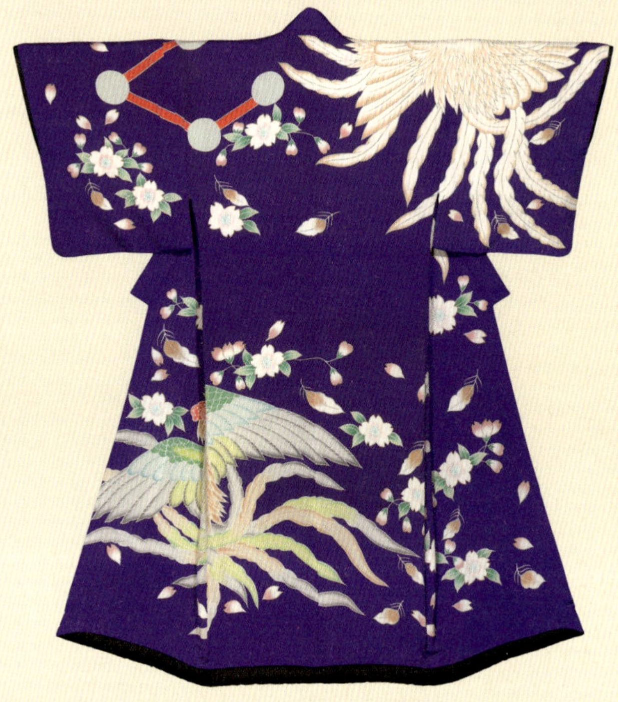

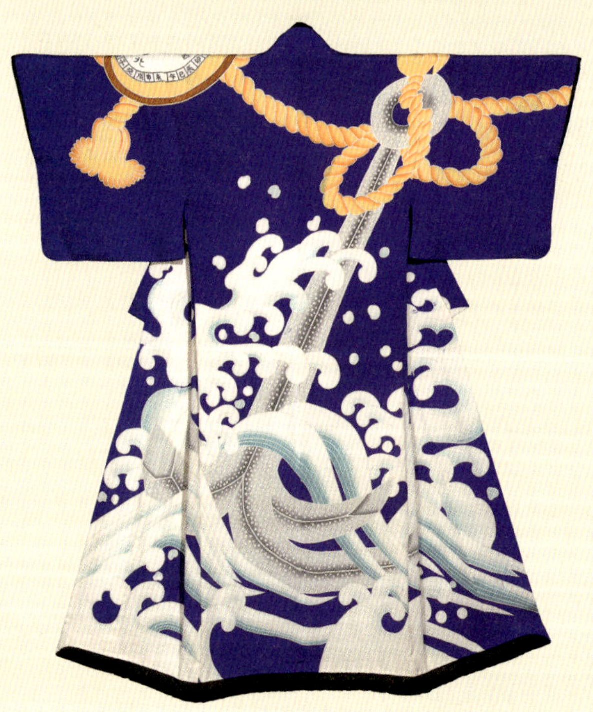

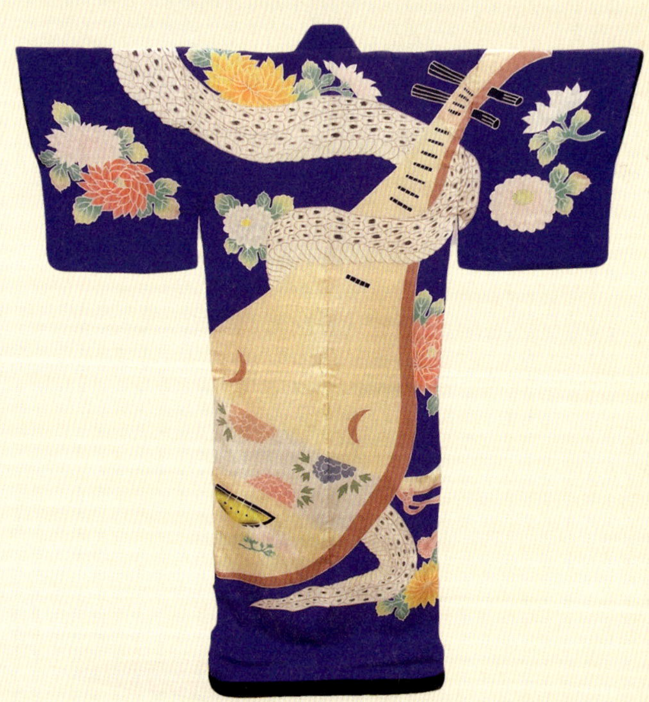

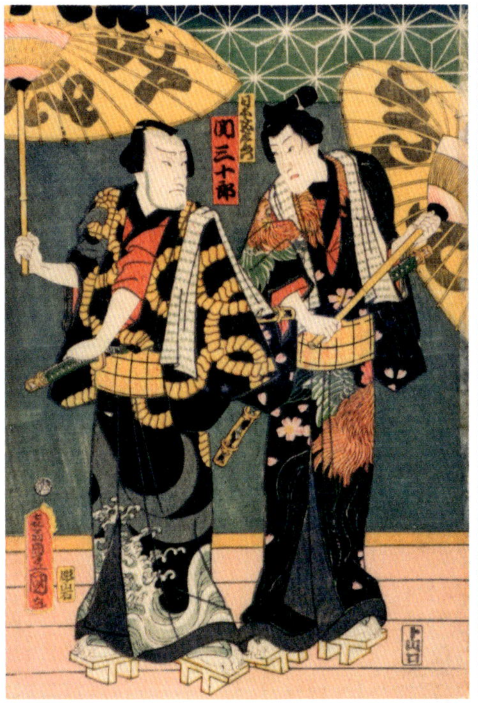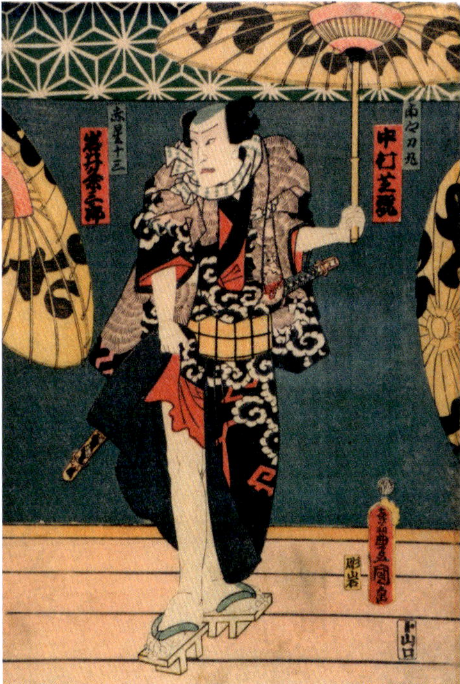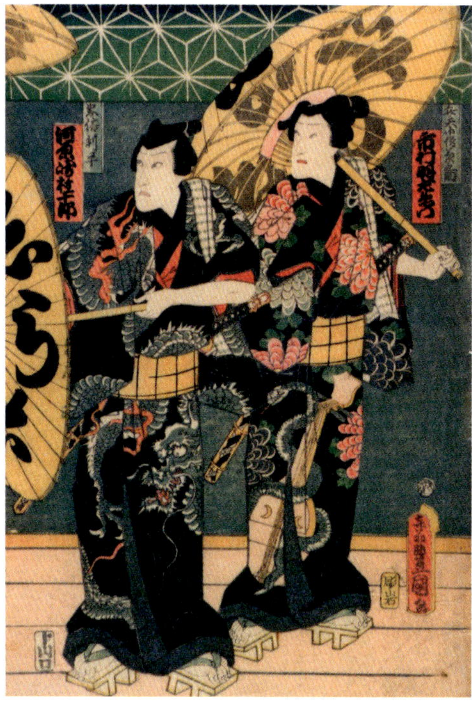

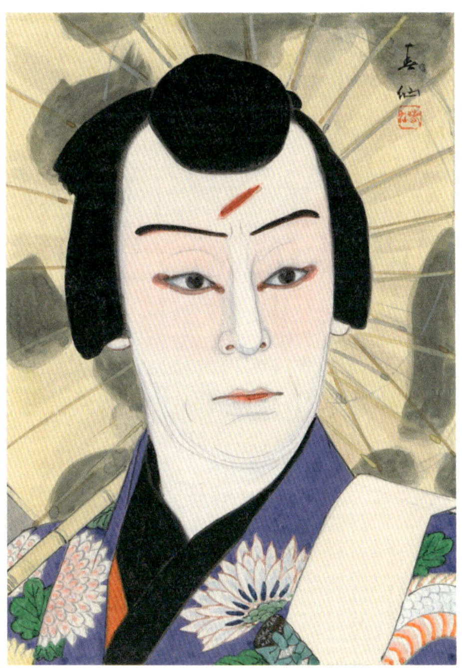

Yet body decoration remained on the kabuki stage and was reinforced as a symbol of the city's brutal elements. Tough urban characters wore tight-fitting vests and leggings decorated with tattoo motifs, which they flashed into view by rolling up their sleeves or kicking up their heels for action. Symbols of the rough men of the cities were also transferred to their kimono. In early-twentieth century productions of *The glorious picture book of Aoto's exploits*, for example, the bandits promenade in robes emblazoned with the same motifs their tattooed predecessors had displayed on their bodies: the dragon, lion dog (or wolf), snake and lute, rooster (or phoenix), rope and anchor (and compass) amid clouds, waves, thunder and lightning. Each of the five bandits came to be identified with a particular motif. Ironically, in feudal times such motifs were associated with powerful rulers. Some also have classical

(above) **Utagawa Kunisada** (1786–1865) *Kabuki actors as the five bandits in 'The glorious picture book of Aotos's exploits'* 1862
woodblock print; ink and colour on paper, 37.4 x 76.0 cm
Tsubouchi Memorial Theatre Museum of Waseda University, Tokyo

(left) **Natori Shunsen** *Ichimura Uzaemon XVI as Benten Kozō in 'The glorious picture book of Aoto's exploits'* 1950 (p 136)

(opposite clockwise from top left) **Shōchiku Costume Company** *Kabuki robes for Nangō Rikimaru, Akaboshi Jūzaburō, Benten Kozō and Nippon Daemon in 'The glorious picture book of Aoto's exploits'* c 2000
silk; appliqué, rice-paste resist, hand painting, 168.0 x 151.0 cm each
National Gallery of Australia, Canberra, Pauline and John Gandel Fund, 2011

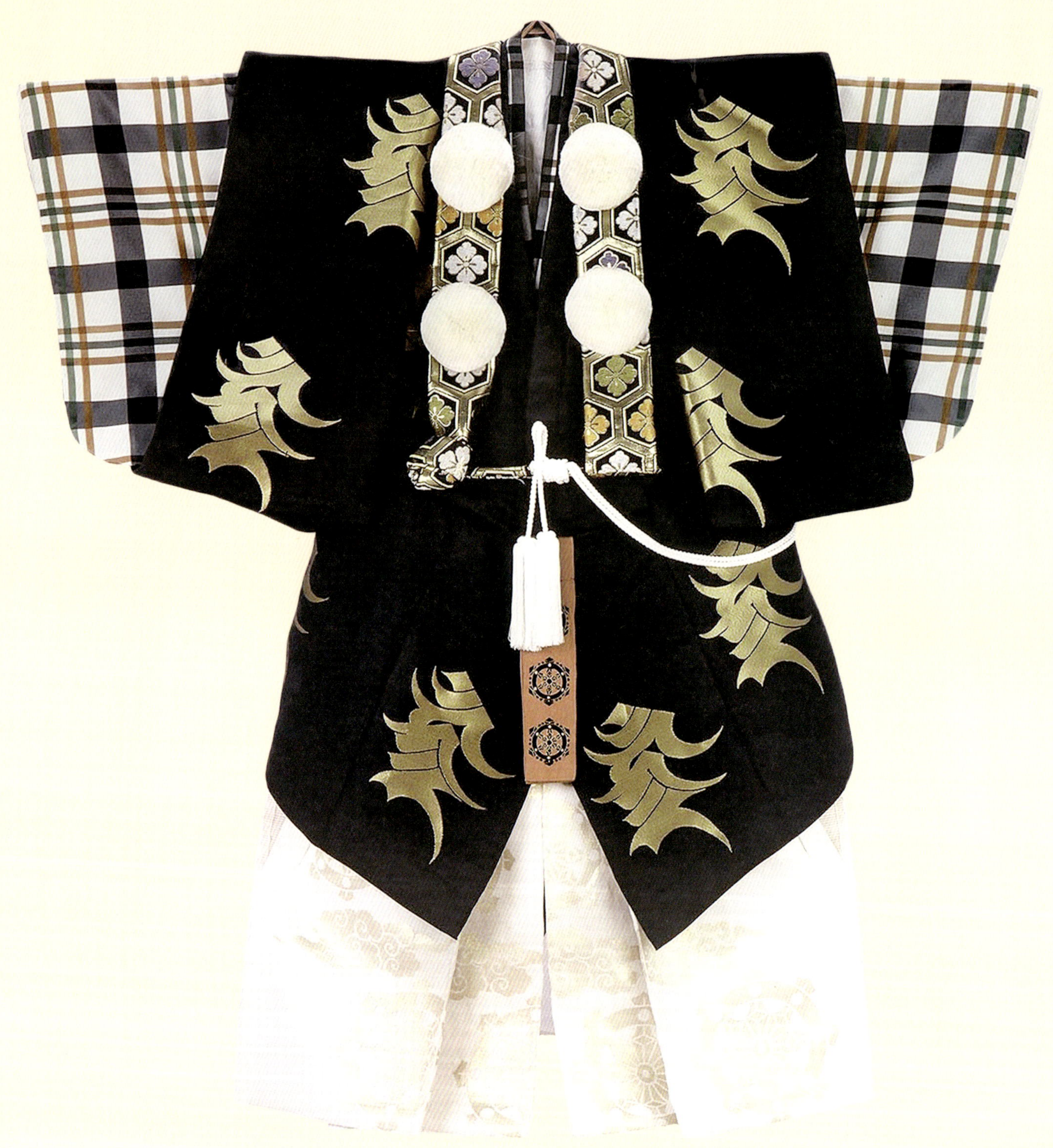

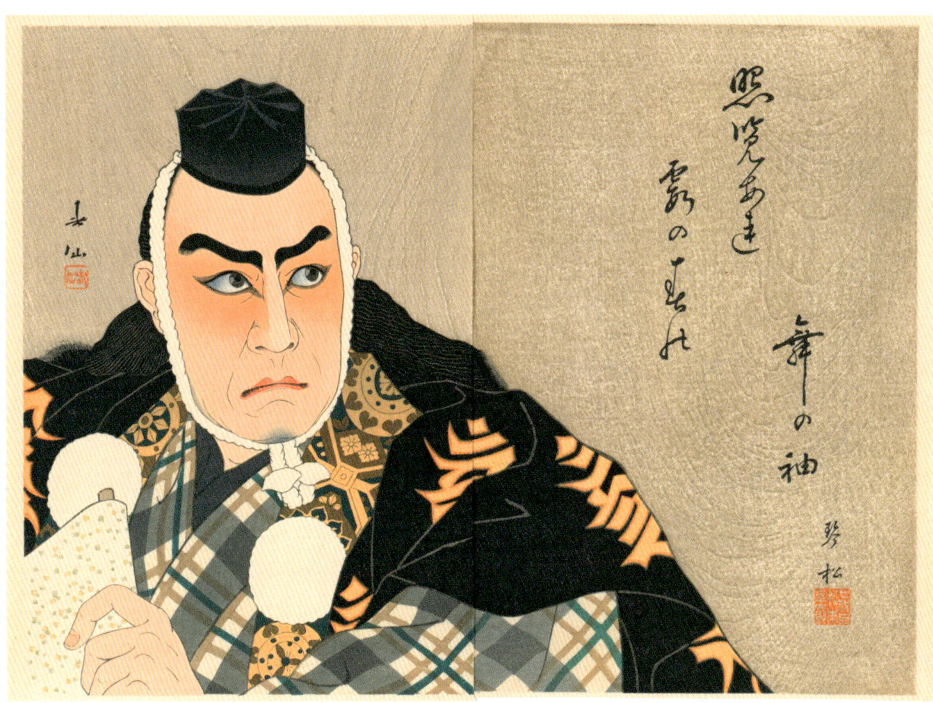

(left) **Natori Shunsen** *Matsumoto Kōshirō VII as Benkei in 'The subscription list'* 1935 (p 130)

(below) Matsumoto Koshiro VII as Musashibō Benkei in 'The subscription list', published in Zöe Kinkaid, *Kabuki: the popular theatre of Japan*, 1925

(opposite) **Shōchiku Costume Company** *Kabuki costume for Benkei in 'The subscription list'* c 2000
silk and gold thread brocade; embroidery, laid couching, pompons, plaited cord, tassels, twill woven plaid,
176.0 x 161.5 cm
National Gallery of Australia, Canberra,
Pauline and John Gandel Fund, 2011

religious allusions, such as the lute and white snake that were attributes of the Goddess of Music, Benten, and feature on the robe of the bandit Benten Kozō.

The late-nineteenth century gentrification of kabuki to present a flattering image of a modern yet quintessentially Japanese nation—a theatre respectable enough for the Emperor himself to attend—included government promotion of historical dramas. Their sustained appeal throughout the twentieth century saw major roles based on samurai-class figures. Such plays provided the opportunity to adopt the costume styles and designs of the aristocratic and centuries older *nō* theatre. One of the most impressive *nō*-inspired outfits is worn for the role of Benkei, a renegade samurai. Shunsen catches the character at the moment he must prove himself a Buddhist monk. By the 1920s Benkei's outfit had been refined to what it is today—

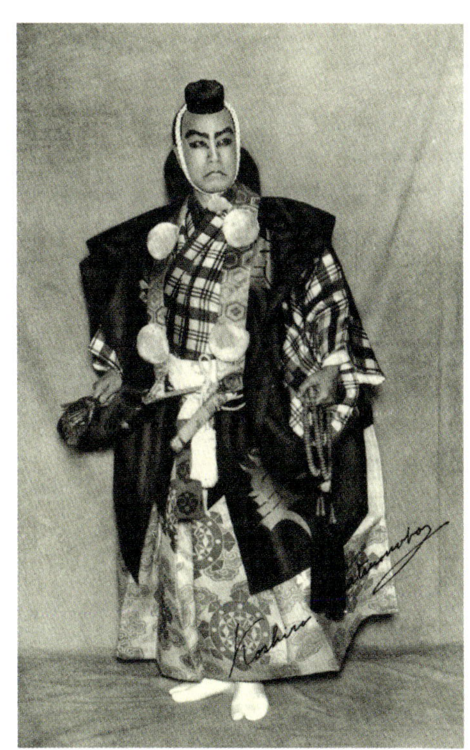

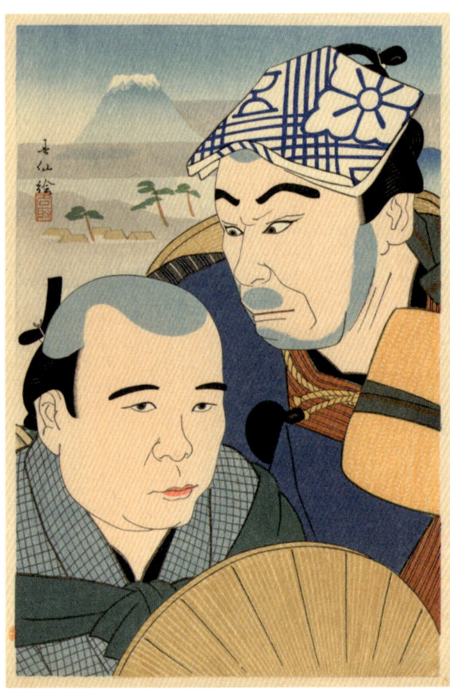

the voluminous *ōguchi* (wide-legged) form of *nō*'s classical stiff, pleated *hakama* trousers, with auspicious Buddhist wheel and cloud motifs; a dark *happi* outer garment emblazoned with large gold stylised kanji characters; and a checked twill under-robe. The accoutrements of pompon, brocade and tasselled neckpiece and small Buddhist cap are also essential elements of the Benkei costume in the modern kabuki era.

Benkei's magnificent clothing is largely created from gold brocade *kinran*, a classical aristocratic handwoven fabric (from the Meiji period the rich brocades for kabuki outfits were woven on modern jacquard looms). Well-to-do commoners wore silk *chirimen* crepe and *rinzu* satin, embellished with bold hand-painted *yūzen* (paste-resist dyed) designs as well as with silk embroidery and gold. In contrast, kabuki's humble origins can still be recognised in the outfits of characters of lowly birth. Indigo-dyed homespuns and striped and checked fabrics in drab hues are the substance of the robes and short jackets of both villagers and common townspeople, of petty rogues, honest magistrates and lowly retainers. The unassuming garb of farmers and fishermen also provides an effective disguise for an itinerant well-born hero. For kabuki's urban audiences in the 1920s, such styles were fast becoming historical yet the message was and still is well understood. Shunsen's portraits of the two bumbling travellers in the picaresque adventure *Shank's mare,* and Bandō Mitsugorō as Farmer Manbei, are good examples of this type of clothing.

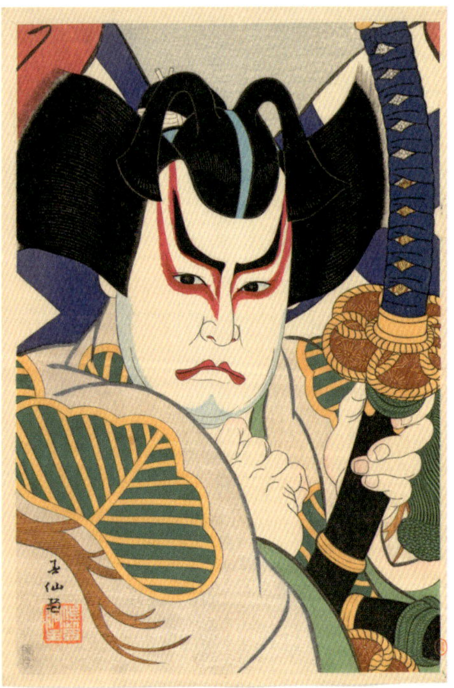

Crucial to the development of kabuki costume in the twentieth century has been the growth of the Shōchiku Costume Company, established by the Shōchiku Theatre Company (founded in 1895). Renting out costumes to the burgeoning

number of kabuki troupes, Shōchiku gradually expanded to control the repertoire and details of kabuki costume throughout Japan. Into the twenty-first century, kabuki costume is still tightly controlled by the company and the superb costumes recorded by Shunsen continue to symbolise familiar characters and dramas. Moreover, specific character outfits can often be identified with the particular actor dynasties specialising in the role. The costumes of the great stars of the 1920s are largely unchanged today except for personal, often superstitious, touches contributed by actors. Nevertheless, the possibility appears to remain open for a luminary to collaborate with a costumier in enacting more radical change in costume or fabric design.

Shunsen's lavish portraits are remarkable records of a period of rapid transformation in kabuki theatre. They not only illustrate the wide range of kabuki characters and costumes, but also capture the moment of invention that preceded kabuki's elevation into a revered national art form.

(above left) **Natori Shunsen** *Soganoya Gorō and Choroku as Tochimen Yajirobei and Kitahachi in 'Shank's mare'* 1928 (p 116)

(below left) **Natori Shunsen** *Bandō Hikosaburō VI as Matsuōmaru in 'Sugawara's secrets of calligraphy'* 1928 (p 62)

(opposite) **Natori Shunsen** *Ichimura Uzaemon XV as Kataoka Naojirō in 'The faithful samurai'* 1925 (detail) (p 106)

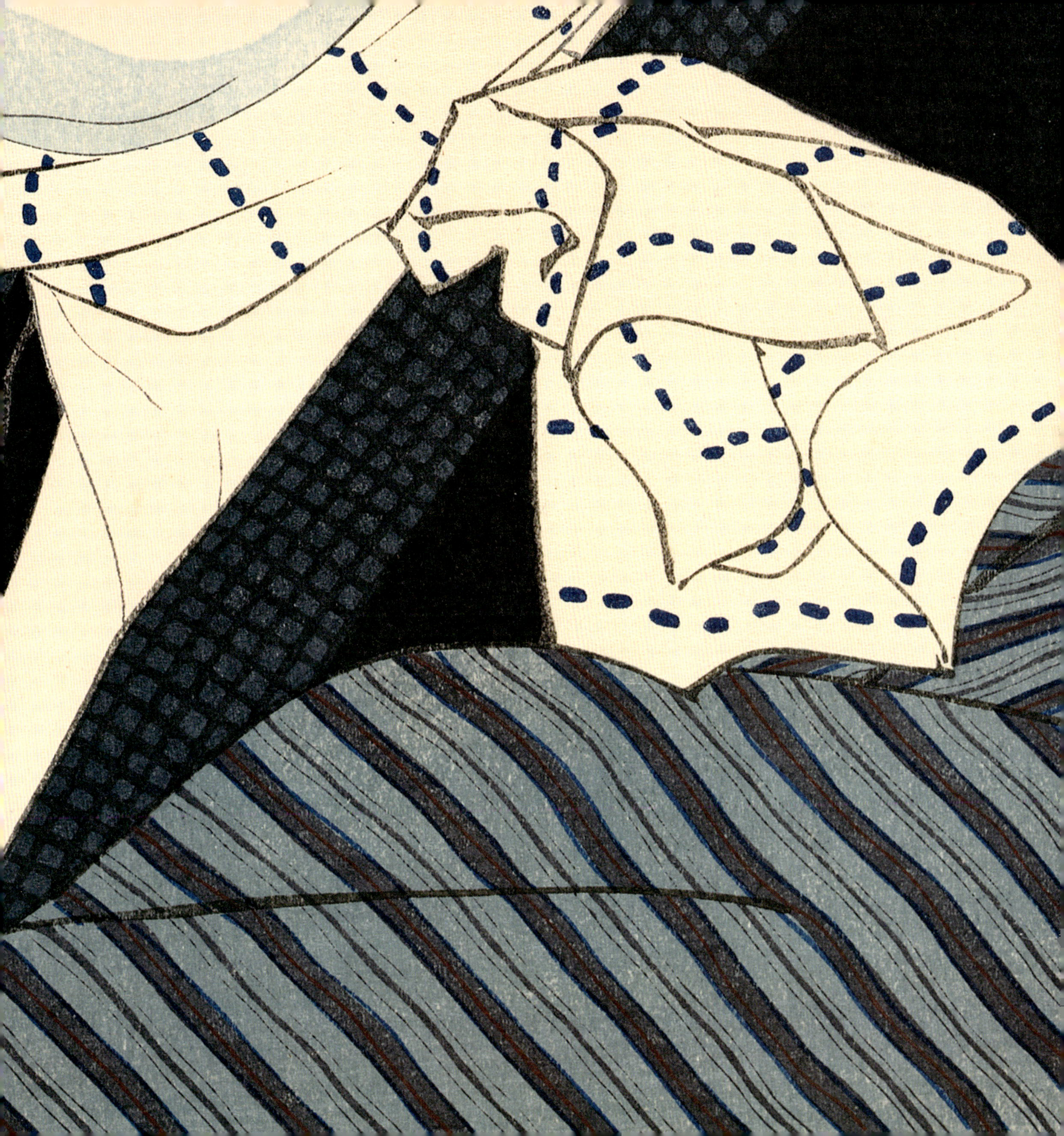

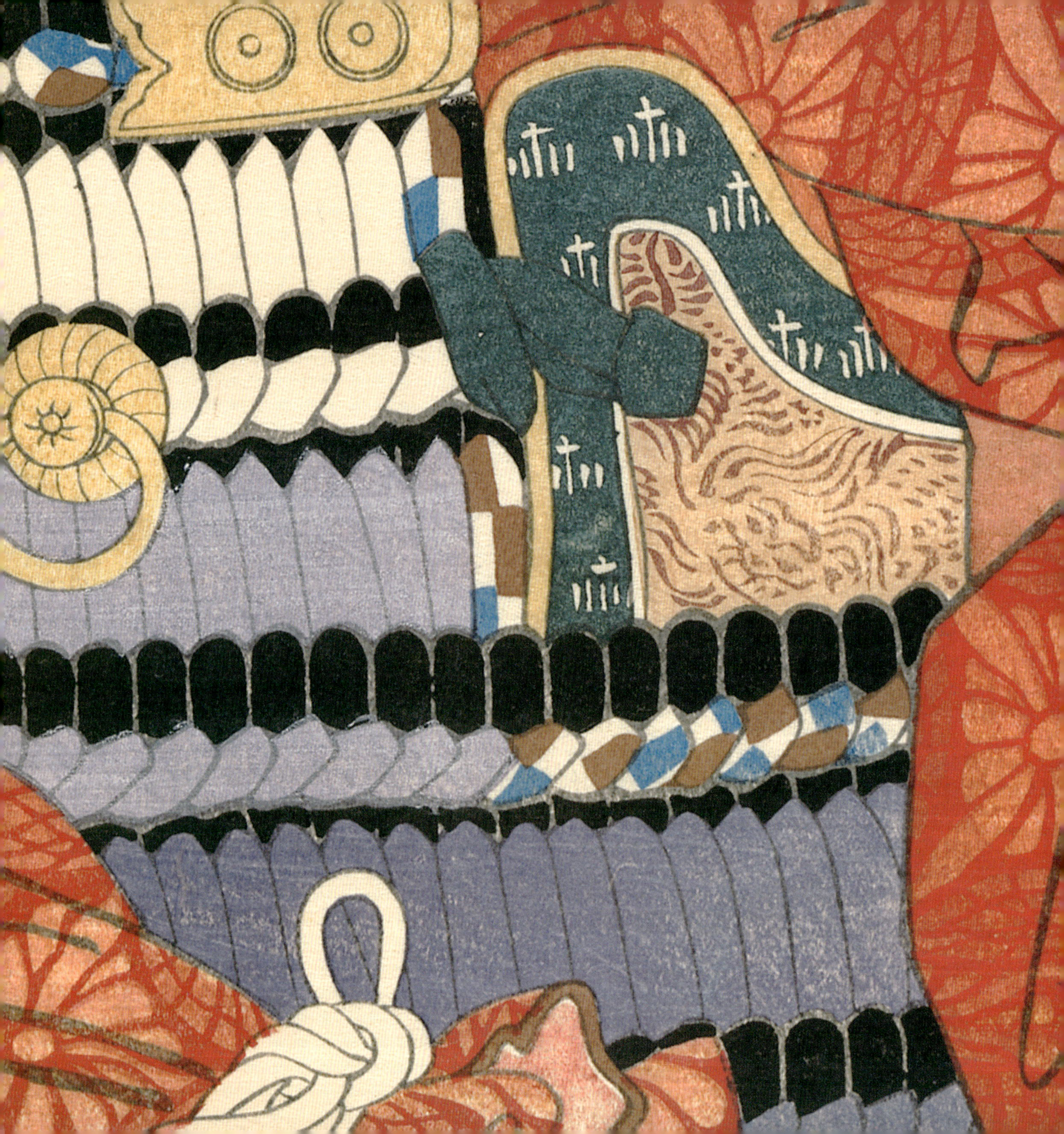

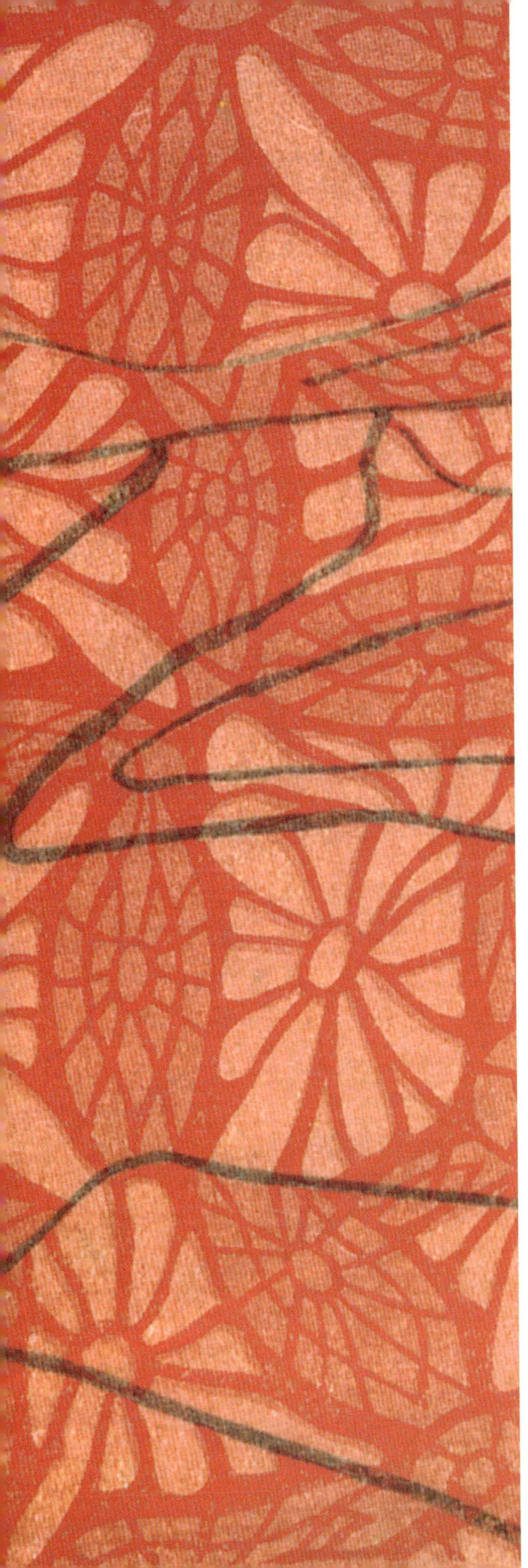

NATORI SHUNSEN'S IMPRESSIONS: PLAYS, PRINTS, ACTORS

Made for kabuki fans, Natori Shunsen's famous prints from the 1920s and early 1930s capture prominent actors of the day performing their most famous roles. The following synopses outline the plots of the plays from which the images derive and the specific scenes they depict. Kabuki audiences are usually very familiar with the characters, who have complex life stories and may appear in a number of interrelated plays as well as in history, literature, legends and popular culture. In order to convey Shunsen's great knowledge of kabuki and the techniques of its actors, relevant background information to each character is provided. The authors are indebted to the various translations of the plays, particularly the works of James Brandon and Samuel L Leiter. Other sources are listed in the bibliography.

For clarity, full character names are used and nicknames explained. Names for characters, actors and playwrights are in Japanese order, with family name first. To avoid confusion, actors—who usually change their names throughout their careers—are referred to by the name held at the time the print was made. Common English translations of play titles are accompanied by phonetically inscribed Japanese. The prints were originally released with sheets bearing the artist's title—generally the actor's name, along with colloquial or shortened names for the characters and plays—and the English transcriptions of these appear in square brackets following the series title for each print.

The banner of rebellion (Toki wa ima kikyō no hataage)

written by Tsuruya Nanboku IV, first kabuki performance in 1808

Commonly known as *Mitsuhide and the horse trough* (Badarai no Mitsuhide), *The banner of rebellion* examines the complexities of samurai loyalty. A classic history kabuki (*jidaimono*), it dramatises Mitsuhide's betrayal of Oda Nobunaga, the powerful sixteenth-century warlord who laid the foundations for the unification of Japan. To comply with government censorship, in the play the historical Oda Nobunaga is renamed Oda Harunaga and Akechi Mitsuhide is Takechi Mitsuhide.

The play begins with Oda Harunaga ordering his loyal retainer Mitsuhide to organise a banquet. Suspicious of Mitsuhide's ambition, Harunaga finds fault with the preparations. Mitsuhide is beaten on the forehead and arrested.

Mitsuhide later protests his punishment at Kyoto's Honnō Temple. Ruthless and paranoid, Harunaga humiliates Mitsuhide by making him drink from a horse-washing trough and confiscating his land and status. Mitsuhide remains emotionless until Harunaga presents him with a box of hair that Mitsuhide's wife had been forced to sell when Mitsuhide was a masterless samurai. Mitsuhide menacingly taps the box as he exits, a sign that he will betray Harunaga.

In the final scene, Mitsuhide is ordered to relinquish his title and property. Samurai who fail their lords are obliged to commit *seppuku*, suicide by disembowelment. Mitsuhide appears in a white death robe, but instead of killing himself he spontaneously murders Harunaga's messenger, and is set to overthrow Harunaga.

The print

The first of the *Collection of creative portraits by Shunsen* published by Watanabe Shōzaburō, the image depicts the Honnō Temple scene of *The banner of rebellion*. Nakamura Kichiemon famously imbued Mitsuhide, traditionally played as a merciless traitor, with heroism, courage and pathos. Shunsen captures Mitsuhide as a man driven to rebellion. His threatening expression and characteristic villain's wig suggest menace, while the prominent scar on his brow recalls his unjust treatment.

Nakamura Kichiemon I (1886–1954)

Kichiemon, son of actor Nakamura Karoku III, was born in Tokyo. His mother's family owned a Tokyo theatre tea-shop. The actor debuted at age 11 and, unusually, never changed his name. Kichiemon quickly became a star, renowned for passionate portrayals of tragic heroes and villains in historical male roles. He was trained by the great Ichikawa Danjūrō IX at Tokyo's Kabuki Theatre, and later achieved enormous success in partnership with artistic rival Onoe Kikugorō VI at the Ichimura Theatre. Kichiemon joined the Shōchiku Theatre Company in 1921, but later formed his own troupe. He was the first living kabuki actor to receive the Japanese Order of Culture.

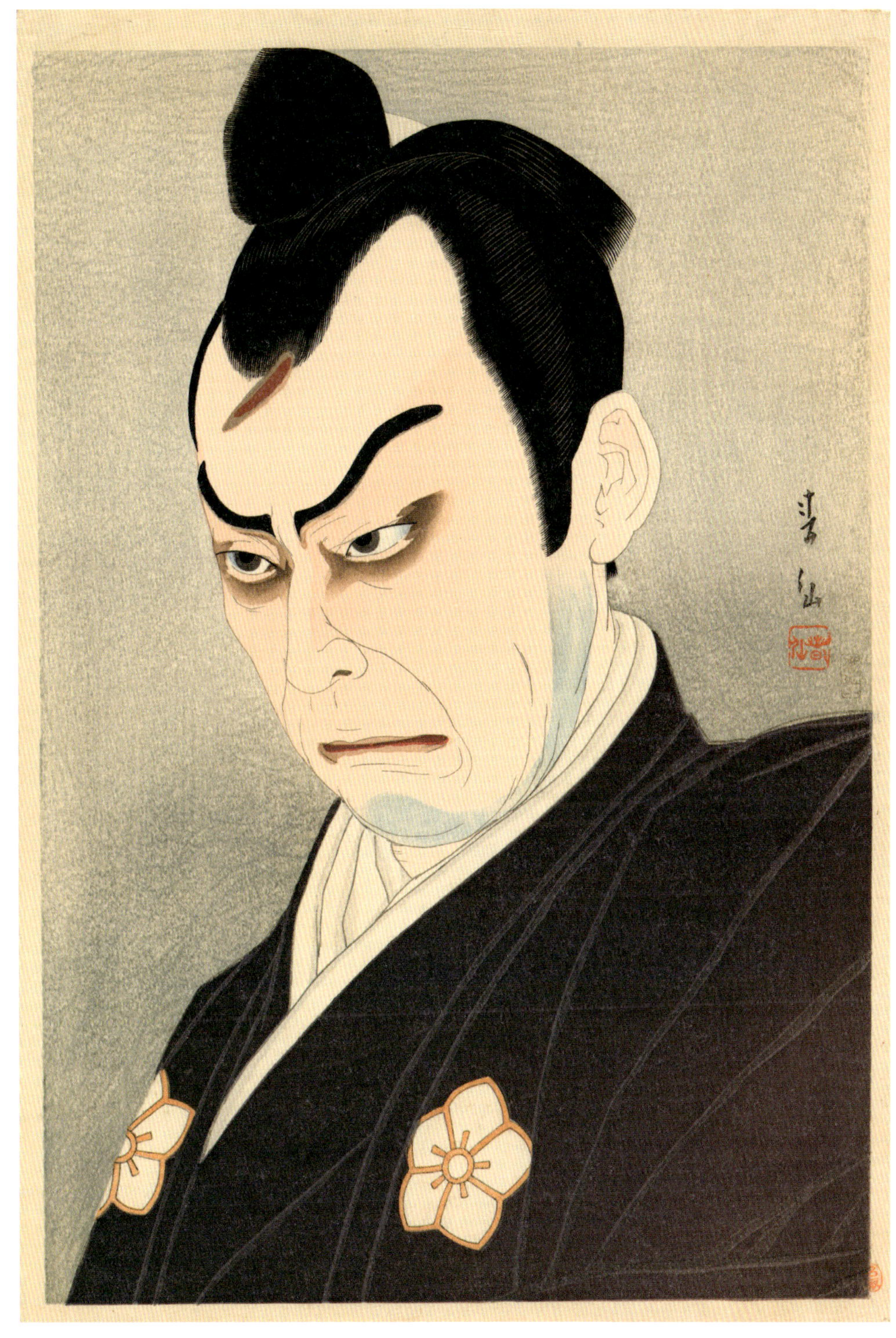

*Onoe Kikugorō VI as Adachi Motoemon in
'The revenge at Tengajaya'* 1925 from the series
Collection of creative portraits by Shunsen
[Onoe Kikugorō VI Tengajaya Motoemon]
woodblock print; ink and colour on paper
sheet: 40.2 x 27.7 cm, image: 37.9 x 25.9 cm
National Gallery of Australia, Canberra,
gift of Jennifer Gordon, 1998

The revenge at Tengajaya (Katakiuchi Tengajaya mura)

written by Nagawa Kamesuke, first kabuki
performance in 1781

Based on a seventeenth-century vendetta,
The revenge at Tengajaya was enthusiastically
appreciated for its gory and comic scenes.

Brothers Genjirō and Iori, with the help of their
servant Yasuke, are searching for Tōma, the
samurai who murdered their father. Another
servant, Yasuke's brother Adachi Motoemon, is
travelling separately to try and recover a lost
scroll painting, a valuable heirloom. Motoemon
arrives on the scene and recognises Tōma's
retainer, Udesuke. While Motoemon interrogates
Udesuke, Tōma creeps up behind him and
knocks him unconscious. Knowing Motoemon's
love of sake, Udesuke revives him with alcohol.
The brothers discover the staggering Motoemon
(who had been too inebriated to prevent their
father's murder), reeking of alcohol. They dismiss
and abandon him.

The action resumes with Motoemon, disguised
as a blind masseur, approaching Iori and
Genjirō's house. Motoemon overhears a former
brothel owner telling Genjirō that the missing
scroll painting has been found at a pawnshop.
The price is extravagant, so Iori's wife sells herself
into prostitution. Motoemon then executes
several outrageous acts of betrayal. He steals the
money raised by Iori's wife and, after a long drink
of sake, tries to murder Genjirō (temporarily
blind from illness) while he sleeps. Motoemon
then slays his own brother and wounds Iori.

The brothers are left destitute, and Iori is crippled
by tetanus. Genjirō, his blindness cured, sets out
to pursue Tōma. Motoemon and Tōma seize the
opportunity to ensure Iori endures a slow and
painful death. In the final act, Genjirō and his
supporters launch a surprise assault on Tōma,
murdering him at Tengajaya village. Pathetically,
the traitorous Motoemon begs for mercy, but is
also killed.

The print

This portrait depicts Onoe Kikugorō VI as arch
villain Adachi Motoemon in *The revenge at
Tengajaya*. Shunsen captures Motoemon at the
height of his treachery, brandishing a sword just
before he murders his former master, Iori.

Onoe Kikugorō VI (1885–1949)

Onoe Kikugorō VI was the son of Onoe Kikugorō
V, one of the greatest Meiji-era actors. He made
his first kabuki appearance as an infant. Kikugorō
VI's versatility became legendary when he
performed seven roles in a single play. During
the 1920s, he was the star of the Ichimura
Theatre and his prestige continued to grow
after the theatre was subsumed by the Shōchiku
Company. In 1945 he famously stated: 'If an air
raid destroys this theatre, I will have the play go
on in the open air. I will die nowhere else but on
stage'. Notoriously excessive, Kikugorō VI died
after a tempura party celebrating two strenuous
days of performance.

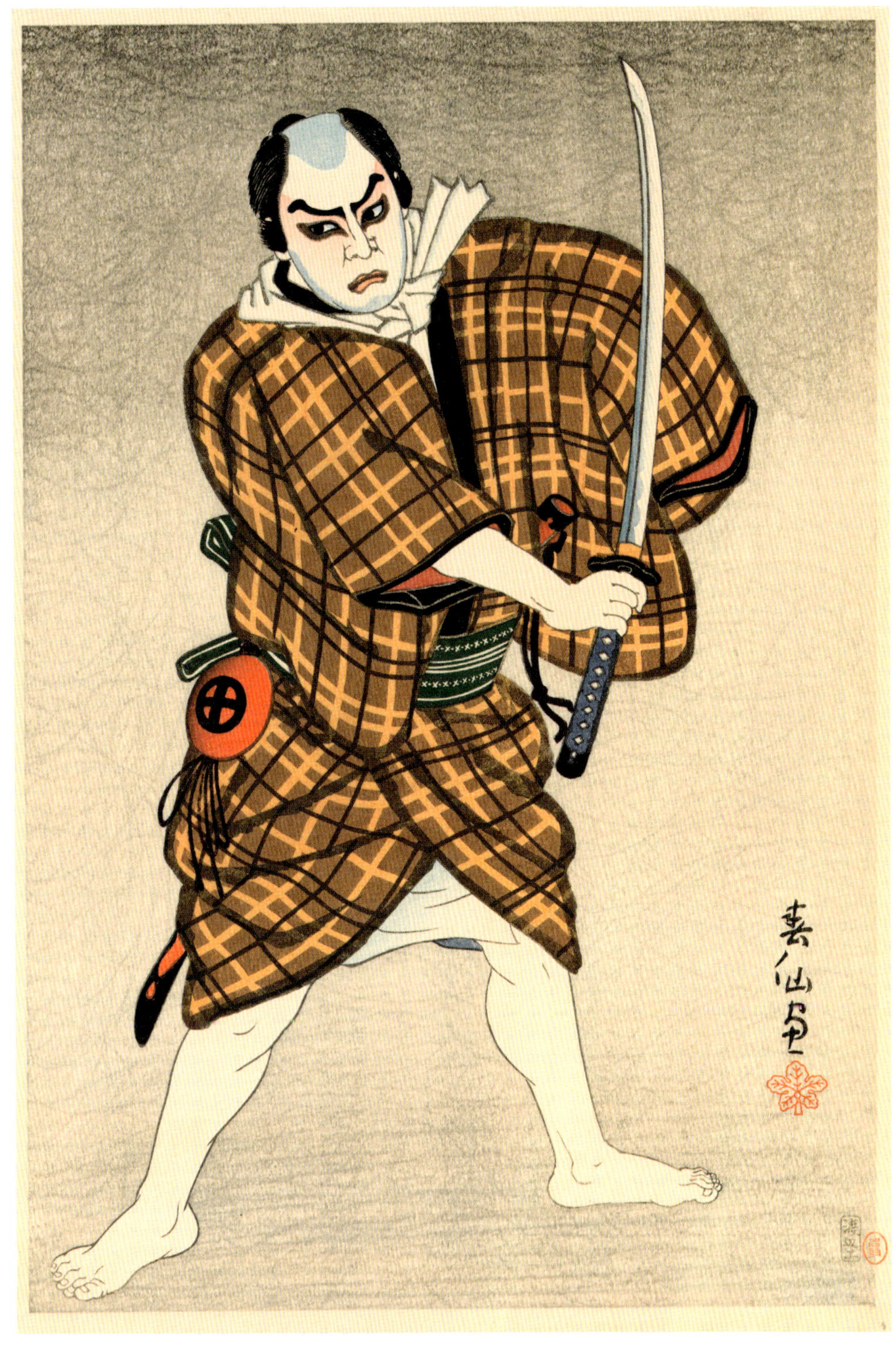

Ichikawa Udanji II as Sukune Tarō in 'Sugawara's secrets of calligraphy' 1928 from the series *Collection of creative portraits by Shunsen*
[Ichikawa Udanji II Dōmyōji no Sukune Tarō]
woodblock print; ink and colour on paper
sheet: 40.3 x 27.7 cm, image: 37.9 x 25.9 cm
National Gallery of Australia, Canberra,
gift of Jennifer Gordon, 1998

Bandō Hikosaburō VI as Matsuōmaru in 'Sugawara's secrets of calligraphy' 1928 from the series *Collection of creative portraits by Shunsen*
[Bandō Hikosaburō VI shajin Matsuōmaru]
woodblock print, embossing; ink, colour and mica on paper
sheet: 40.1 x 27.6 cm, image: 38.0 x 25.6 cm
National Gallery of Australia, Canberra,
gift of Jennifer Gordon, 1998

Matsumoto Kōshirō VII as Umeōmaru in 'Sugawara's secrets of calligraphy' 1926 from the series *Collection of creative portraits by Shunsen*
[Matsumoto Kōshirō VII Umeō]
woodblock print; ink and colour on paper
sheet: 40.6 x 27.4 cm, image: 38.2 x 25.9 cm
National Gallery of Australia, Canberra,
gift of Jennifer Gordon, 1998

Ōtani Tomoemon VI as Kan Shōjō (Sugawara Michizane) in 'Sugawara's secrets of calligraphy' 1927 from the series *Collection of creative portraits by Shunsen*
[Ōtani Tomoemon VI Ankyo no Kan Shōjō]
woodblock print; ink and colour on paper
sheet: 40.4 x 27.6 cm, image: 38.2 x 25.8 cm
National Gallery of Australia, Canberra,
purchased 2001

Sugawara's secrets of calligraphy (Sugawara denju tenarai kagami)

written by Takeda Izumo I, Miyoshi Shōraku, Namiki Senryū and Takeda Koizumo, first kabuki performance in 1746

Sugawara's secrets of calligraphy is an epic history play (*jidaimono*) written for the puppet theatre and quickly adapted for the kabuki stage. The plot was inspired by the historical figure Sugawara Michizane, a ninth-century politician, poet and calligrapher who was banished from the imperial court because of the intrigues of a political rival. Numerous mysterious events were attributed to his exile and, after his death, Sugawara Michizane was deified the God of Calligraphy. Typical of *jidaimono*, the complex plot interweaves history, legend and contemporary events in a story of betrayal and allegiance. The play features triplet characters (Umeōmaru, Sakuramaru and Matsuōmaru), a response to the sensational birth of triplets in Osaka around the time the drama was created.

In the play, Sugawara Michizane is known as Kan Shōjō and shares political power at court with Fujiwara Shihei. Rarely performed, the first scenes of *Sugawara's secrets of calligraphy* introduce a rift developing between the ministers.

Standard versions of the play open with a scene in which Kan Shōjō names his successor in the art of calligraphy. Takebe Genzō, the most talented of Kan Shōjō's pupils, has been dismissed after forming a relationship with one of Kan Shōjō's maidservants. The virtuous Kan Shōjō struggles with the decision but eventually calls Genzō back to court. Despite the scheming of another student, Genzō proves his skill and is given a scroll containing Kan Shōjō's secrets of calligraphy.

Meanwhile, Shihei has poisoned the Emperor against Kan Shōjō by suggesting that, in orchestrating a marriage between the Crown Prince and his own daughter Kariya, the calligrapher was plotting to control the throne. Kan Shōjō is banished and escorted from the palace. Faithful Genzō realises that Kan Shōjō's son, Kan Shūsai, is in danger. With the help of Kan Shōjō's samurai retainer Umeōmaru, Genzō takes the boy to the safety of his village.

Kan Shōjō's daughter Kariya feels responsible for her father's exile. She plans to see him and ask his forgiveness when he stays with her sister Tatsuta. Later it is revealed that Tatsuta's husband Sukune Tarō is secretly allied with Fujiwara Shihei and is plotting to kill Kan Shōjō. After Tatsuta overhears the plan and pleads for her father's life, she is ruthlessly murdered by her husband. He then holds a rooster over her body to make it crow. The noise awakens Kan Shōjō who, thinking his escort has arrived, climbs into a waiting carriage and is taken away by Shihei's henchmen. When Tatsuta's death is discovered, Tarō feigns distress but Tatsuta's aunt sees through his act and stabs him.

The officials who were meant to accompany Kan Shōjō arrive and realise that he has been captured. Then a strange incident occurs, revealing the first hint of Kan Shōjō's supernatural powers. The captors return to report that they had kidnapped a wooden statue, not Kan Shōjō. To everyone's bewilderment, Kan Shōjō emerges from the carriage and Kariya is able to engineer a brief meeting with her father.

The subsequent *kuruma biki* (literally 'pulling the carriage apart') scene, the most famous of the play, was created specifically for kabuki. It involves the triplet retainers—the heroic Umeōmaru, the romantic Sakuramaru and the roguish Matsuōmaru—their distinct personalities expressed through stylised acting techniques, costume and makeup.

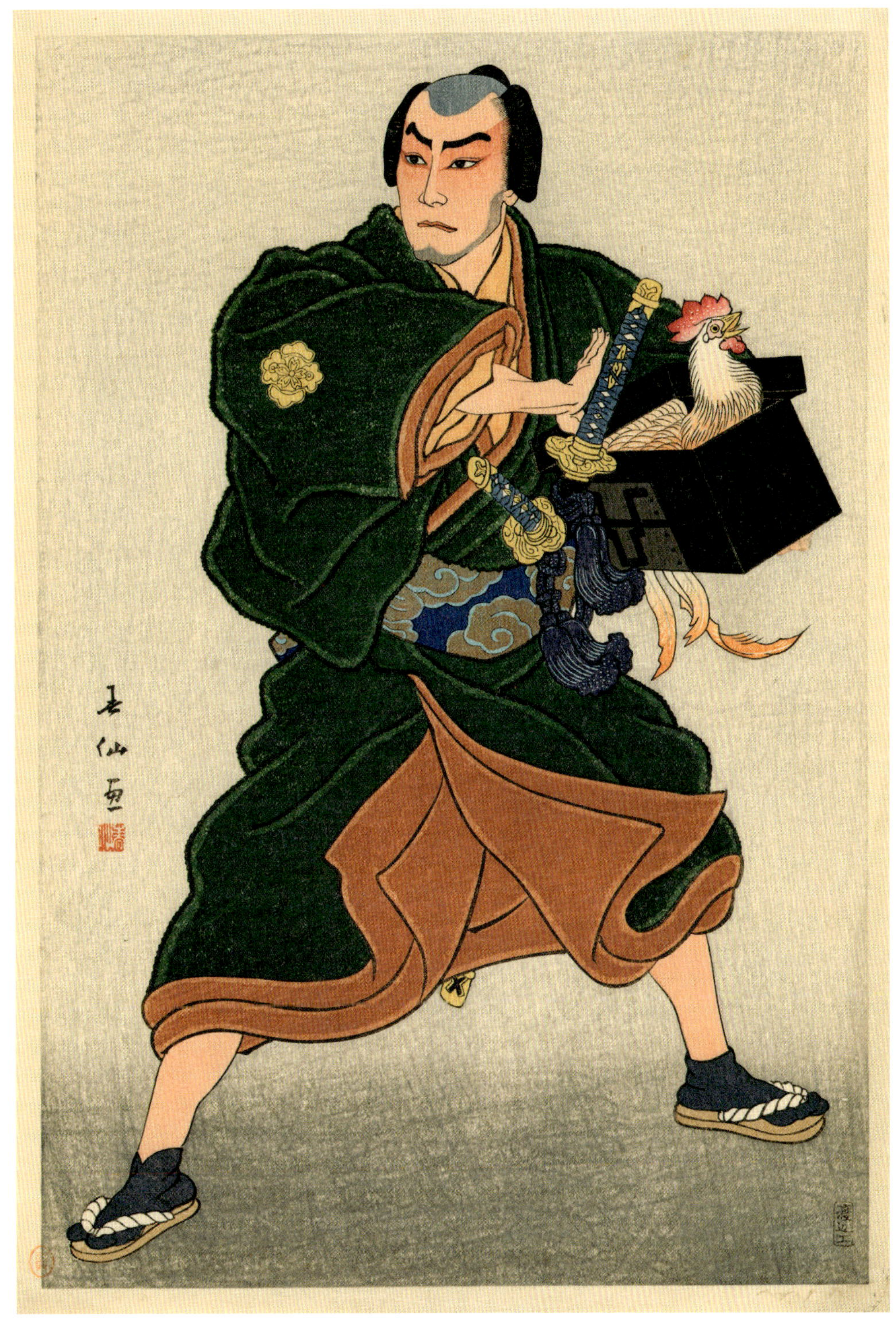

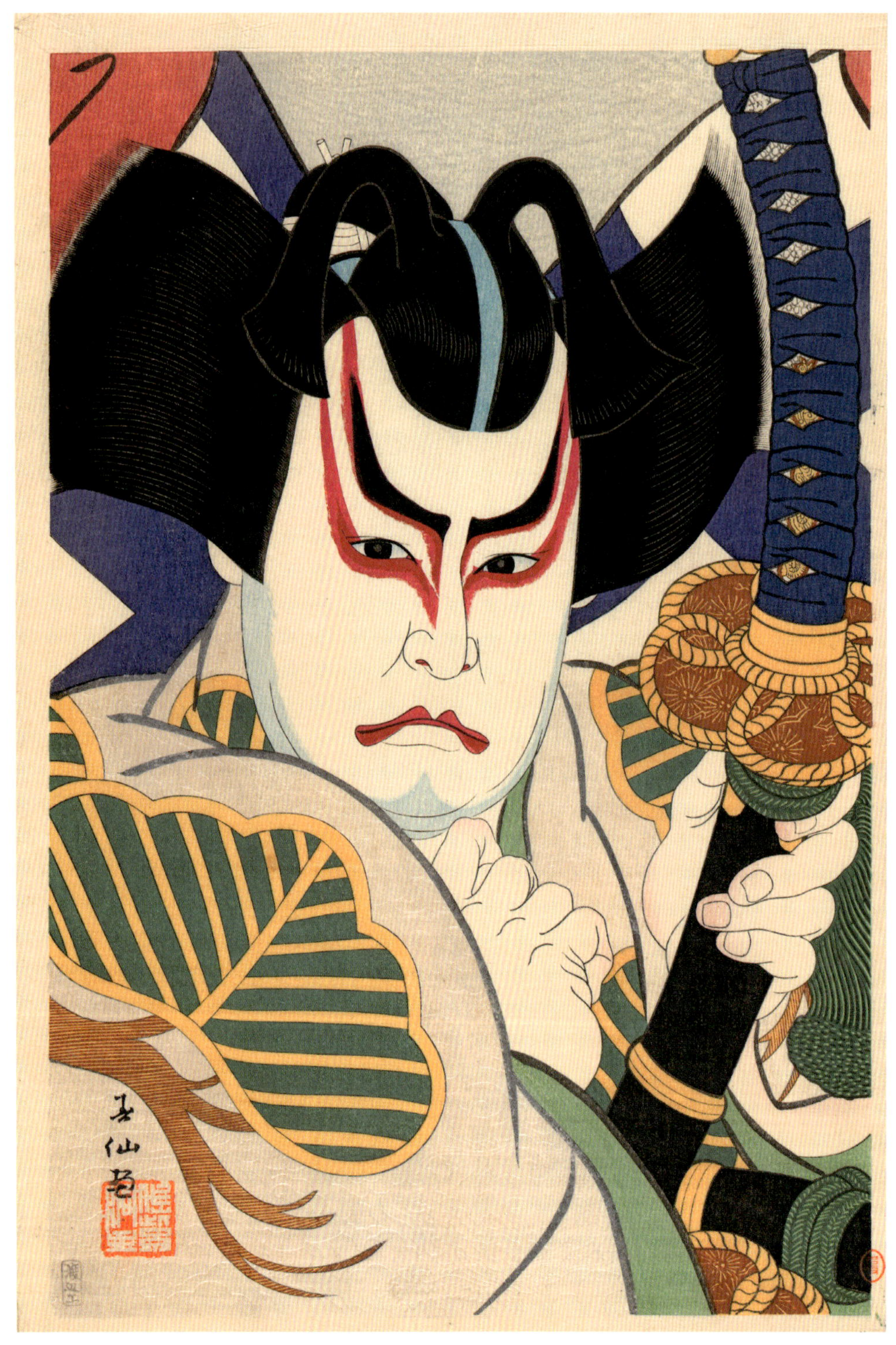

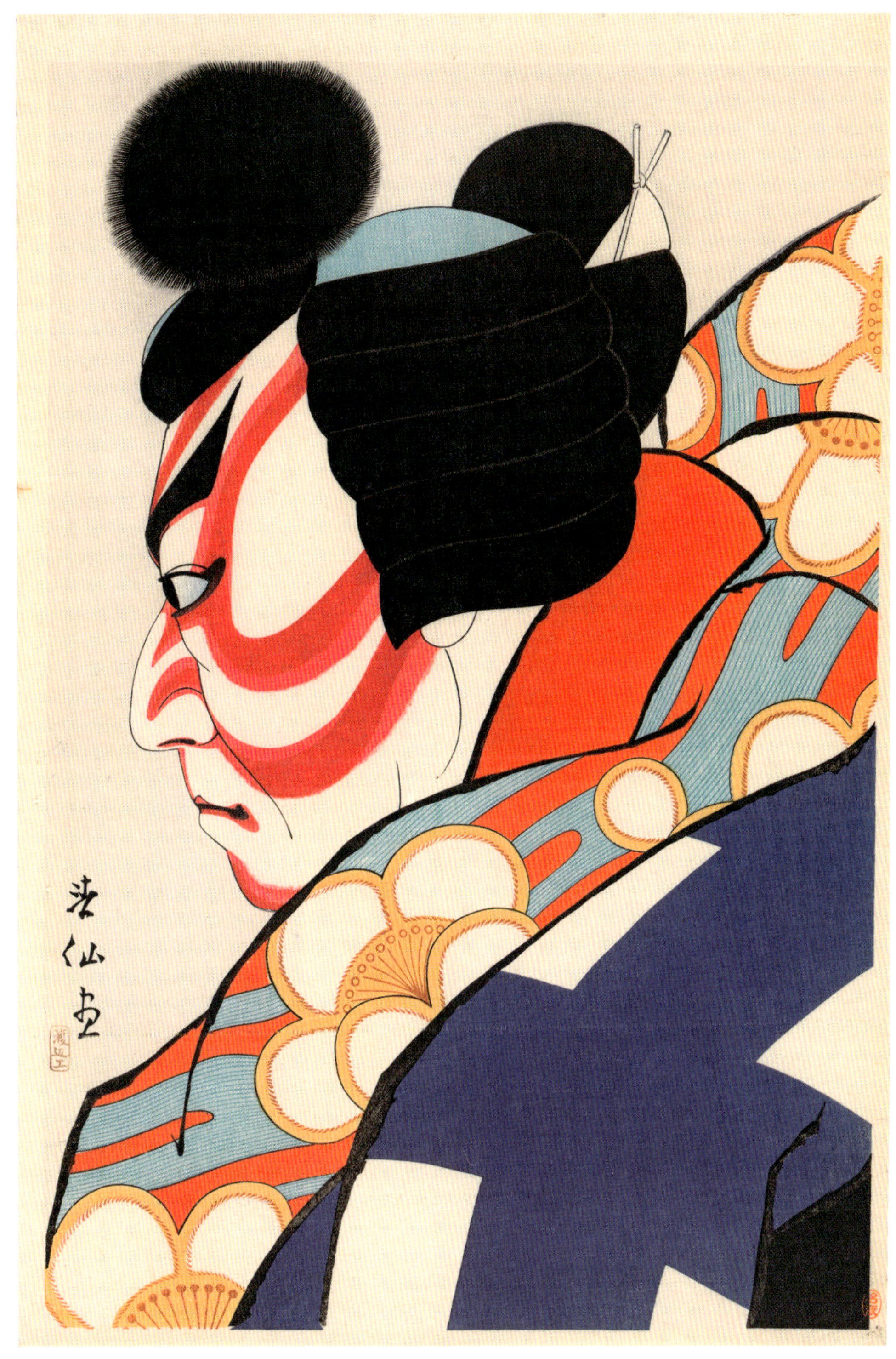

Sakuramaru and Umeōmaru, both rendered masterless samurai or *rōnin* with Kan Shōjō's exile, meet to bemoan their fate. Matsuōmaru, a servant of Shihei, arrives. Unlike his brothers, Matsuōmaru's fortunes are improving. The siblings argue until Shihei's carriage draws up before them. Umeōmaru and Sakuramaru pull the carriage apart in anger. The sequence is a piece of kabuki magic—as parts of the carriage are removed, Shihei materialises wearing blue makeup and ceremonial dress, posed to express formidable evil. He condemns his enemy Kan Shōjō, leaving the brothers cowering in fear.

The triplets' quarrel is revived at their father's birthday celebration when Umeōmaru and Matsuōmaru come to blows. Their father Shirodayū encourages Umeōmaru to stay and protect Kan Shōjō's son rather than follow his master into exile. He then disinherits Matsuōmaru because of his allegiance to Fujiwara Shihei. Matsuōmaru sorrowfully departs. Ashamed that his own negligence contributed to Kan Shōjō's exile, Sakuramaru decides to kill himself. In a poignant scene, his father expresses his heartbreak and leaves to join Kan Shōjō.

A year later Kan Shōjō has a dream that directs him to a nearby temple, which he visits with Shirodayū. They find Umeōmaru engaged in a swordfight with one of Shihei's followers, who is conspiring to assassinate Kan Shōjō. Kan Shōjō again displays supernatural powers, cutting the man's head off with a tree branch. The statesman then ascends to heaven, seeking divine intervention to defeat Shihei.

The next scene is set in the village where Genzō has been sheltering Kan Shōjō's son, Kan Shūsai. Shihei has been trying to capture and kill the young boy, and has just discovered where to find him. Genzō is ordered to present Kan Shūsai's head, while Matsuōmaru is sent to confirm that this takes place.

Meanwhile Genzō's wife is teaching at the local school. Of noble birth, Kan Shūsai is clearly distinguishable from the other children in the class. Matsuōmaru's wife enters the school to enrol her son, Kotarō. Like Shūsai, Kotarō has the appearance of an aristocrat and the boys are of the same age. Kotarō's mother sadly parts with her son. Preoccupied with how he will save Kan Shūsai, Genzō approaches with the box in which he must place the young prince's severed head. When he sees Kotarō, he decides the boy will make a suitable substitute.

Shihei's men arrive with Matsuōmaru. The children leave the school, but must pass Matsuōmaru's inspection to ensure Genzō does not try to smuggle Kan Shūsai out. The box containing the head is brought before Matsuōmaru who identifies the head as that of Kan Shūsai. He then resigns from Shihei's service. Genzō is relieved that his plan has worked— Kan Shūsai is alive and the head presented to Matsuōmaru was that of Kotarō.

Later Matsuōmaru and his wife tell of their complicity in the ruse, having intentionally placed their son in the school to allow Genzō to protect Kan Shūsai. The parents grieve and glorify their son's death as a noble sacrifice, dropping their outer robes to reveal white funeral clothing.

In the rarely staged final act, Kan Shōjō utters a curse on Shihei as he dies. The Imperial Palace suffers a number of catastrophes and Kan Shōjō's ghost reveals that Shihei's evil deeds have brought disaster on the throne. Kan Shūsai murders Shihei to avenge his father's exile. Kan Shōjō's name is cleared and he is declared a deity.

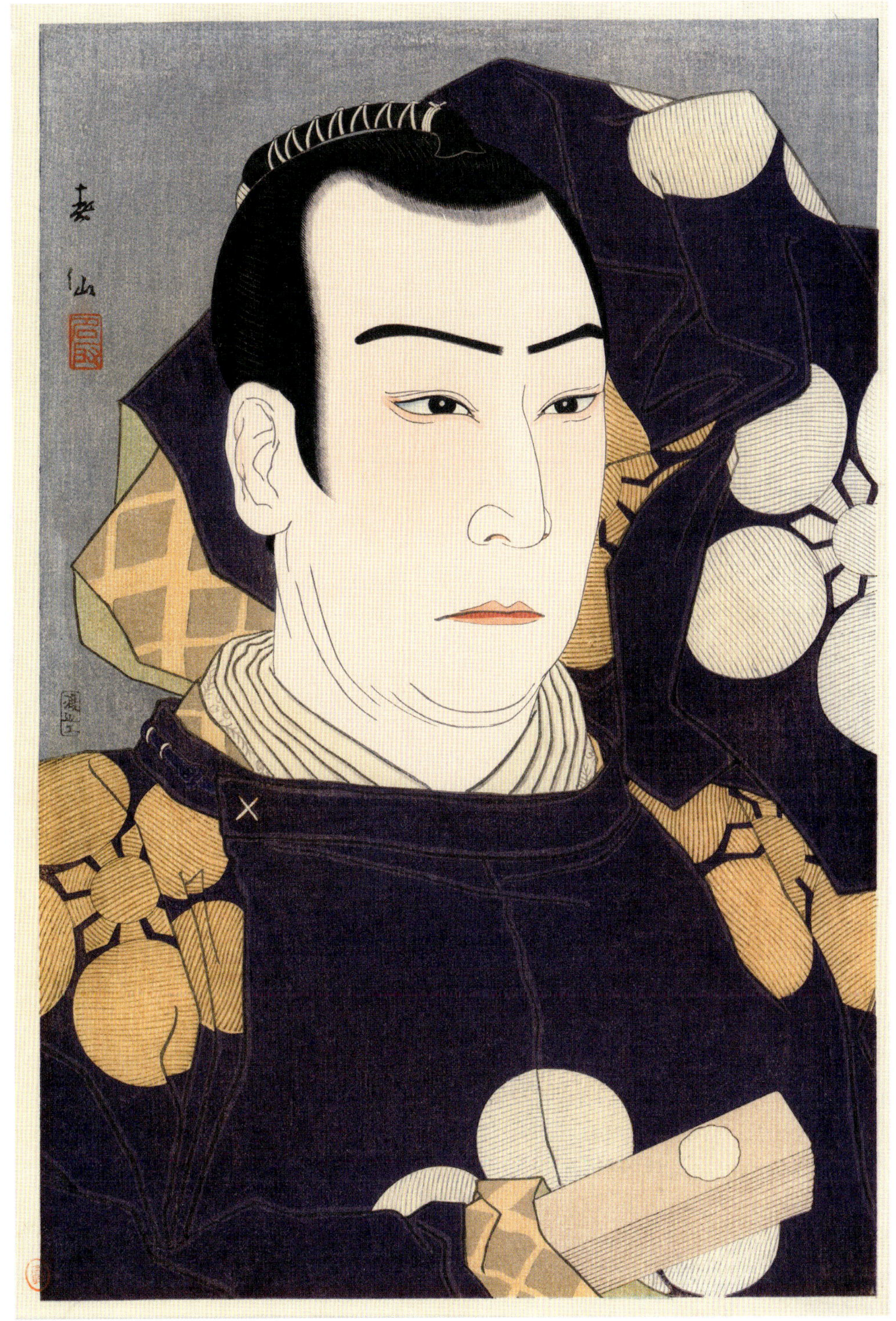

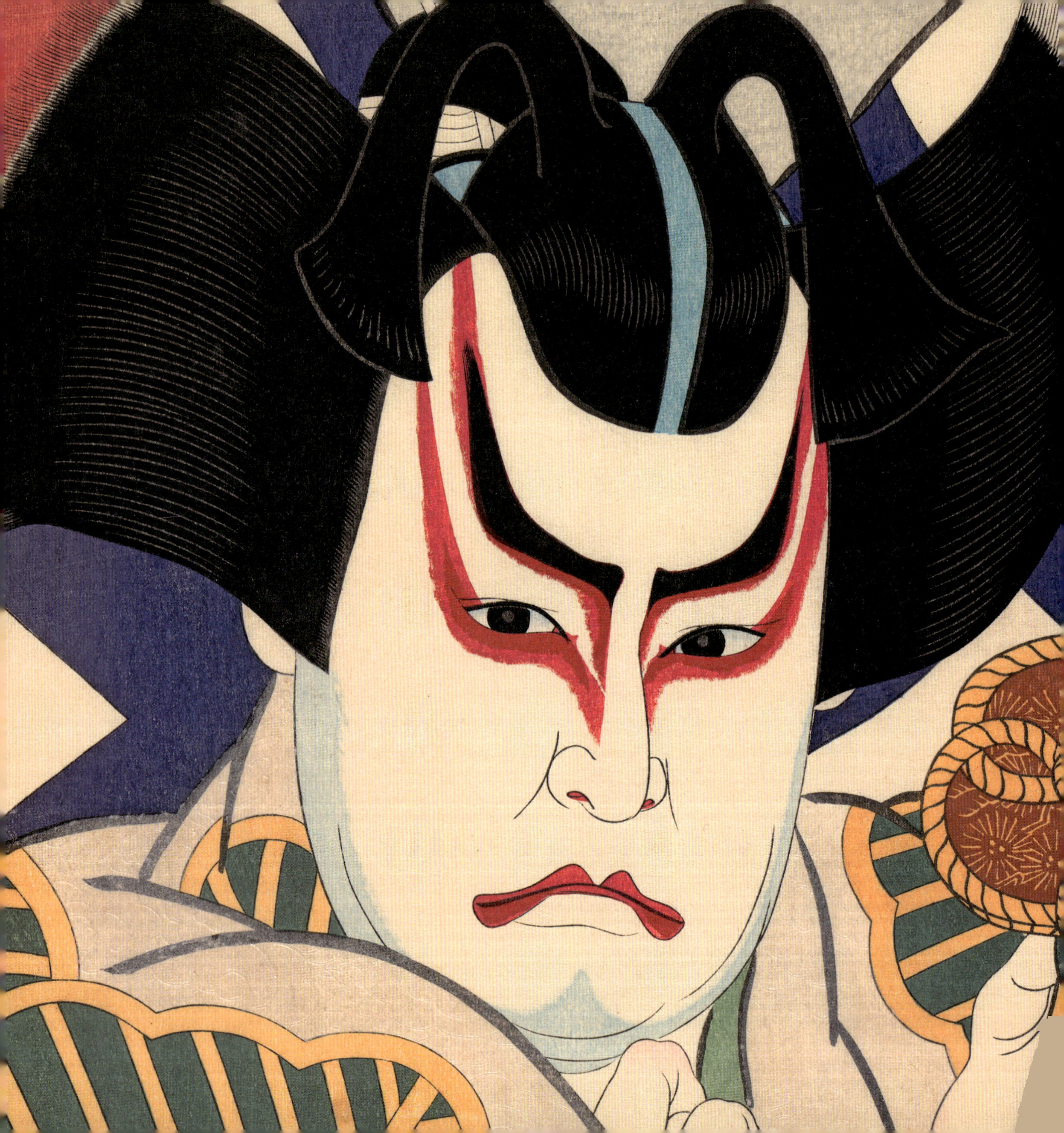

The prints

Of the 36 prints in the series *Collection of creative portraits by Shunsen,* four depict characters from different productions of the great kabuki epic *Sugawara's secrets of calligraphy*.

Shunsen's print of Kan Shōjō (Sugawara Michizane) conveys the statesman's solemn dignity. His precious calligraphy scroll can be seen in his right hand. The image of Sukune Tarō depicts the pivotal moment of betrayal when, having just murdered his wife, he clutches the rooster with which he will trick his father-in-law Kan Shōjō.

The bold portraits of Umeōmaru and Matsuōmaru illustrate the characters in the iconic *kuruma biki* scene in which Shihei's carriage is dismantled. Shunsen presents the talented actor Matsumoto Kōshirō VII in profile as Umeōmaru. The character is the quintessential heroic, masculine *aragoto* (rough thing), epitomised by loud bombastic speech, exaggerated movements, oversized costumes and wigs, and bold red makeup. The print of Matsuōmaru, the villain who ultimately becomes the play's great hero, is similarly powerful. Matsuōmaru is distinguishable from his brother by his characteristic wig and the prominent pine-tree motifs on his sleeves.

Ōtani Tomoemon VI (1886–1943)

Tomoemon VI studied with Nakamura Utaemon V and began his stage career in 1891. He was a well-regarded actor, especially famous for his portrayal of old men and scoundrels.

Ichikawa Udanji II (1881–1936)

From an Osaka kabuki family, Udanji II started performing at the age of five. According to a newspaper poll, he was the region's most popular young star of 1899. Udanji II was celebrated for his stage tricks, dance and acrobatic skills.

Matsumoto Kōshirō VII (1870–1949)

Matsumoto Kōshirō VII was widely acknowledged to be the greatest kabuki star of his generation. As a child he was adopted by prominent Tokyo dance-master Fujima Kanemon II. Ichikawa Danjūrō IX saw him perform and, recognising his talent, trained him to be a kabuki actor from the age of 11. He quickly gained popularity, earning praise for his expressive movements, innovation and ability to credibly transform himself into a variety of characters. Kōshirō particularly excelled in powerful male roles, and famously played Benkei in *The subscription list* 1600 times. Kōshirō joined the newly established Imperial Theatre in 1911 and the Shōchiku Theatre in 1929. He preserved traditional kabuki styles but also embraced modern ideas, starring in the first Japanese opera, in mixed-gender kabuki productions and in film.

As a young man, Kōshirō's imprudent offstage behaviour angered Danjūrō IX, and was apparently the reason he did not ascend to the name of Ichikawa Danjūrō X after his former master's death. Kōshirō's son, however, became Ichikawa Danjūrō XI.

Bandō Hikosaburō VI (1868–1938)

Adopted by the Bandō family in 1909, Hikosaburō VI mainly worked for the Ichimura Theatre, where he performed with his older brother Onoe Kikugorō VI. He was most successful portraying comic villains or feudal lords.

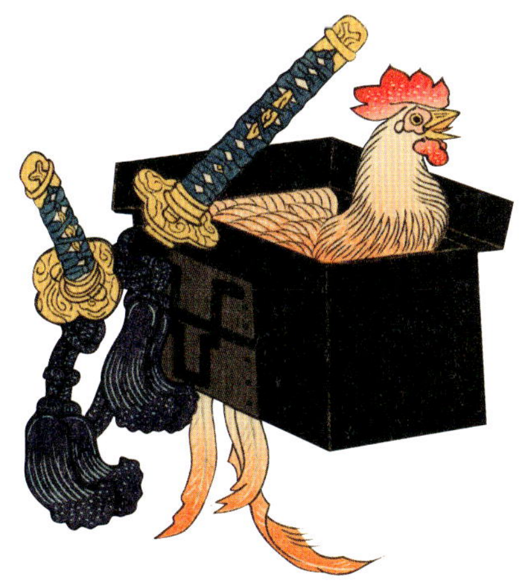

Onoe Baikō VI as Sayuri in 'Bridge of Return' 1925
from the series *Collection of creative portraits
by Shunsen*
[Onoe Baikō VI Modori Bashi Sayuri]
woodblock print; ink and colour on paper
sheet: 39.4 x 27.4 cm, image: 37.5 x 25.5 cm
National Gallery of Australia, Canberra,
gift of Jennifer Gordon, 1998

Bridge of Return (Modori Bashi)

written by Kawatake Mokuami, first kabuki
performance in 1890

According to legend, the Modori Bridge in
Kyoto's Ichijō area is a portal between the human
and spirit realms. The dance-drama *Bridge of
Return* opens on an eerie, moonlit night. Stage
effects—wind rustling the leaves of willow
trees, ghostly lighting and music—enhance
the sinister atmosphere. The heroic samurai
Watanabe Tsuna nears the bridge and notices
Sayuri, a seemingly demure and beautiful young
woman. She approaches and tells him that
she is afraid to walk home alone. Allured, he
accompanies her.

Uncannily Sayuri seems to know Tsuna, and
the samurai realises she is a demon in disguise
when he glimpses her reflection in the water. In
Japanese ghost stories, evil spirits can magically
change their appearance but their true nature is
exposed when reflected. The actor playing Sayuri
gives the audience hints of her supernatural
status through mysterious changes in voice,
posture and facial expressions.

When Tsuna accuses Sayuri of being a demon,
she attacks him and a wild fight ensues with
actors flying through the air on wires. Sayuri
dramatically metamorphosises into her true form
(the actor momentarily disappearing off stage
and returning wearing a fearsome mask with
horns and mane). Tsuna eventually succeeds in
cutting off the devil-woman's arm, just before
she flees.

The print

In the subscription series, Shunsen's print of
Onoe Baikō VI followed his portrait of Baikō's
great stage partner Ichimura Uzaemon XV
(see page 106). The image emphasises Onoe
Baikō VI's renowned elegance and delicate
beauty by presenting the actor as an unearthly
woman, his most celebrated role type, before
her demonic nature is revealed.

Onoe Baikō VI (1870–1934)

Born in Nagoya, Onoe Baikō VI was the son of
Onoe Asajirō (although there were rumours
that Onoe Kikugorō V may have been his
natural father) and grandson of the eccentric
Onoe Kikugorō III. Onoe Kikugorō V adopted
Baikō VI in 1882, after seeing him perform in
Nagoya, and prepared him for the Tokyo stage.
Baikō VI became one of the principal *onnagata*
(female-role specialists) of his time, admired
for his emotional range. He was very successful
in domestic plays and historical dramas, and
legendary for playing supernatural female
characters. Productions in which Baikō starred
opposite Ichimura Uzaemon XV as the romantic
male lead were sensational hits. In 1911 Baikō
became artistic director of Tokyo's Imperial
Theatre. The actor died after suffering a stroke
on the Kabuki Theatre stage. Baikō VI's legacy
survives through his memoir of life in the
theatre, *The wind beneath the plum blossoms*,
published in 1934.

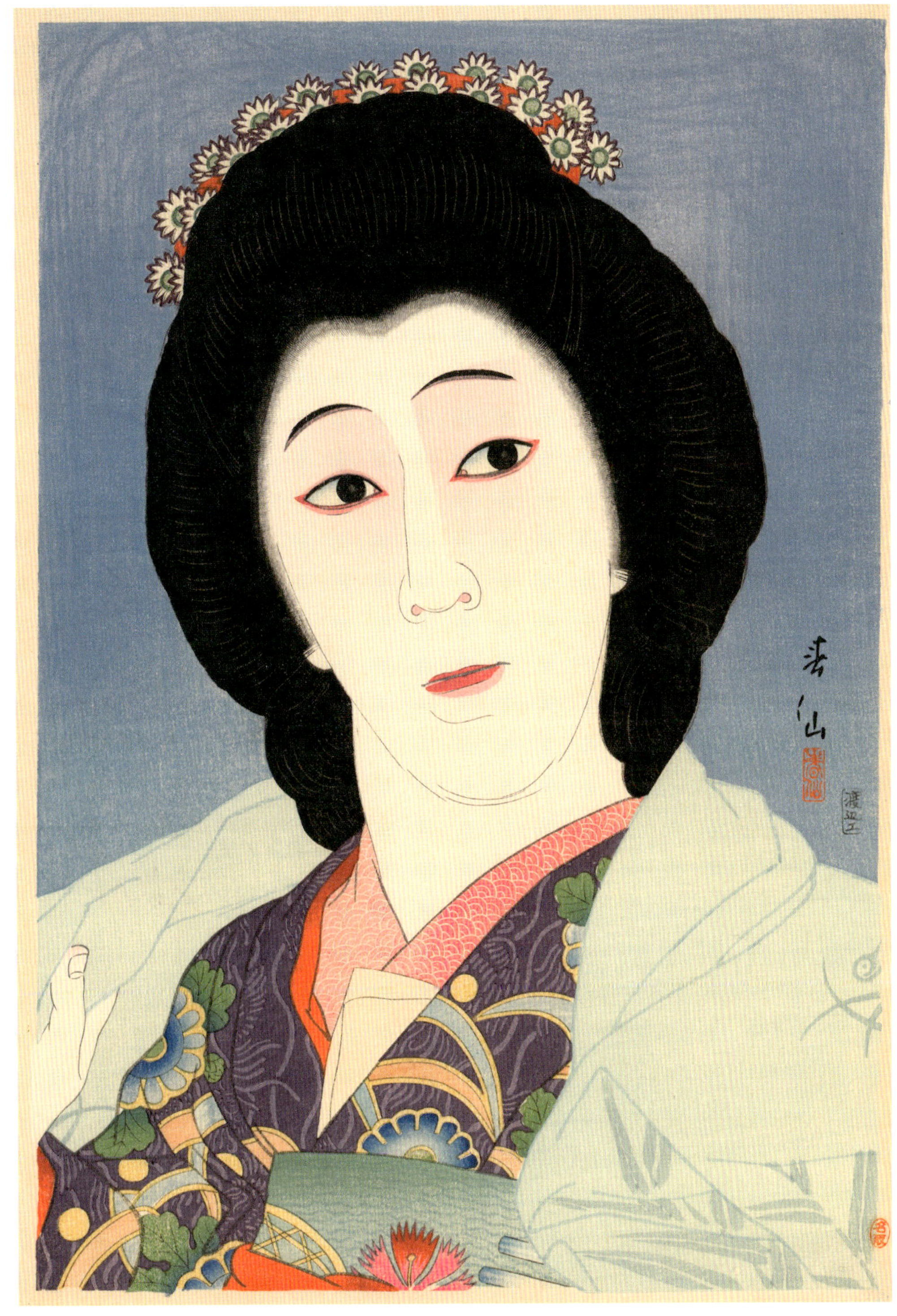

Onoe Matsusuke IV as Nozarashi Kobei in 'The freak show producer' 1925 from the series *Collection of creative portraits by Shunsen* [Onoe Matsusuke IV Ingamonoshi Kobei]
woodblock print; ink and colour on paper
sheet: 39.7 x 27.9 cm, image: 37.9 x 25.7 cm
National Gallery of Australia, Canberra,
gift of Jennifer Gordon, 1998

The freak show producer (Ingamonoshi)

written by Kawatake Mokuami, first kabuki performance in 1875

The freak show producer, also known as *Fate* (Inga kozō), is a bandit play that developed out of the unsuccessful drama *The dragon-shaped clouds over the high summit (*Ryō to mimasu takane Kumokiri*).* Set in the brothels and ghettos of Tokyo, it explores the concept of fate and portrays the living conditions of the poor in late-nineteenth century Japan.

Nozarashi Kobei, a freak show producer, witnesses the grisly murder of a town clerk, arranged by his disowned son Rokunosuke. A member of a notorious criminal gang, Rokunosuke has absconded with his lover Osono. Gonji is pursuing the lovers as Osono is a prostitute indentured to him. The play represents the chase in a distinctive *danmari* scene, enacted without dialogue and set in the dark, with the actors miming exaggerated dance-like actions. Osono's hairpin is dropped during the pursuit and retrieved by Kobei. Later Gonji finds Kobei's tobacco pouch near the body of the murdered clerk.

A gravely ill Kobei languishes at the house of his other son Shichinosuke, located in an entertainment quarter. Shichinosuke sells Osono's hairpin to raise money to pay their rent. This results in Gonji linking Kobei to Osono and the crime of harbouring a wayward prostitute. Inadvertently, Shichinosuke reveals that the tobacco pouch in Gonji's possession belongs to Kobei. The old man is accused of the town clerk's murder. Mortified for causing the false indictment, Shichinosuke and his pregnant lover commit suicide.

Kobei later welcomes Osono and Rokunosuke. He tells of Shichinosuke's death and his own imminent arrest. He then displays his tattoo, a skull (*nozarashi*) symbolising courage and his debt to a man who forgave him for a crime years before. Osono is astonished because that generous man was her father. In atonement for his many past sins, Kobei promises to save Osono and Rokunosuke. The play closes with the lovers' escape and Kobei's arrest.

The print

Shunsen's print of the elderly actor Onoe Matsusuke IV illustrates the great intensity and expressiveness that is characteristic of kabuki acting. The image depicts the popular star in one of his most celebrated roles, the ill-fated Nozarashi Kobei, the title character of *The freak show producer*.

Onoe Matsusuke IV (1843–1928)

Onoe Matsusuke IV was the Osaka-born son of one of Matsumoto Kōshirō V's stage assistants. He first performed kabuki in 1848 under the name Matsumoto Tatsusuke and became a highly regarded and enduringly popular supporting actor.

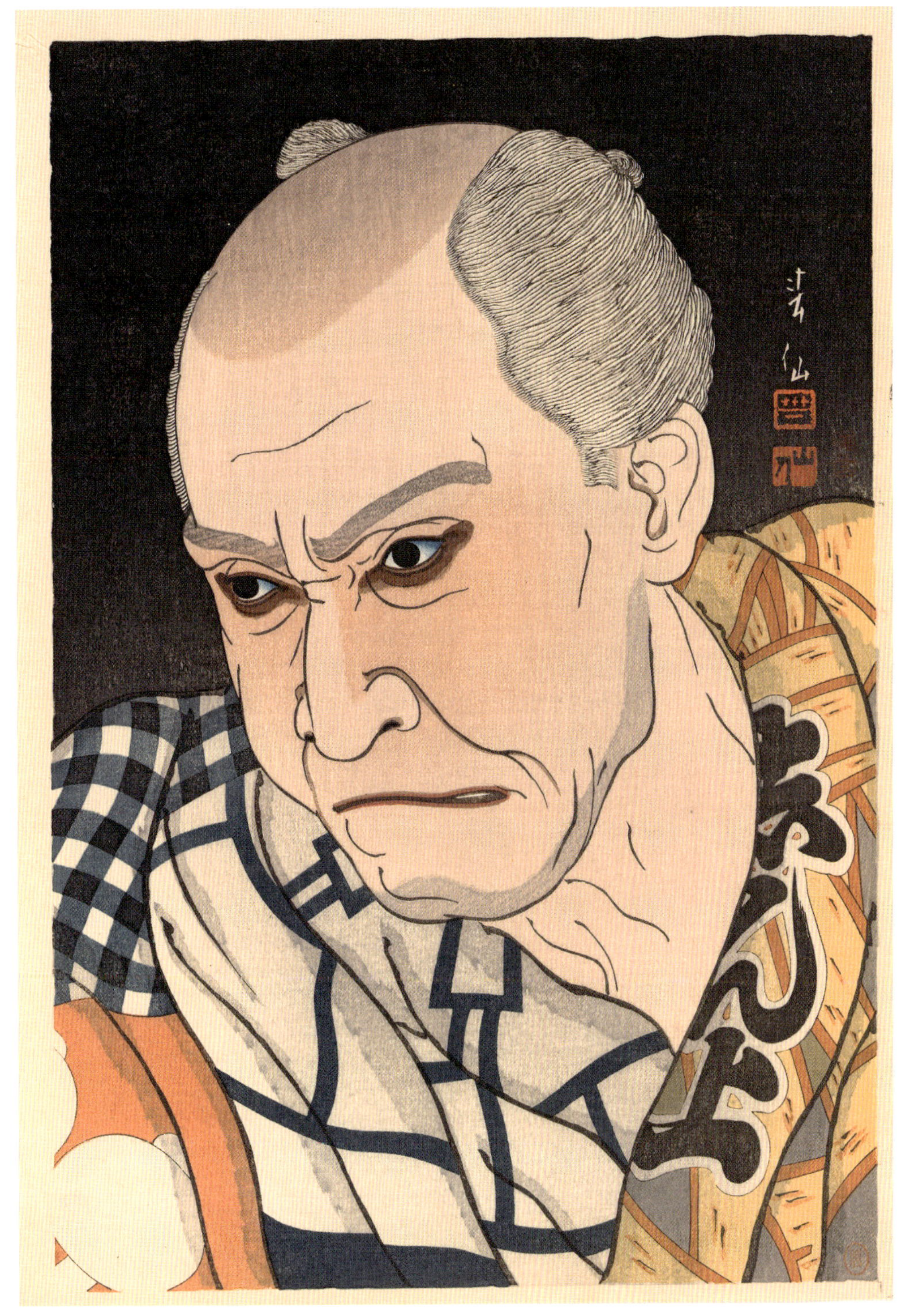

*Nakamura Ganjirō I as Sakata Tōjūrō in
'Tōjūrō's love'* 1925 from the series *Collection
of creative portraits by Shunsen*
[Nakamura Ganjirō Sakata Tōjūrō]
woodblock print; ink and colour on paper
sheet: 39.5 x 27.7 cm, image: 38.1 x 26.0 cm
National Gallery of Australia, Canberra,
gift of Jennifer Gordon, 1998

Tōjūrō's love (Tōjūrō no koi)

written by Kikuchi Kan, first kabuki performance
in 1919

Tōjūrō's love was inspired by tales of Sakata
Tōjūrō I, a seventeenth-century kabuki actor with
an unrelenting dedication to his art. The play is
based on an anecdotal incident in which Tōjūrō
became romantically involved with the wife of a
theatre tea-house owner in order to inform his
portrayal of an adulterer. Tea houses were closely
connected with the staging of performances and
the kabuki experience. Patrons visited before
and after the entertainment, and were served
food and drinks during the plays. Reliant on the
success of theatres, tea-house owners often
financed or advised on productions.

The first scene of *Tōjūrō's love* is set in a Kyoto
theatre tea-house. The handsome young Tōjūrō
appears preoccupied while his troupe enjoys
a feast. He is concerned about an upcoming
performance, playing a seducer, as he has no life
experience to draw on. When Tōjūrō is served by
Okaji, the owner's wife, he assumes his character
and woos her. Okaji is unaware that she is being
exploited, and Tōjūrō convincingly plays out
the role. When she returns his advances, Tōjūrō
makes a hasty exit.

Tōjūrō's performance is a huge success, at
the expense of Okaji who is heartbroken and
ashamed. The play magnifies reality, culminating
with Okaji's suicide backstage. Tōjūrō, concerned
only with acting, looks dispassionately at
Okaji's body.

The print

Incorporating modern design elements into
a traditional Japanese actor image, this print
exemplifies the refined and decorative elements
of the *shin-hanga* (new print) movement. It also
expresses the delicate characteristics of kabuki's
wagoto acting style, a gentle mode of portraying
male characters obsessed by romance. Nakamura
Ganjirō I, a leading *wagoto* actor, is illustrated
as Sakata Tōjūrō. Ganjirō was the first actor to
perform the role.

Nakamura Ganjirō I (1860–1935)

Ganjirō was born in Osaka's Shinmachi pleasure
district, the son of actor Nakamura Ganjaku III.
He first took to the stage at age three but
his kabuki training was disrupted for almost
a decade. Unusually, he also worked as a
puppeteer. Ganjirō became famous for
exemplifying the traditions originated in
the Kyoto-Osaka area. From 1906 he found
widespread fame as a star of Tokyo's Kabuki
Theatre. Reputedly very attractive, Nakamura
Ganjirō I played female and male roles, especially
wagoto. He retained traditional techniques,
but also explored new theatrical forms such
as *shinpa* (new school, Western-influenced
drama), political plays and dramatisations of
contemporary novels.

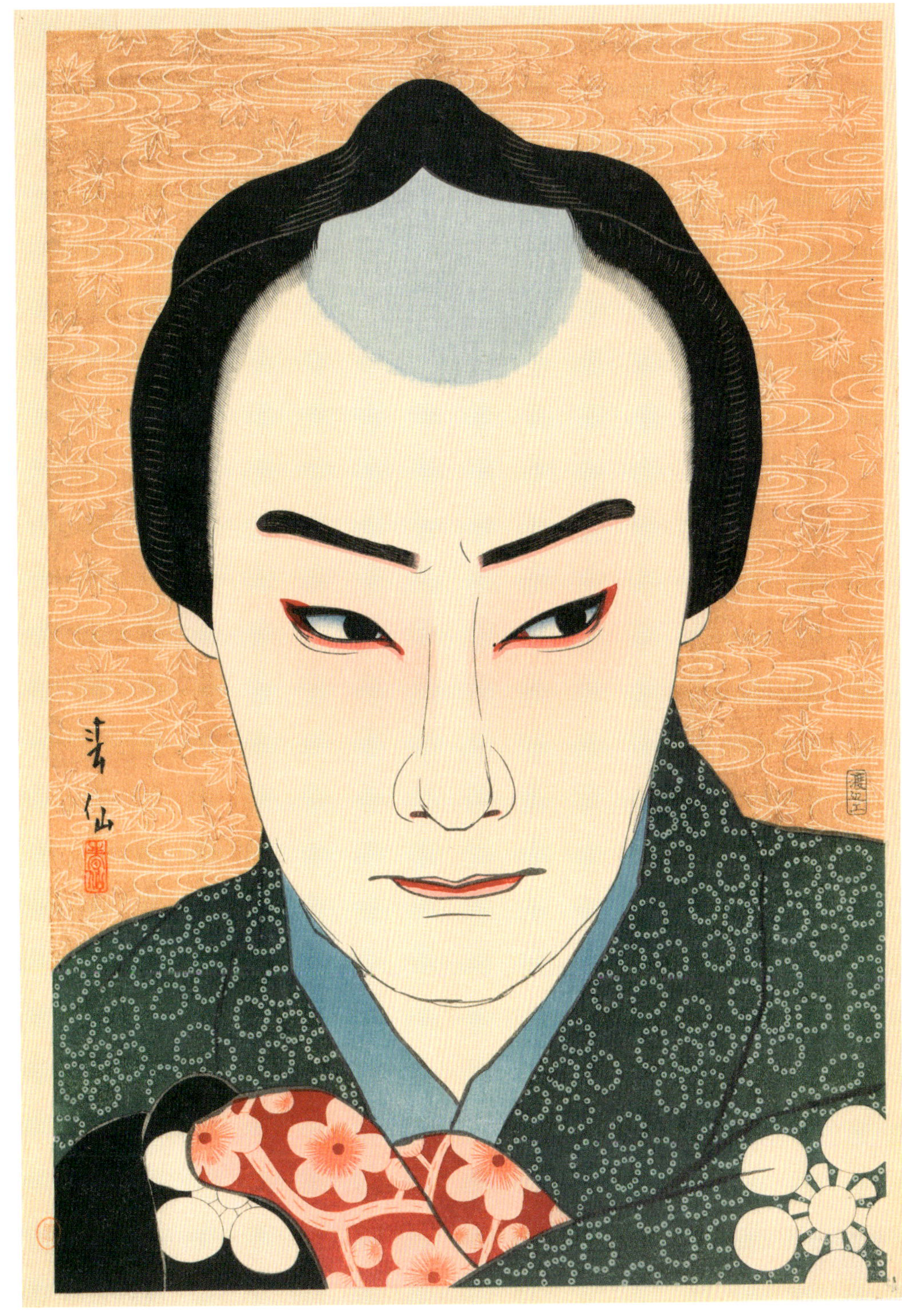

*Nakamura Shikaku II as Shizuka Gozen in
'Yoshitsune and the thousand cherry trees'* 1926
from the series *Collection of creative portraits
by Shunsen*
[Nakamura Shikaku II Horikawa Gosho Shizuka
Gozen]
woodblock print, embossing; ink and colour
on paper
sheet: 39.7 x 27.2 cm, image: 38.2 x 25.6 cm
National Gallery of Australia, Canberra,
gift of Jennifer Gordon, 1998

*Bandō Shūchō III as Shizuka Gozen in
'Yoshitsune and the thousand cherry trees'* 1925
from the series *Collection of creative portraits
by Shunsen*
[Bandō Shūchō III Shizuka]
woodblock print; ink, colour and mica on paper
sheet: 42.3 x 28.2 cm, image: 38.0 x 25.9 cm
National Gallery of Australia, Canberra,
gift of Jennifer Gordon, 1998

**Yoshitsune and the thousand cherry trees
(Yoshitsune senbon zakura)**

written by Takeda Izumo II, Namiki Sōsuke,
Miyoshi Shōraku, first kabuki performance
in 1748

An epic history play centring on vengeance and
loyalty, *Yoshitsune and the thousand cherry trees*
is an imaginary account of events following the
twelfth-century conflict between the powerful
Minamoto and Taira clans. The play was banned
as an undemocratic glorification of feudalism
during the American occupation after the
Second World War.

Yoshitsune and the thousand cherry trees is set
after a Minamoto victory. Yoritomo is shogun
and increasingly jealous of his younger brother,
military hero Yoshitsune. Antagonised by several
misunderstandings, Yoritomo sends troops to
capture his brother. Some productions open
with Shizuka Gozen, Yoshitsune's mistress and
a distinguished court dancer, performing for
Yoshitsune's wife and followers, including the
impulsive and fiercely loyal warrior-priest Benkei.
Suddenly, an imminent attack by Yoritomo's
forces is announced. Yoshitsune's wife and
Shizuka, who puts on a suit of armour, restrain
Benkei from rushing into the fray. Tragedy
unfolds with Yoshitsune's wife killing herself
in the belief that she caused the rift between
the brothers. Benkei compounds the situation
by killing some of Yoritomo's commanders.
Yoshitsune is forced to flee.

Yoshitsune and his men meet at the Inari Shrine,
near Kyoto. Cherry trees in full bloom give the
scene an elegant beauty belying the dangerous
situation. Performed in a distinctive *aragoto*
(literally 'rough thing') style of exaggerated
masculinity, Benkei explodes onto the stage
begging forgiveness for his rash behaviour.
Shizuka unexpectedly appears, hoping to join

her lover. After much melodramatic weeping,
Benkei is pardoned. Shizuka's tears are not so
effective and she is ordered to return to Kyoto.
She refuses and is tied to a tree. As a symbol of
his love, Yoshitsune gives her a cherished drum
presented to him by the former emperor, and
tells her to beat it when she is in danger.

An inconsolable Shizuka weeps and sadly plays
the drum. The noise alerts Yoritomo's men who
are hiding nearby. Recognising Yoshitsune's
mistress, they attempt to kidnap her. Satō
Tadanobu, another of Yoshitsune's retainers,
rescues her and kills some of Yoritomo's men in
an acrobatic swordfight. Yoshitsune, watching
nearby, praises Tadanobu and asks him to escort
Shizuka to safety.

After several acts of revenge by the rival
Taira and Minamoto factions, Shizuka and
Tadanobu return to the stage. They are following
Yoshitsune. Pining for her lover, Shizuka plays the
drum. Tadanobu's demeanour changes uncannily
with the drumbeats and he dances in strange
nimble steps reminiscent of the movements
of a fox.

Meanwhile, Yoshitsune is sheltering at the palace
of a powerful priest. He questions Tadanobu
about Shizuka and is bewildered that he has not
seen her for weeks. The confusion intensifies
when Shizuka arrives. After reuniting with
Yoshitsune, she realises that Tadanobu is not
the person who has been accompanying her.
Tadanobu is seized by Yoshitsune's guards.

Suspecting the occult, Shizuka arms herself
with a dagger and begins to play the drum.
Tadanobu miraculously appears, strangely
transformed—his long hair tied to resemble a
fox's ears—and dances as if entranced. Shizuka
attacks Tadanobu, but he evades her. On
interrogation he reveals that he is a fox posing
as Tadanobu to be close to Yoshitsune's drum,

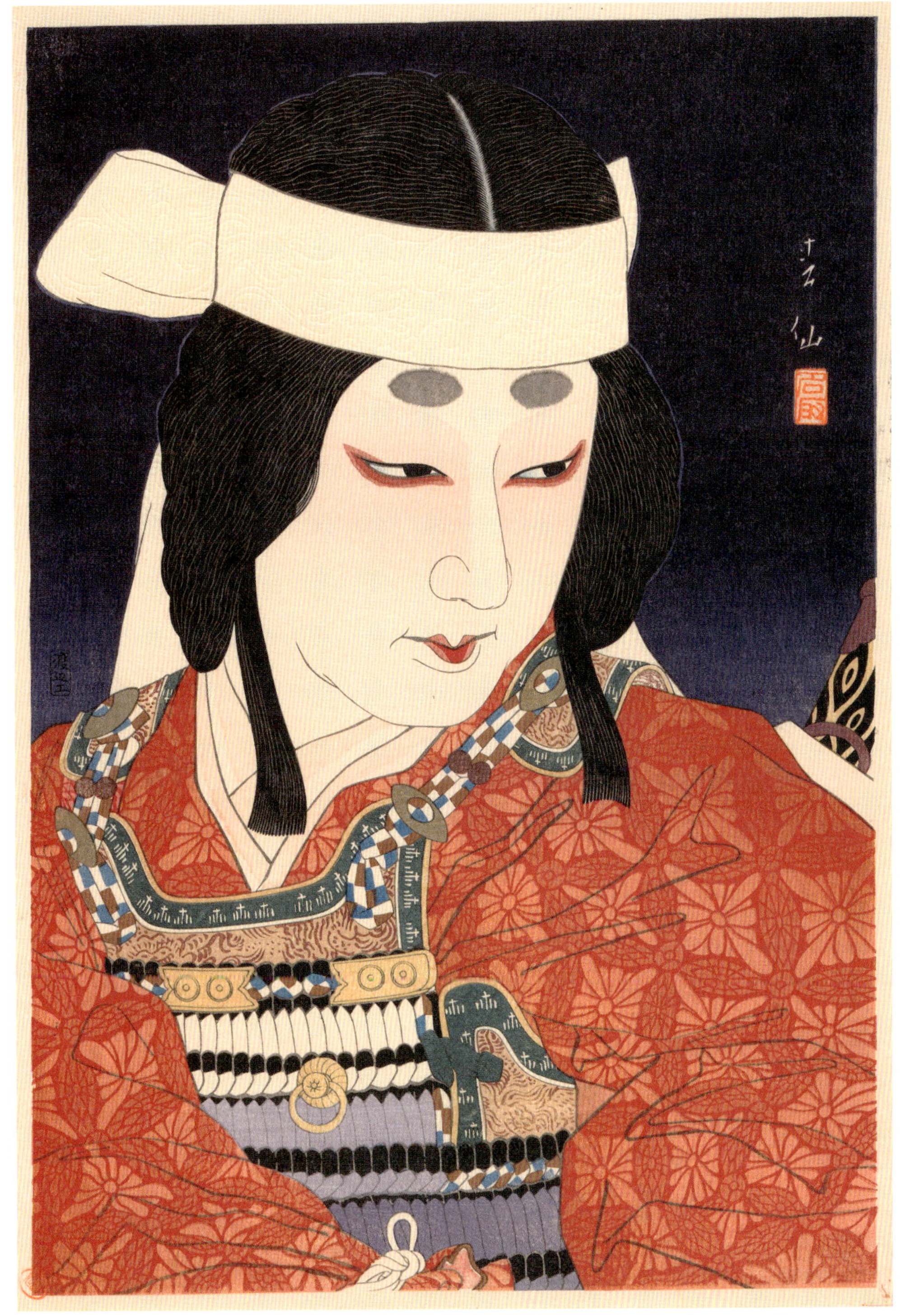

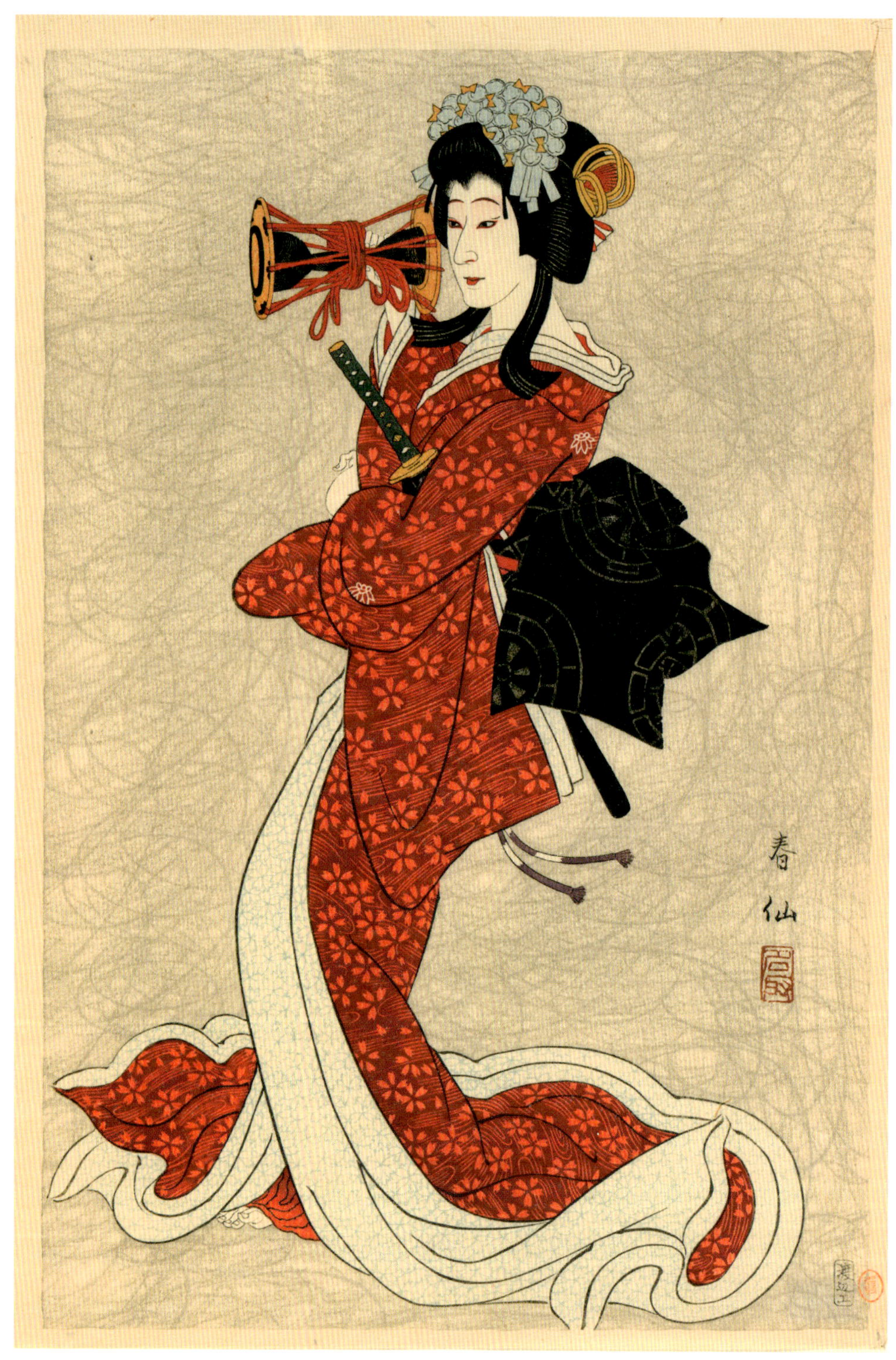

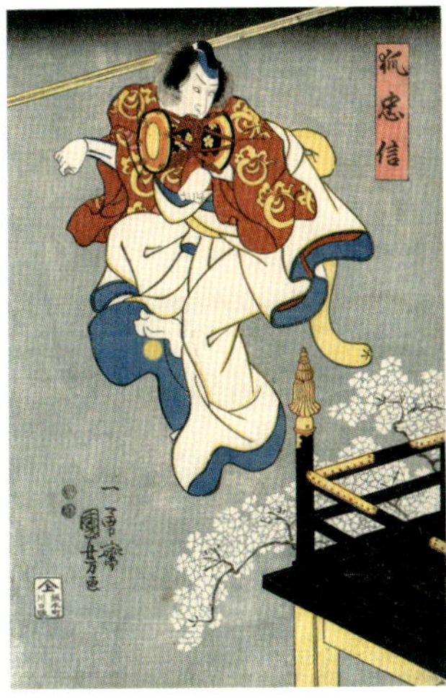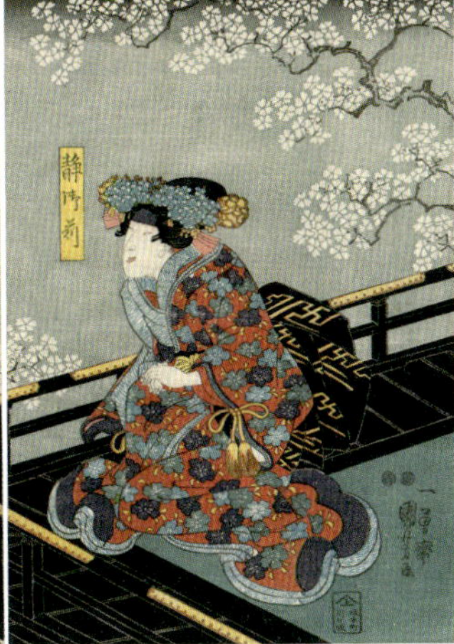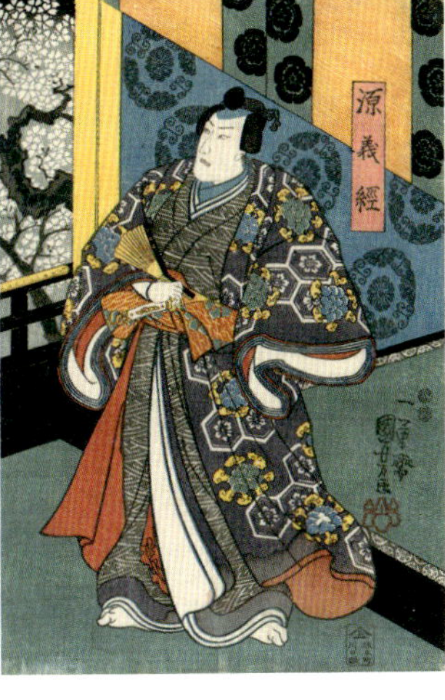

(left) **Utagawa Kuniyoshi** (1797–1862) *Kabuki actors as Minamoto Yoshitsune, Shizuka Gozen and Tadanobu* 1847–52 woodblock print; ink and colour on paper, 36.6 x 73.7 cm Museum of Fine Arts, Boston, William Sturgis Bigalow Collection

made from the skins of his parents. (In Japanese folklore the fox, *kitsune*, is a magical spirit able to assume human form.) In performance, Tadanobu vanishes through a trapdoor and reappears wearing a furry white costume decorated with orange flames, signifiers of the supernatural. Shizuka and Yoshitsune free the real Tadanobu and release the fox from his parents' spell. The fox exits, dancing or spectacularly flying up over the audience.

In the play's remaining scenes, often not performed, Yoshitsune and the magical fox slay surviving leaders of the Taira clan.

The prints

Shunsen included two images of Shizuka, heroine of *Yoshitsune and the thousand cherry trees*, in his series of actor portraits. The print of Nakamura Shikaku II as Shizuka relates to an early scene when she pulls on armour to stop Benkei from attacking Yoritomo's men. Shunsen captures the moment in a dramatically cropped portrait, emphasising Shizuka's determined warrior-like expression. The full-length portrait of Bandō Shūchō III represents the famous

fox-charming scene. Shizuka appears as an elegant dancer, dressed in an *akahime* (red princess) robe, holding the drum with a dagger at her side.

Nakamura Shikaku II (1900–81)

Born in Tokyo, Nakamura Shikaku II was the son of Kabuki Theatre actor Nakamura Denkurō VI. A popular and skilled supporting *onnagata* (female-role actor), Shikaku wrote a number of books describing traditional acting styles and techniques.

Bandō Shūchō III (1880–1935)

Bandō Shūchō III began his career as a *nagauta* singer. *Nagauta* literally means 'long song', and is the term given to the singing and instrumental music used in kabuki to enhance dramatic scenes. Shūchō III married the daughter of Bandō Shūchō II and started acting after studying with Ichikawa Danjūrō IX, the leading actor of the Meiji period. He debuted in Tokyo in 1896 and became a respected *onnagata* performer, both in kabuki and *shinpa* (new school, Western-influenced) theatre.

Kataoka Nizaemon XI as Kakogawa Honzō in 'The treasury of the loyal retainers' 1925
from the series *Collection of creative portraits by Shunsen*
[Kataoka Nizaemon XI Kudanme Honzō]
woodblock print; ink, colour and mica on paper
sheet: 40.0 x 27.2 cm, image: 37.8 x 25.5 cm
National Gallery of Australia, Canberra,
gift of Jennifer Gordon, 1998

Onoe Kikugorō VI as Hayano Kanpei in 'The treasury of the loyal retainers' 1931
from the series *Supplement to collection of portraits by Shunsen*
[Onoe Kikugorō VI Hayano Kanpei]
woodblock print; ink and colour on paper
sheet: 37.5 x 24.8 cm, image: 35.1 x 23.5
National Gallery of Australia, Canberra,
Pauline and John Gandel Fund, 2011

Onoe Eizaburō VII as Okaru in 'The treasury of the loyal retainers' 1926 from the series *Collection of creative portraits by Shunsen*
[Onoe Eizaburō VII Okaru]
woodblock print; ink and colour on paper
sheet: 40.0 x 27.6 cm, image: 38.1 x 25.9 cm
National Gallery of Australia, Canberra,
gift of Jennifer Gordon, 1998

The treasury of the loyal retainers (Kanadehon Chūshingura)

written by Takeda Izumo II, Miyoshi Shōraku and Namiki Sōsuke, first kabuki performance in 1748

In 1703 a group of fiercely loyal samurai exacted revenge on the enemy of their master Asano Naganori, the lord of Japan's Akō domain. Rich in samurai honour, violence and sacrifice, the historical incident became the basis for numerous plays, of which the most famous is the marathon 11-act drama known as *The treasury of the loyal retainers* or *The forty-seven samurai*. The play is set in the mid-fourteenth century and the protagonists' names have been altered, to comply with regulations forbidding the realistic dramatisation of history.

A ceremony takes place to open a shrine at Kamakura, near Tokyo. Several important men are in attendance including the shogun's brother, Moronao governor of Kamakura, and the feudal lords (*daimyō*) Wakasanosuke and Enya Hangan (representing the historical Asano Naganori). Hangan's wife Kaoya is also summoned. When the officials depart, Moronao is left alone with Kaoya. He propositions her, threatening her husband's position if she does not submit to his lust. Wakasanosuke returns, allowing Kaoya to slip away. Moronao admonishes the *daimyō* for his intrusion. The samurai prepare to duel, but are interrupted by the return of the shogun's retinue.

Act two introduces a retainer of the impetuous Wakasanosuke, the wise and moderate Kakogawa Honzō. Wakasanosuke is preoccupied with Moronao's insults and vows to kill the governor, given the slightest provocation. Honzō professes encouragement but privately hopes to deter any violence.

In an attempt to calm the situation Honzō meets Moronao and presents him with gifts, ostensibly

from Wakasanosuke. Moronao accepts and enters the shogun's palace. Hangan arrives on the scene with his retainer Hayano Kanpei, who notices one of Moronao's henchman making amorous advances towards his love, Okaru, a woman in service to Kaoya. The chivalrous Kanpei protects Okaru and the couple disappear together.

A placated Moronao behaves with great humility, apologising to Wakasanosuke for their altercation. Unable to engage Moronao in a fight, Wakasanosuke leaves frustrated. Moronao feels he has lost face in the interaction and, still smarting from Kaoya's rejection, takes out his annoyance on Hangan. Moronao taunts the *daimyō* and questions the fidelity of his wife. Hangan lashes out, striking Moronao with his sword. Honzō quickly intervenes to avert further bloodshed. Palace guards arrest Hangan.

Kanpei is engaged in a tryst with Okaru when he hears of his master's predicament. Having deserted Hangan, Kanpei holds himself responsible and prepares to commit suicide. Okaru, however, implores him to go into hiding until the time is right to return.

At his mansion, Hangan is given the shogun's verdict: for committing violence within the palace, Hangan will lose land and title and be forced to commit *harakiri* (ritual suicide). Dressed in a white death robe, Hangan kneels, takes a dagger and stabs himself in the abdomen. Hangan's beloved retainer Yuranosuke arrives on the scene as his master dies. Understanding Hangan's desire for retribution, Yuranosuke collects the dagger. Hangan's men, now *rōnin* (masterless samurai), gather to plan a vendetta against Moronao under Yuranosuke's leadership.

Meanwhile, Okaru and Kanpei have been living in the country. One night Kanpei comes across one of Hangan's men, Yagorō. Kanpei learns

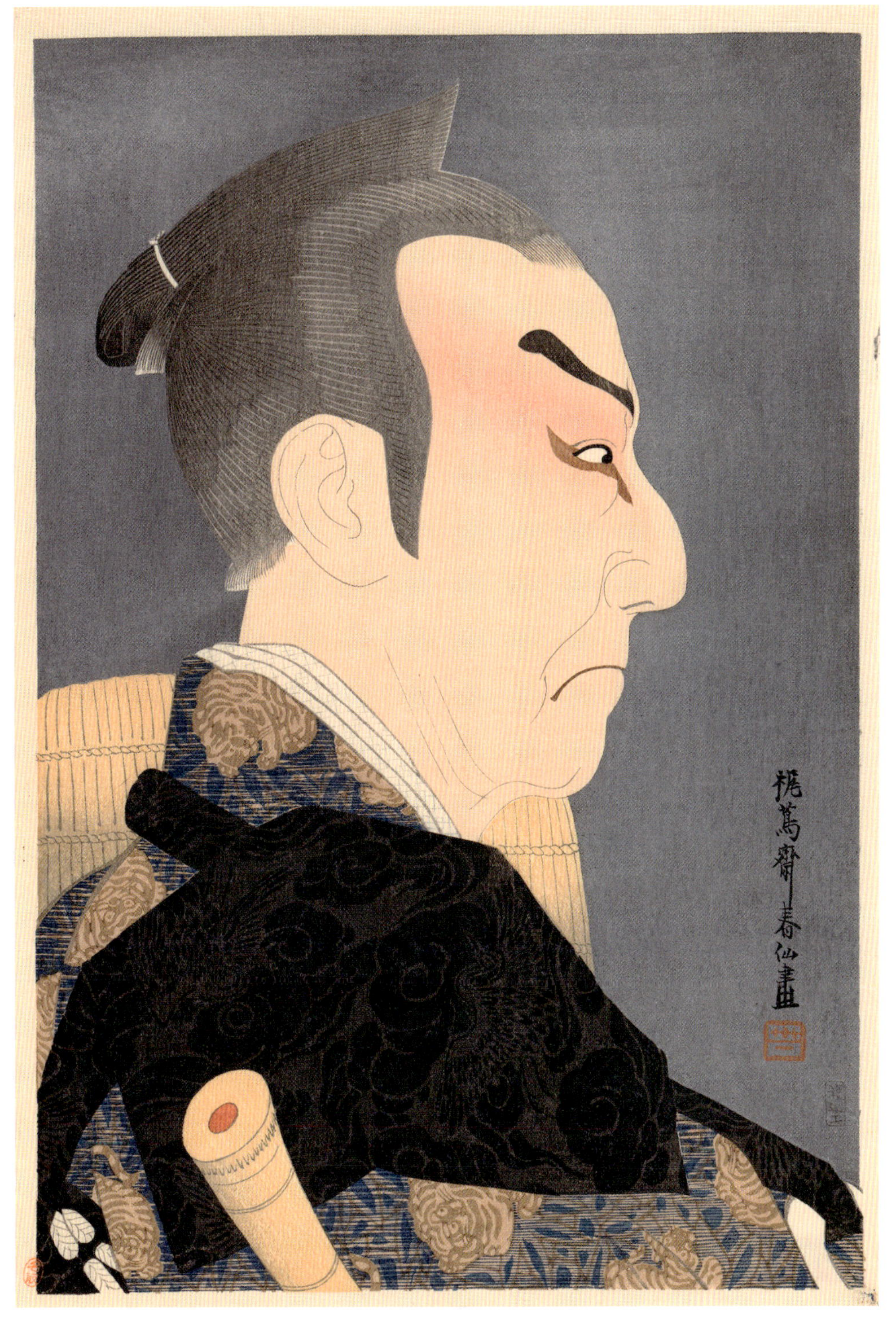

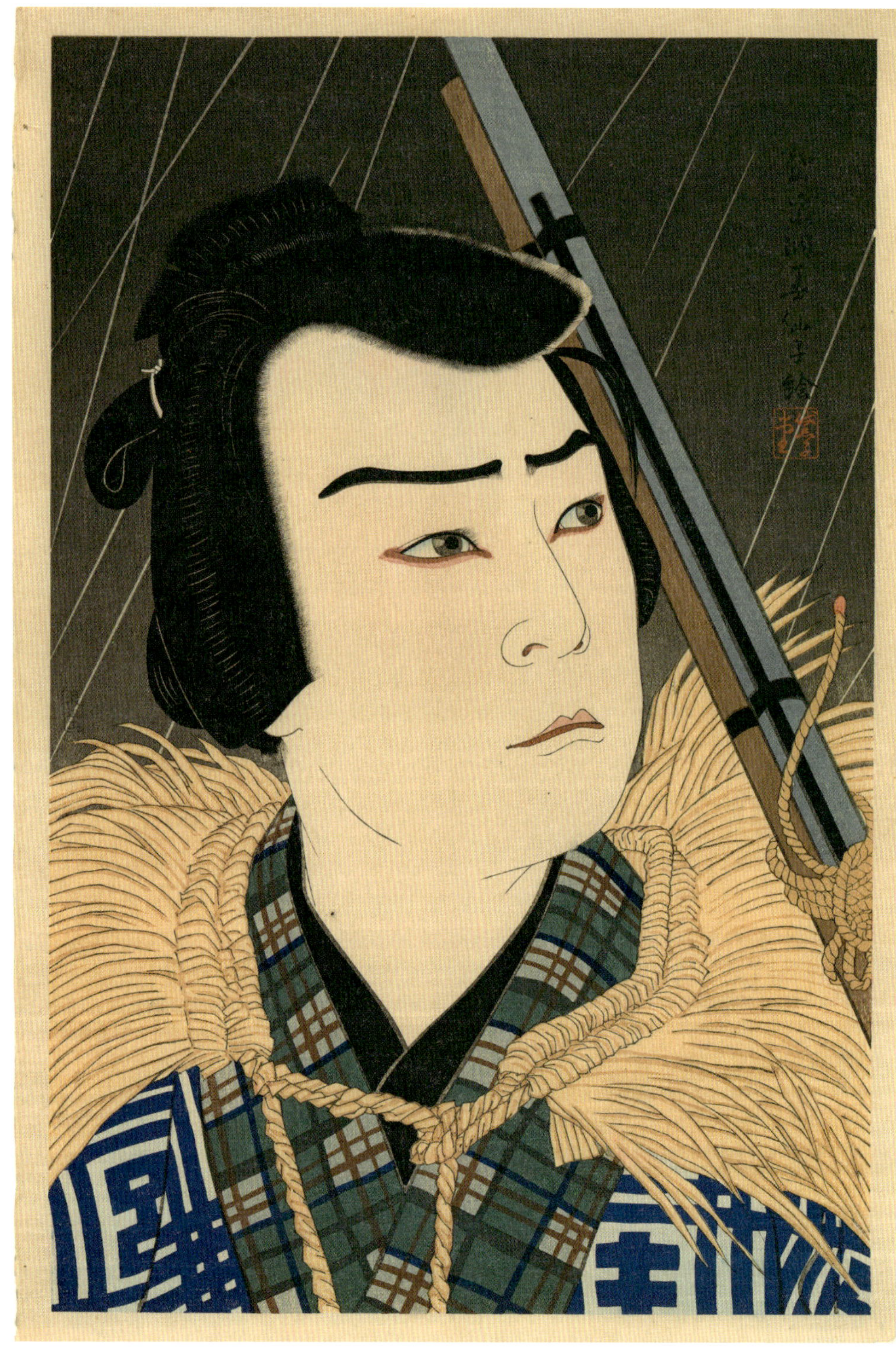

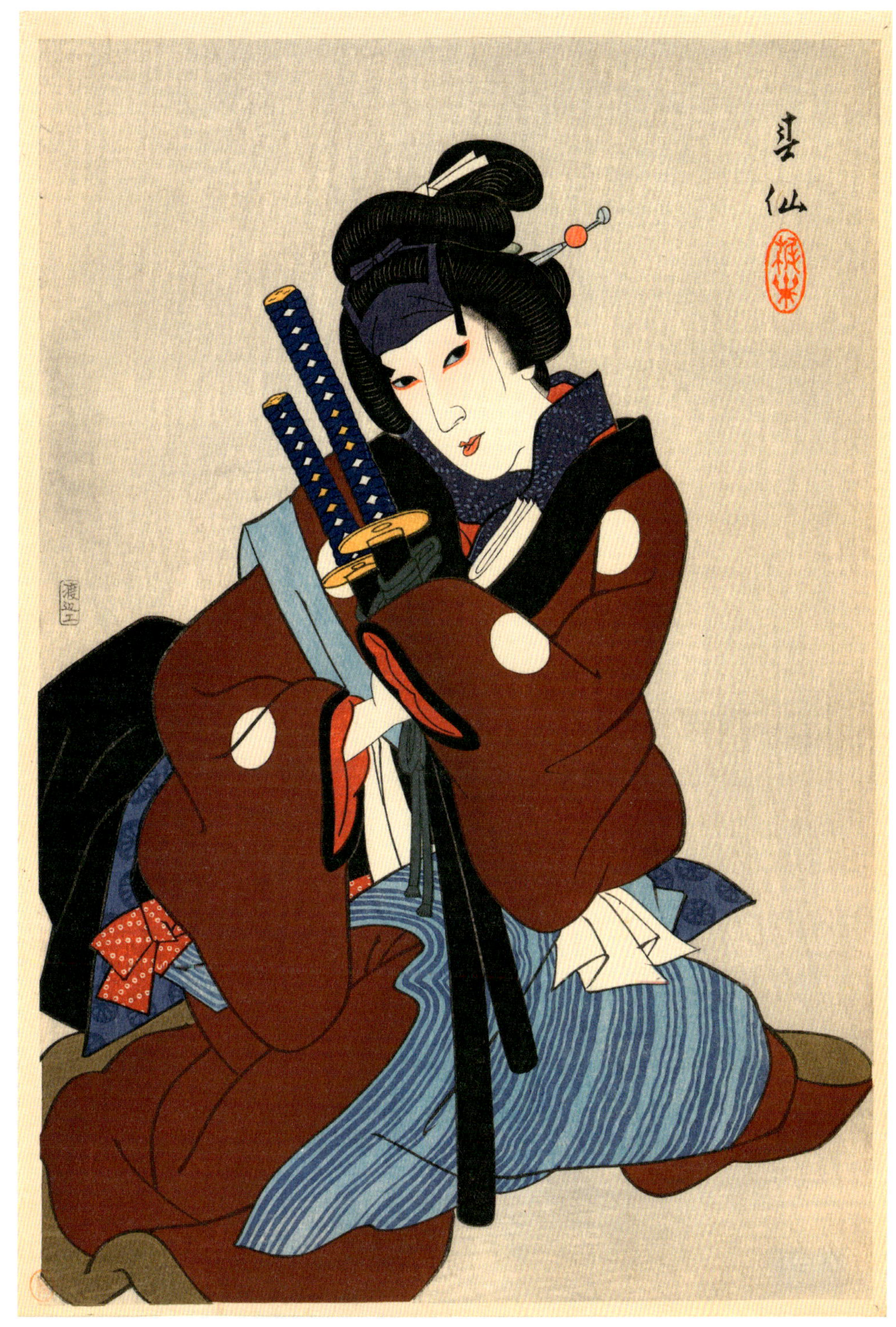

of Hangan's death and the intentions of the loyal retainers. He hopes to join the posse, but Yagorō asks him to instead sponsor a memorial to Hangan. Kanpei resolves to find the money. Later, Okaru and her father Yoichibei secretly organise for Okaru to be sold into prostitution to raise the funds.

Having received money for promising Okaru to a Kyoto brothel, Yoichibei rests in the countryside before returning home. During the night he is stabbed and robbed. Meanwhile, Kanpei is out hunting. A wild boar rushes past and Kanpei shoots, accidentally executing Yoichibei's murderer. Unable to identify his victim in the dark, Kanpei panics, takes the man's purse and flees. In the morning, the brothel owner arrives to collect Okaru and is surprised to find that Yoichibei has not yet returned. Kanpei enters and is told that Okaru has been sold. He reaches for his purse, planning to pay Okaru's bond, and is horrified to see that the stolen purse matches exactly the one held by the brothel's madam. Kanpei concludes that the man he shot was Yoichibei, and guiltily encourages Okaru away.

Soon Yoichibei's body is brought to the house. Okaru's mother Okaya confronts Kanpei, who is acting suspiciously, and discovers the blood-stained purse. Yagorō arrives and informs Kanpei that his donation will not be accepted because of his neglect of Hangan at the palace. Okaya compounds Kanpei's shame by accusing him of murder. Kanpei is mortified. He explains the accidental shooting and, to restore his honour, commits *seppuku*. Yagorō examines Yoichibei's corpse, sees that he died from a knife wound, and realises that Kanpei had inadvertently avenged his father-in-law's murder. Still breathing, Kanpei is able to sign his name in blood on the scroll, pledging vengeance on behalf of Hangan. Kanpei dies with his good name restored.

On the anniversary of Hangan's suicide, Yuranosuke visits the brothel where Okaru is working. Anxious to dispel any suspicion that he might be planning an attack on Moronao, Yuranosuke blithely feasts, drinks sake and enjoys the entertainers. Kudayū, once a follower of Hangan but now a spy for Moronao, is convinced that Yuranosuke is no longer dedicated to his deceased *daimyō*. Later, Yuranosuke offers to pay for Okaru's release. Her joy turns to heartbreak, however, when she learns of Kanpei's death. Yuranosuke gives her his sword, but instead of directing her to commit suicide he asks her to slay the traitor Kudayū.

Yuranosuke and his fellow *rōnin* travel to their hideaway. Yuranosuke rolls a large snowball and delivers a rousing speech, reminding the men that, like the snowball, they will only survive in the shadows. Earlier a marriage had been arranged between Yuranosuke's son Rikiya and Konami, the daughter of Honzō. It is declared that the union will be nullified unless the couple kill Honzō, who is in disgrace for his cowardice in bribing Moronao and preventing Hangan from assassinating the evil governor. On cue, Honzō arrives and is stabbed by Rikiya. Honzō begs forgiveness for his actions and gives Yuranosuke a detailed plan of Moronao's mansion.

Hangan's 47 retainers, in matching costumes, break in to the mansion. A series of spectacular fight scenes ensue, with Hangan's men eventually defeating Moronao and dragging the villain out into the snow. Yuranosuke stabs Moronao, using Hangan's dagger. Moronao's head is severed and carried off in victory.

The prints

Shunsen's actor prints include three portraits of characters from *The treasury of the loyal retainers*. The image of the highly respected actor

Kataoka Nizaemon XI as Honzō is a particularly fine print, with mica-flecked background and superb embossing. It presents the elderly samurai, reviled for his conservative approach to honourable samurai conflicts, in profile as he prepares to die at the hands of his daughter's fiancé. Another print illustrates Onoe Eizaburō VII as Okaru in the scene where she prepares to kill herself, having just found out that her father and her lover Kanpei are both dead, but instead attacks an enemy of Kanpei's former lord. From the *Supplement to collection of portraits by Shunsen*, the image of Onoe Kikugorō VI illustrates the actor in the role of the loyal yet ill-fated samurai Kanpei. The rifle with which Kanpei accidentally kills his father-in-law's murderer is slung over his shoulder. The print's dark background represents the night sky.

Kataoka Nizaemon XI (1857–1934)

Son of Nizaemon VIII, Kataoka Nizaemon XI was born into a large, successful kabuki family in Tokyo and took to the stage as an infant. He spent his early years training in the Kyoto-Osaka area. In 1867 he moved to Tokyo and became a popular *wagoto* (romantic male) actor, but played a great range of roles. Nizaemon XI's most highly acclaimed characters were the old men of classic kabuki plays.

Onoe Eizaburō VII (1900–26)

The son of Onoe Baikō VI, Eizaburō VII began acting as a child. Considered one of the most promising *onnagata* (female-role specialists) of the early-twentieth century, he died very young. Shunsen's print was released in the year of the actor's death.

Onoe Kikugorō VI (1885–1949)

See page 58 for actor's biography.

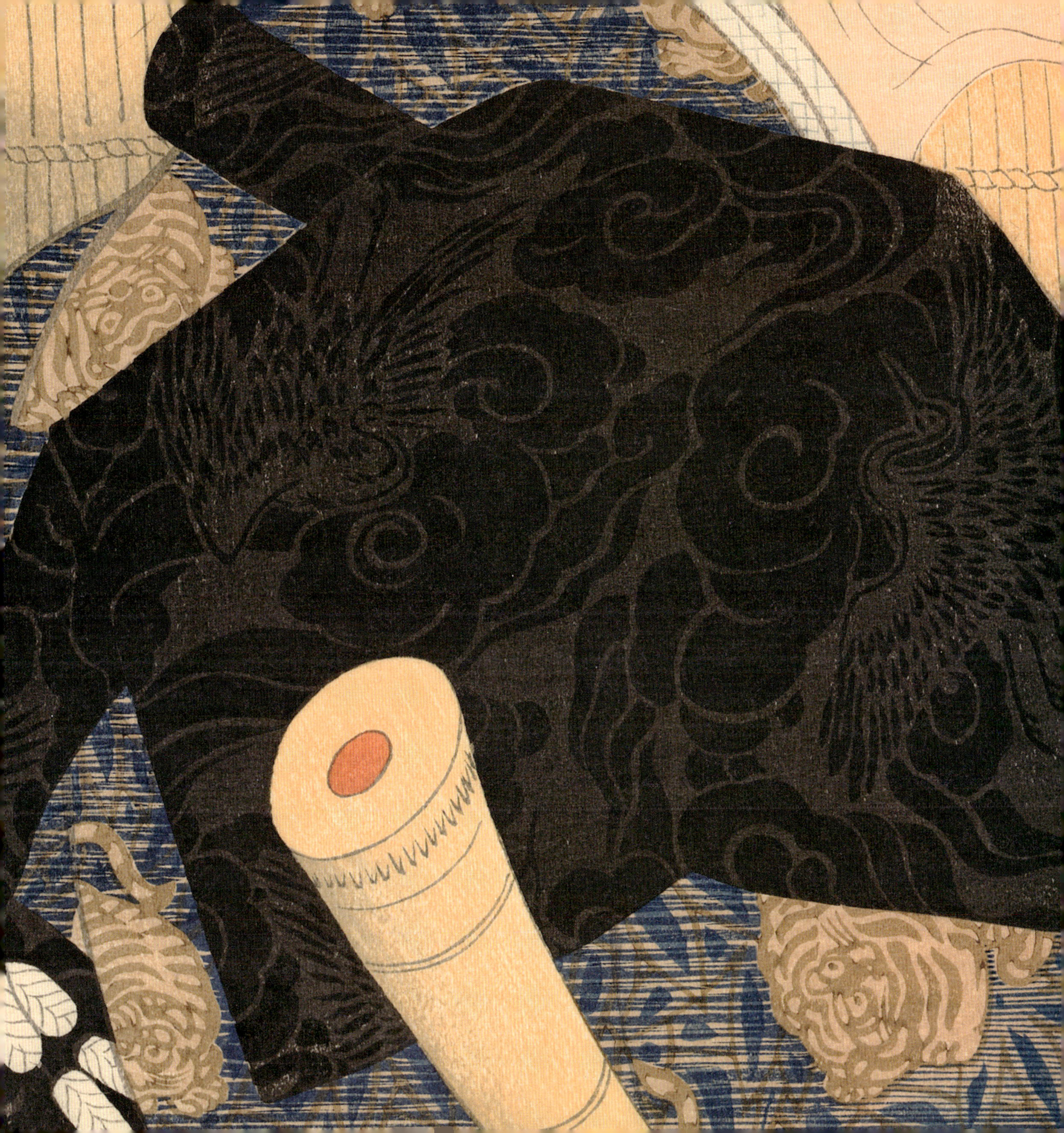

Nakamura Utaemon V as Yodogimi in 'A sinking moon over the lonely castle where the cuckoo cries' 1926 from the series *Collection of creative portraits by Shunsen*
[Nakamura Utaemon V Yodogimi]
woodblock print, embossing; ink, colour and mica on paper
sheet: 40.0 x 27.0 cm, image: 37.6 x 25.6 cm
National Gallery of Australia, Canberra,
gift of Jennifer Gordon, 1998

A sinking moon over the lonely castle where the cuckoo cries (Hototogisu kojō no rakugetsu)

written by Tsubouchi Shōyō, first kabuki performance in 1905

Tsubouchi produced a number of *shin* (new) kabuki dramas in the early-twentieth century. *Shin* kabuki employed modern Western theatrical styles to achieve historical and psychological realism. The plays are typically rich in dialogue and retain kabuki staging and costumes, but eschew symbolic posing, stage tricks, traditional music and distinctive makeup.

The central character in *A sinking moon*, Yodogimi, is based on a Japanese historical figure but closely resembles Shakespeare's Lady Macbeth. The real Yodogimi was left a widow after Toyotomi Hideyoshi, overlord of Japan, died in 1598. A council was appointed to rule for their infant son, Hideyori. Tokugawa Ieyasu usurped power, partly by arranging for Hideyori to marry his granddaughter Princess Sen. Ieyasu became shogun, but Hideyori threatened his legitimacy.

The play is set in 1615, with Ieyasu poised to take Hideyori's Osaka stronghold. Inside, Princess Sen's attendants scheme to spirit the princess out of the castle. Yodogimi is becoming increasingly paranoid. She discovers the plot and kills one of the conspirators. Another commits suicide. Yodogimi hysterically attacks the princess for betraying Hideyori. The battle rages outside—signified by gongs, wild music, explosions, smoke and clashing swords. Princess Sen escapes in the chaos.

Yodogimi's distress escalates as the castle burns. She tears at the princess' discarded robe, lashes out in confusion and laughs manically. Amid impassioned arguing, Hideyori surrenders. He later commits suicide, while his deranged mother is killed to prevent her capture.

The print

Shunsen presents Nakamura Utaemon V as Yodogimi—a role created especially for him—as she descends into madness. With contorted facial features and unkempt hair, Yodogimi clutches the weapon with which she murdered Princess Sen's lady-in-waiting.

Nakamura Utaemon V (1865–1940)

Tokyo actor Nakamura Shikan IV adopted Nakamura Utaemon V, the son of a government official, in 1875. He debuted in 1877 and was popular in Tokyo and Osaka for his intelligence and beauty. Utaemon V rose to be one of the great *onnagata* (female-role specialists) of his generation, performing opposite experienced stars including Ichikawa Danjūrō IX and Onoe Kikugorō V. In his later years, Utaemon V was partially paralysed due to lead poisoning from kabuki makeup. Despite this, he continued to perform from seated or kneeling poses.

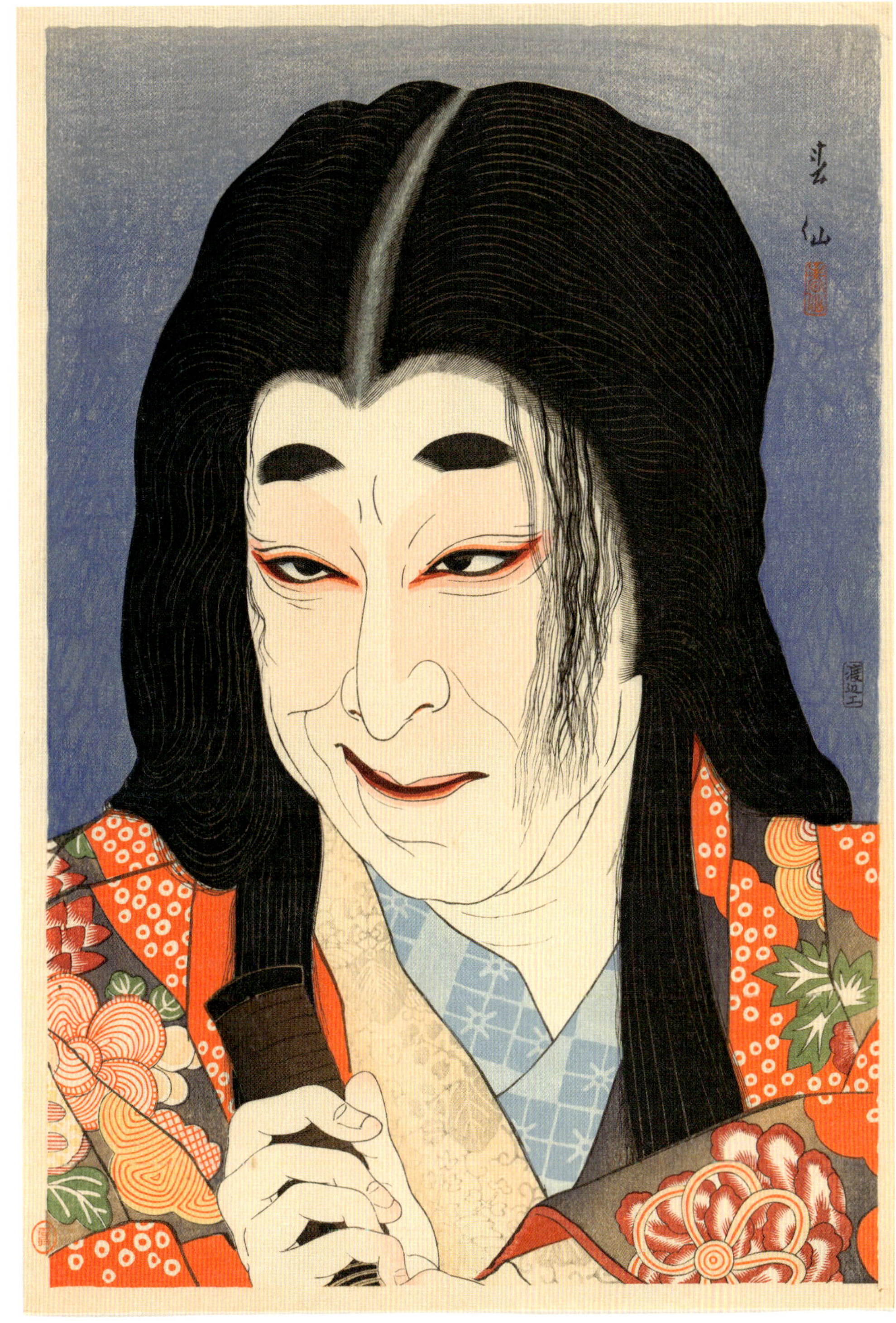

Sawamura Gennosuke IV as Nikki Danjō in 'The precious incense and autumn flowers of Sendai' 1928 from the series *Collection of creative portraits by Shunsen* [Sawamura Gennosuke IV Yukashita no Nikki] woodblock print; ink and colour on paper sheet: 40.2 x 27.9 cm, image: 38.0 x 25.6 cm National Gallery of Australia, Canberra, gift of Jennifer Gordon, 1998

(below) **Utagawa Kunisada** (1786–1865)
Kataoka Nizaemon VIII as Matsugae Matonosuke and Bandō Hikosaburō V as Nikki Danjō 1861
woodblock print; ink and colour on paper, 37.5 x 51.3cm
Museum of Fine Arts, Boston, William Sturgis Bigelow Collection

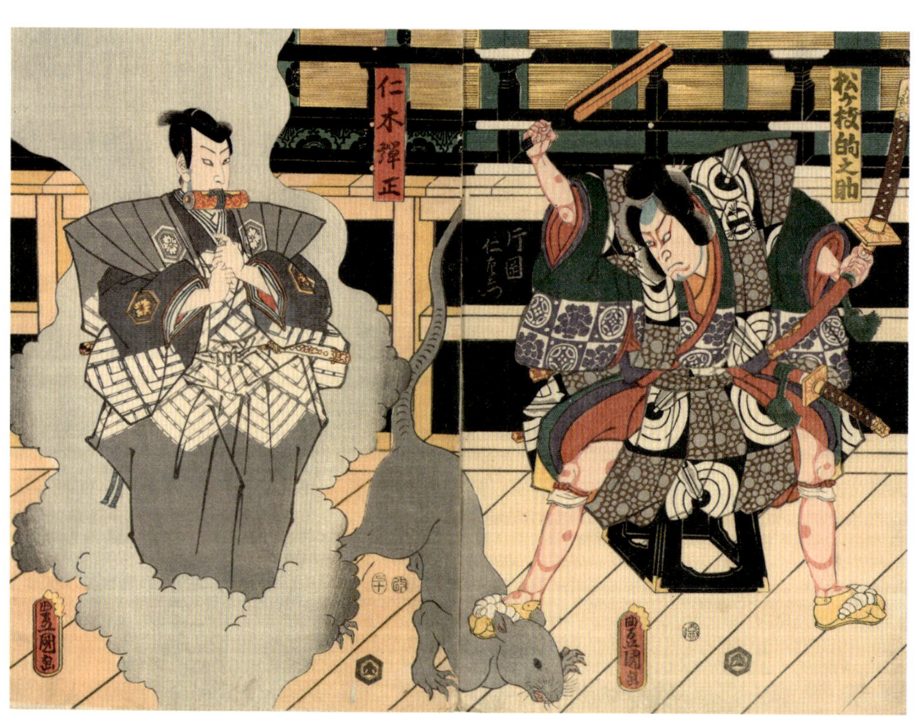

The precious incense and autumn flowers of Sendai (Meiboku Sendai hagi)

written by Nagawa Kamesuke, first kabuki performance in 1777

The precious incense and autumn flowers of Sendai is based on the scandalous historical power struggle brought about by an affair between the leader of the Date family and a prostitute. The play uses the name Ashikaga instead of Date.

The head of the Ashikaga family is too ill to rule and his brother Yorikane is preoccupied with his mistress. Oe Onitsura senses a power vacuum and conspires to seize control with the help of his nephew, the evil sorcerer Nikki Danjō. Meanwhile Nikki Danjō's sister, Yashio, plots to kill Yorikane's son Tsurukiyo. She enters Tsurukiyo's chambers with her retinue and presents Tsurukiyo with some cakes. But the boy's dutiful nurse, Masaoka, tests all Tsurukiyo's food on her own son, Senmatsu. When Senmatsu eats a cake, Yashio cuts his throat to conceal that it was poisoned. Masaoka masks her emotions so well that one of the conspirators assumes that the boy who died must be Tsurukiyo. He gives Masaoka a scroll listing those in league against Yorikane. Alone, Masaoka expresses the depth of her grief. Yashio returns to murder Masaoka, but is overpowered and stabbed. In the chaos, a rat (an actor) carries off the scroll.

The scene changes, revealing a samurai loyal to Yorikane in a cellar room. The rat scurries in and is struck on the head. Magically, the animal transforms into Nikki Danjō. (On stage, the rat disappears down a trapdoor and the sorcerer rises up in a cloud of smoke.) The sorcerer evades the samurai by vanishing.

The play resumes in a courtroom, with Nikki Danjō challenging the young Tsurukiyo's legitimacy as clan leader. The complex scene— rich in deception, forgery and blackmail—ends with Nikki Danjō and Onitsura found guilty of an attempted coup. Eventually, Nikki Danjō is killed.

The print

Shunsen illustrates Sawamura Gennosuke IV, a senior actor of the 1920s, portraying the climactic moment when Nikki Danjō emerges from beneath the stage. The sorcerer holds a scroll in his mouth, and his forehead bears a fresh gash, to convey his transformation from the rat. The grey kimono mimics the colour of the rat.

Sawamura Gennosuke IV (1859–1936)

The adopted son of actor Sawamura Gennosuke III, Gennosuke IV debuted in 1870 and spent many years playing supporting roles alongside the leading Meiji-era stars. He was considered a talented and versatile actor, especially in *onnagata* (female) roles.

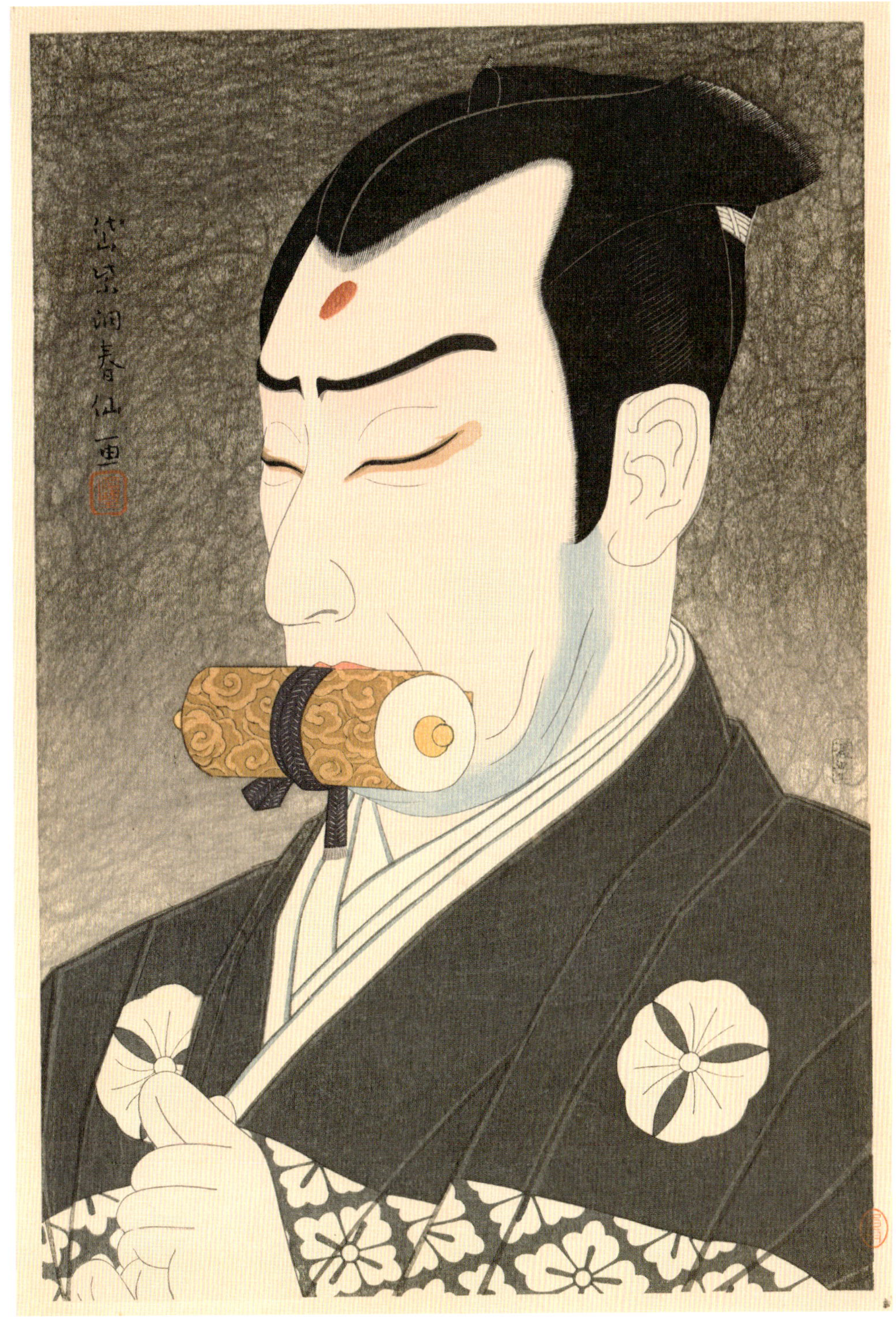

*Ichikawa Sanshō V as Soga Gorō in
'The medicine peddler'* 1926 from the series
Collection of creative portraits by Shunsen
[Ichikawa Sanshō V Uirō uri]
woodblock print; ink and colour on paper
sheet: 39.7 x 27.5 cm, image: 37.9 x 25.7 cm
National Gallery of Australia, Canberra,
gift of Jennifer Gordon, 1998

The medicine peddler (Uirō uri)

written by Ichikawa Danjūrō II, additional
material by Kawajiri Seitan and Noguchi Tatsuji,
first kabuki performance in 1718

Loved for its vibrancy and entertaining word
play, *The medicine peddler* was originally part of
a New Year play created by Ichikawa Danjūrō II
to showcase his fabulous elocution. The main
character, Soga Gorō, is disguised as a seller of
the Chinese medicine *uirō,* which is promoted as
a cure for all ills. Danjūrō II apparently took the
remedy and, pleased with the results, offered to
create a kabuki to advertise the product. The play
also includes brazen promotions of the Ichikawa
family line.

The background to the play, well known in
Japan, can be found in history, legends, literature
and plays about Soga Gorō and Soga Jūrō,
brothers who became famous for an audacious
vendetta in the twelfth century.

A celebration is held for Kudō Saemon
Suketsune, the powerful statesman who
engineered the murder of Soga Gorō's father.
Suketsune and his attendants are drinking
sake when Soga Gorō calls out, hawking *uirō*.
Suketsune invites him in to entertain the party
with his spiel. He hesitates, then perfectly
delivers the tongue-twisting pitch, speaking
faster and faster to the delight of his audience.
Suketsune's attendants enjoy trying out his
tricky rhymes. In the playful atmosphere,
Gorō is able to push aside the retainers and
threaten Suketsune.

Soga Gorō's identity is revealed, but he is
prevented from killing Suketsune when someone
reminds him that the proper way to carry out
the revenge murder is alongside his brother.
A frustrated Gorō agrees. In admiration of Gorō's
samurai values, Suketsune throws him a map
to help him in his quest.

The print

Shunsen's image of Ichikawa Sanshō V as Soga
Gorō in *The medicine peddler* shows the character
as the quintessential *uirō* seller, dressed in a bold
costume adorned with lucky coin motifs. He
holds the remedy he is selling in his left hand.
His fan bears a Japanese character for longevity.

Ichikawa Sanshō V (1882–1956)

The son of a banker, Ichikawa Sanshō V married
the daughter of Ichikawa Danjūrō IX, kabuki's
highest-ranking actor. He began studying the
art as a young man, unlike most performers who
are trained virtually from birth. When Danjūrō
IX died, Sanshō V inherited the leadership of the
Ichikawa family and began his stage career with
modest supporting roles. He was not a great
star but achieved some recognition, particularly
for staging classic plays by past actors of the
Ichikawa line. Sanshō V revived *The medicine
peddler* in 1922. Not considered sufficiently
talented to bear the title during his lifetime,
he was given the name of Ichikawa Danjūrō X
after his death.

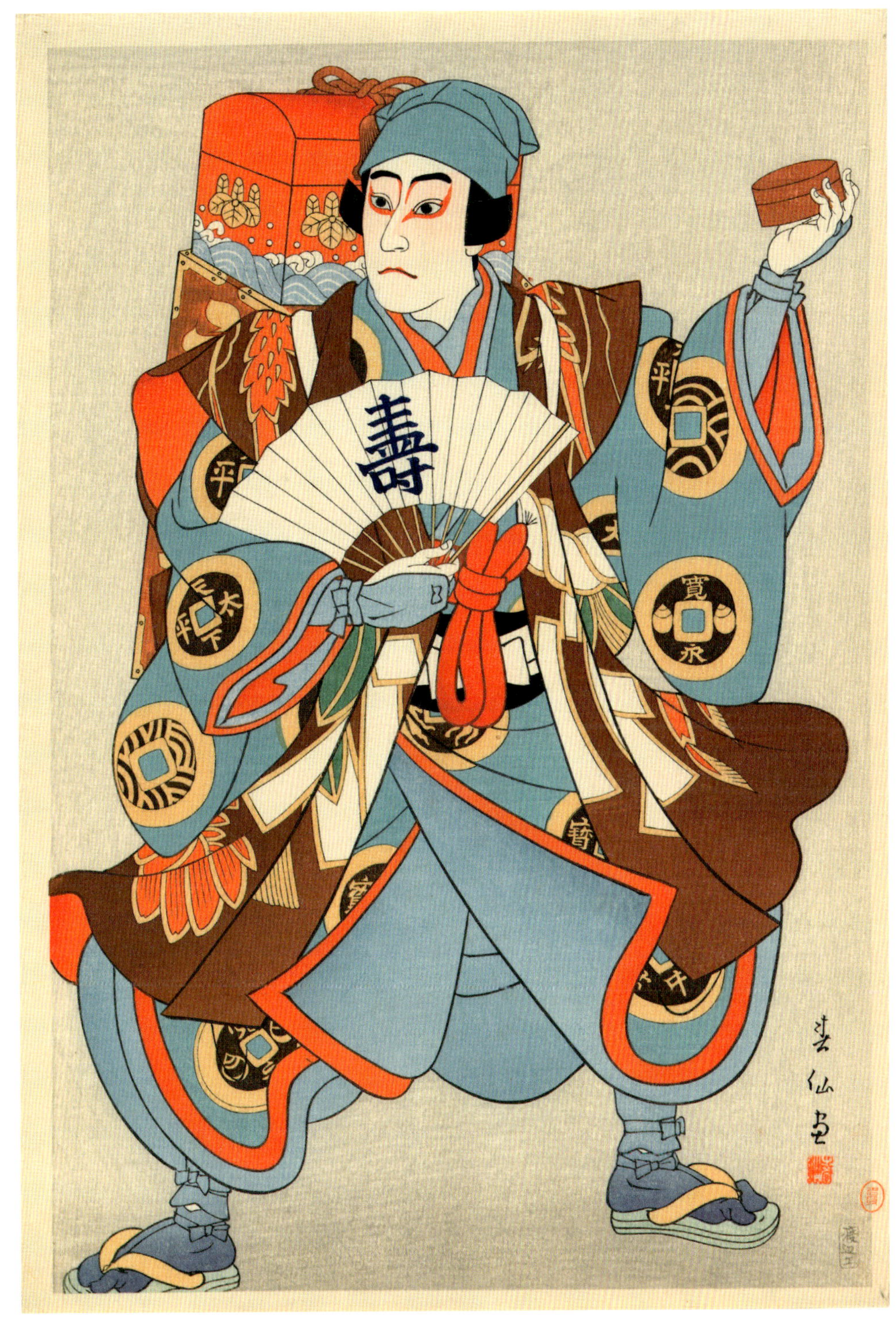

The picture book of the Taikō (Ehon Taikōki)

written by Chikamatsu Yanagi, Chikamatsu Kosui and Chikamatsu Chibai, first kabuki performance in 1800

The original version of *The picture book of the Taikō* follows an unusual format. It concerns a period of 13 days, from the rebellion of Takechi Mitsuhide (the historical figure Akechi Mitsuhide) until his death. Each day is represented by its own act. The background to the betrayal is covered by *The banner of rebellion*, which dramatises Mitsuhide's betrayal of his master Oda Harunga (see page 56).

The only part of *The picture book of the Taikō* performed regularly is act ten. The scene is a cottage in Amagasaki where Mitsuhide's mother Satsuki has taken refuge, appalled by her son's treachery. An itinerant priest calls at the house and Satsuki invites him in, even though she recognises him to be Mitsuhide's rival, Hisayoshi, in disguise. Satsuki later farewells her grandson Jūjirō in a poignant scene. Jūjirō knows that his father's troops are likely to be defeated, but joins them out of filial piety.

Hiding in bamboo groves outside the house is Mitsuhide, disguised as a farmer, who has been secretly following Hisayoshi. He shapes a spear from bamboo and uses it to stab at the figure he believes is Hisayoshi, but who tragically turns out to be his own mother. In her death throes, she begs Mitsuhide to end the rebellion. Jūjirō returns from combat wounded and tells of Mitsuhide's defeat. In some productions, a large circular stage turns on a concealed axis to reveal a battle scene, enabling Mitsuhide to look upon his defeated armies. Back at the cottage, Jūjirō and his grandmother die together. Hisayoshi resolves to vanquish Mitsuhide in battle. Later, poetic justice prevails and a farmer murders Mitsuhide with a bamboo spear.

The print

This bold print illustrates Ichikawa Chūsha VII as Mitsuhide in the guise of a farmer lifting his bamboo hat in the most famous *mie* (pose) of *The picture book of the Taikō*. Chūsha VII was the great master of this role.

Ichikawa Chūsha VII (1860–1936)

Born in Kyoto, Ichikawa Chūsha VII debuted at the age of four. Like many actors of his generation, Chūsha VII was a disciple of Ichikawa Danjūrō IX. He regularly worked in Tokyo and Osaka and was celebrated as a great actor of historical roles, particularly complex characters. Chūsha VII took ill from lead poisoning while performing at the Kabuki Theatre in 1931 and rarely performed again.

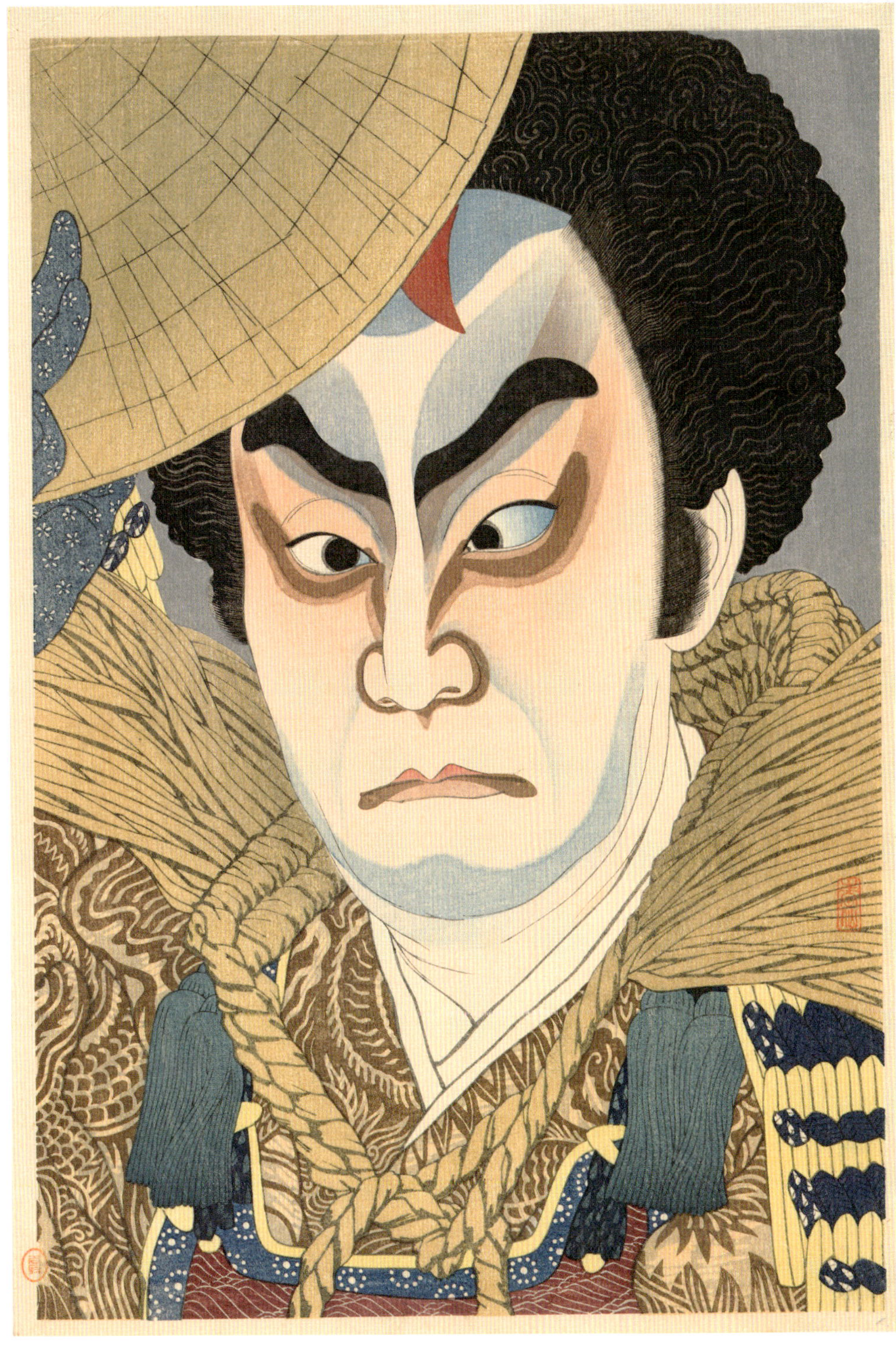

*Jitsukawa Enjaku II as Danshichi Kurōbei in
'Summer festival: mirror of Osaka'* 1926
from the series *Collection of creative portraits
by Shunsen*
[Jitsukawa Enjaku II Danshichi]
woodblock print; ink and colour on paper
sheet: 40.3 x 27.4 cm, image: 38.2 x 26 cm
National Gallery of Australia, Canberra,
gift of Jennifer Gordon, 1998

(below) **Utagawa Kunisada** (1786–1865) *Clearing weather
in the back field* from the series *Eight views of the floating
world* 1855
woodblock print; ink and colour on paper 35.5 x 50.6 cm
Museum of Fine Arts, Boston, William Sturgis Bigelow
Collection

Summer festival: mirror of Osaka (Natsu matsuri naniwa Kagami)

written by Namiki Sōsuke, Miyoshi Shōraku,
Takeda Izumo II, first kabuki performance in 1745

The enduringly popular *Summer festival: mirror
of Osaka* centres on the *otokodate* Danshichi.
Translated as 'chivalrous commoner', *otokodate*
are delinquents glorified for protecting the
people from the abuses of corrupt samurai.

The play begins with Danshichi in prison
for injuring a servant of evil samurai Ōtori
Sagaemon, but due to be pardoned through
the assistance of Tamashima Hyōdayū. Sabu, a
reformed *otokodate*, and Danshichi's wife, Okaji,
travel to meet Danshichi. Okaji goes into the
Sumiyoshi Shrine just as Tamashima Hyōdayū's
son, Isonojō, arrives. Sabu settles a dispute for
Isonojō and directs him to Okaji.

Danshichi is released into exile and vows to
protect Isonojō. Sabu greets his friend and
treats him to a shave and haircut at a nearby
barbershop. A young woman, Kotoura, suddenly
enters, chased by Danshichi's enemy Ōtori

Sagaemon. Kotoura, a former prostitute, is
Isonojō's lover and the object of Sagaemon's
lust. Danshichi trounces Sagaemon in a comical
slapstick sequence, before reuniting with his wife
and son.

The next act opens on the night before the
summer festival. Sabu has been sheltering Isonojō
and Kotoura. Isonojō is accused of stealing and
forced to flee, while Sabu chases after henchmen
who threaten to alert Sagaemon to Kotoura's
presence. Left unprotected, Kotoura is deceived
and captured by Danshichi's devious father-in-law,
Giheiji, who conspires to sell her to Sagaemon.

Danshichi reaches Giheiji and offers to pay
for Kotoura, who is freed. Giheiji discovers that
Danshichi has no money and beats his son-in-
law, who accidentally wounds him. Doomed
for this grave crime, Danshichi murders Giheiji
to silence him. In performance, the characters
grapple in real mud and water as the lively
festival passes by. The stylised movements of
Danshichi, his bare torso covered in bold tattoos,
are spectacular.

The print

Shunsen captures the heroic *otokodate* essence of
the handsome Danshichi Kurōbei as he swaggers
out of the barbershop in a clean red-and-blue
checked kimono. The characteristic curtains of
the barbershop can be seen in the background.

Jitsukawa Enjaku II (1877–1951)

A charismatic and well-loved star, Jitsukawa
Enjaku II began acting in Osaka in 1886. He
first appeared on the Tokyo stage in 1899.
Performances in which he co-starred with
Nakamura Ganjirō I were particularly popular.
Enjaku II was adept at a number of male-role
acting styles, and the hero Danshichi was one of
his finest. Offstage he was a notorious womaniser.

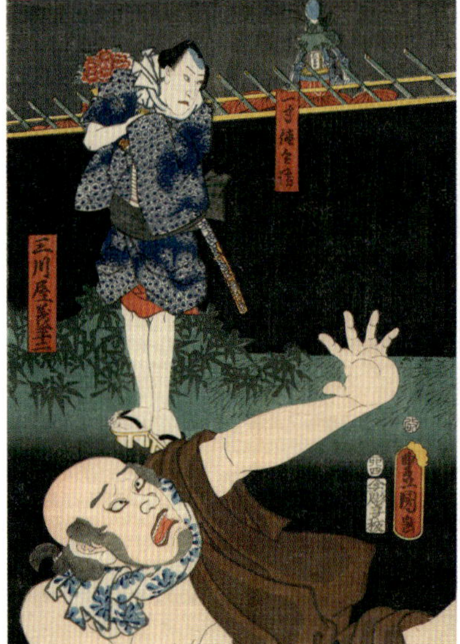
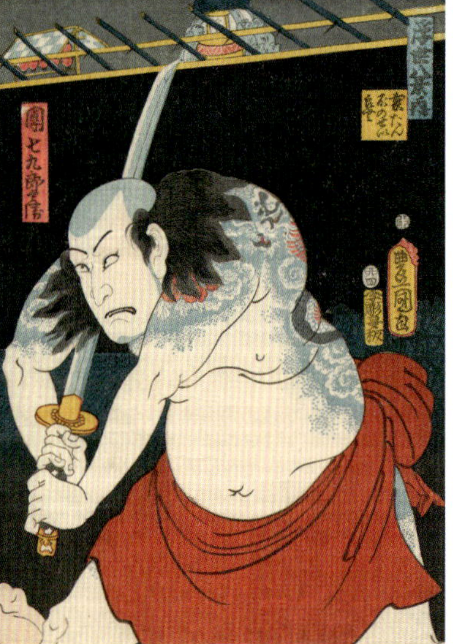

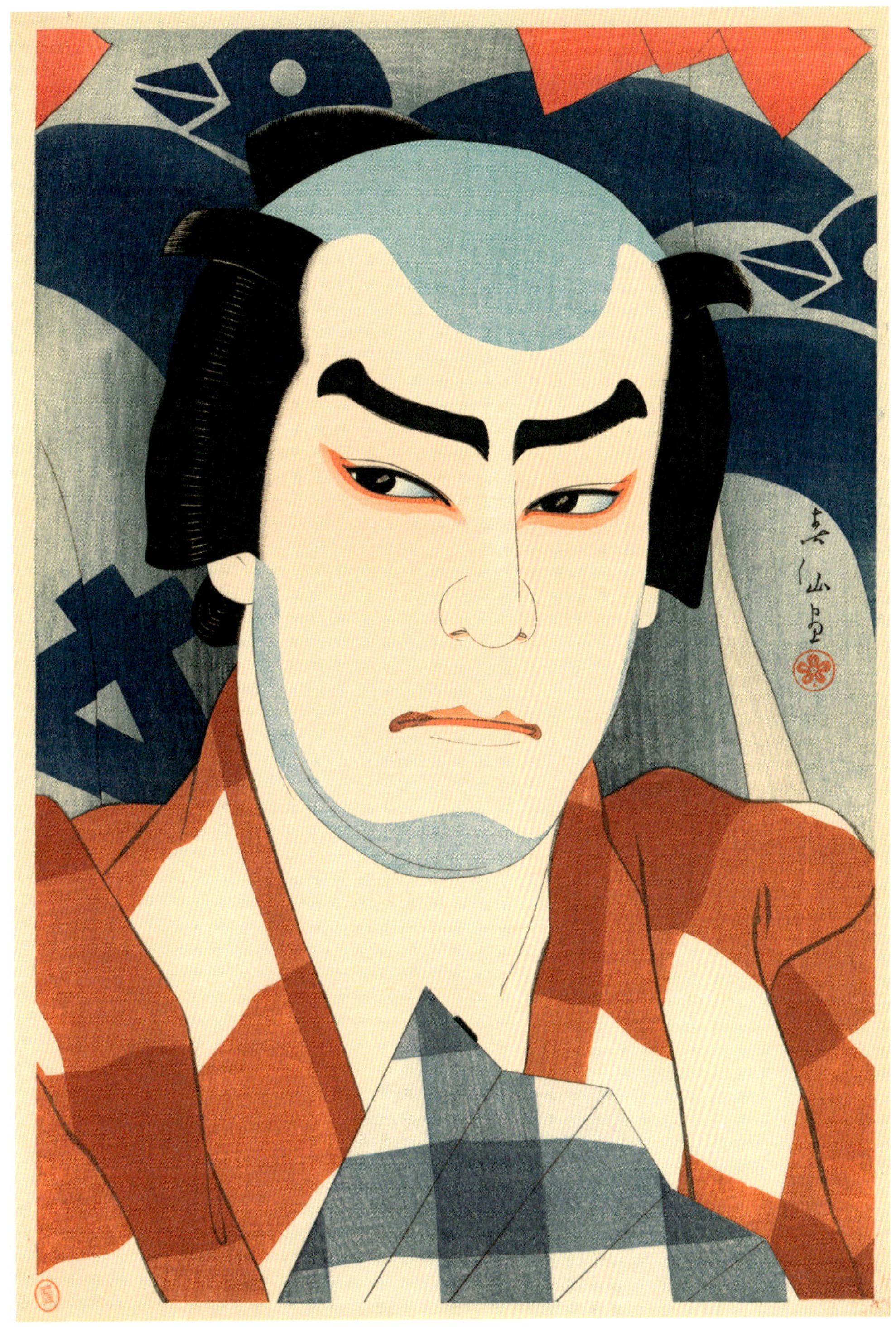

Kataoka Ichizō IV as Benkei in 'The cherry trees of the Imperial Palace' 1927 from the series *Collection of creative portraits by Shunsen* [Kataoka Ichizō IV jōshi no Benkei] woodblock print; ink and colour on paper sheet: 40.2 x 27.8 cm, image 38.2 x 25.7 cm National Gallery of Australia, Canberra, gift of Jennifer Gordon, 1998

The cherry trees of the Imperial Palace (Gosho zakura Horikawa youchi)

written by Matsuda Bunkodō and Miyoshi Shōraku, first kabuki performance in 1755

The cherry trees of the Imperial Palace is an epic drama set during the twelfth-century war between the Minamoto and Taira families. Minamoto leader Yoritomo has become shogun, but remains under threat from the Taira. His brother Yoshitsune, one of the most revered heroes of Japanese history, is a brilliant Minamoto commander. The play's most famous scene is 'Benkei the envoy' (Benkei jōshi), which centres on Yoshitsune's devoted retainer.

Yoritomo sends Benkei to kill Yoshitsune's wife, Kyō no Kimi, the daughter of a Taira general. Benkei goes to the mansion where she is under the care of Jijū Tarō and demands her head. Torn between obeying the shogun and protecting his master's wife, Tarō decides to find a stand-in for Kyō no Kimi and chooses Shinobu, one of her attendants. Shinobu is prepared to give her life to protect her mistress but her mother, Owasa, protests that she cannot die before meeting her father. Owasa describes the fleeting encounter, 18 years earlier, with a mysterious man who left her with child and the memento of his red kimono sleeve. Benkei impatiently stabs the startled Shinobu from behind a paper screen. He steps out to reveal the sleeve of his kimono. It matches the one Owasa has long treasured. Owasa and Benkei weep over the dying Shinobu. Tarō then cuts off Shinobu's head and commits suicide. As he dies, he explains that his death will appear as proper samurai atonement for murdering his master's wife.

To maintain the subterfuge of her death, Yoshitsune's wife is disguised as Shinobu while his mistress Shizuka has taken her place in the household. One day Shizuka's devious brother Tōyota calls on his sister and recognises Kyō no Kimi. Shizuka catches Tōyota writing a letter revealing that she is alive, and the siblings argue furiously. Their mother overhears the altercation and stabs her traitorous son. Tōyota repents and is forgiven after exposing a plot to attack Yoshitsune. Tōyota then fights the men sent to slay Yoshitsune before dying from the wound inflicted by his mother. In the final scenes Yoritomo acknowledges Yoshitsune's loyalty and the brothers reconcile.

The print

Shunsen illustrates the actor Kataoka Ichizō IV as Benkei. Shunsen captures the moment after Benkei fatally wounds Shinobu, when he reveals himself to be her father. The print was published after the actor's death.

Kataoka Ichizō IV (1880–1926)

Born in Tokyo, Ichizō IV was adopted by the actor Kataoka Ichizō III and debuted at the age of seven. He was conscripted in 1900 and fought in the Russo-Japanese War (1904–05). In 1906 he returned and starred in plays glorifying Japan's military victory. Famous for his fabulous stage presence and commanding voice, the actor appeared in the first kabuki play staged in Tokyo after the Great Kantō earthquake of 1923.

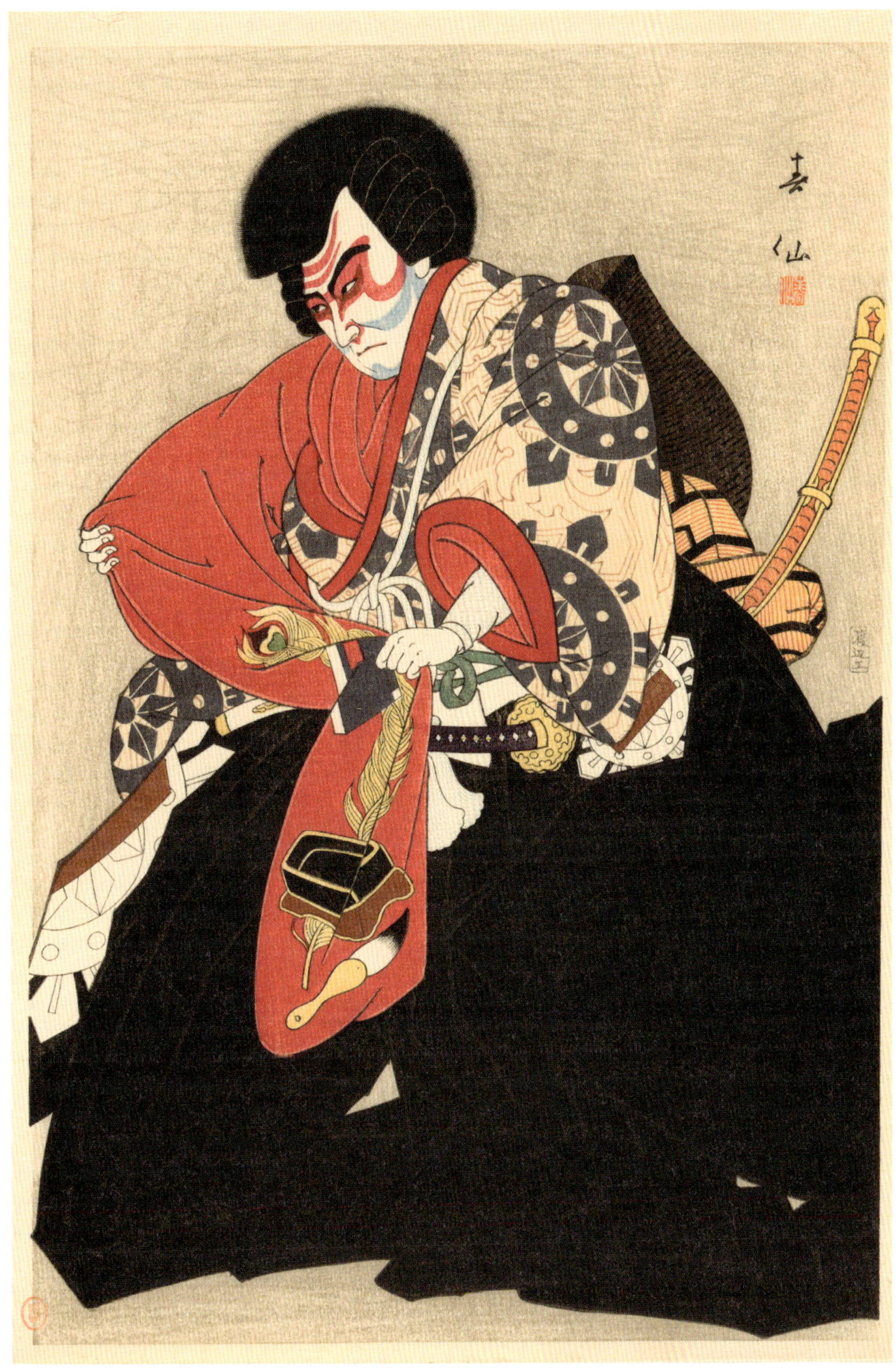

*Ichikawa Ennosuke II as Ikeda Kakutayū in
'The diary of Tōyama, the cherry-blossom tattooed
magistrate' 1927 from the series Collection
of creative portraits by Shunsen*
[Ichikawa Ennosuke II Tōyama seidan no
Kakutayū]
woodblock print; ink and colour on paper
sheet: 39.2 x 27.6 cm, image: 37.6 x 25.8 cm
National Gallery of Australia, Canberra,
gift of Jennifer Gordon, 1998

The diary of Tōyama, the cherry-blossom tattooed magistrate (Tōyama zakura Tenpō nikki)

written by Takeshiba Kisui, first kabuki
performance in 1893

The diary of Tōyama features the mid-nineteenth
century magistrate and playboy Tōyama no
Kinsan in a play about Tokyo criminals. Tōyama
was famous for his distinctive cherry-blossom
tattoos, and has been immortalised in literature,
kabuki, television and film. Set in the Tenpō era
(1830–44), the play reflects the dissatisfaction
with policing and justice in the late-nineteenth
century, when it was written.

A merchant plans to kill himself with his lover,
Nobuwaka, but cannot go through with it.
He turns instead to a life of crime, renaming
himself Yūten Kozō. Meanwhile on his way to
the entertainment quarter, the priest Tengaku
is mistaken for wanted criminal Ikeda Kakutayū
and arrested. Strangely, Tengaku befriends the
real Kakutayū in prison and the pair escape
together. The fugitives later meet up with Yūten
Kozō and swear to be brothers for life.

Some years later, Kakutayū has been thieving
disguised as a blind masseur. When his ex-wife
discovers this, she admonishes him. Kakutayū,
dressed as the masseur, murders her. He is later
captured during a robbery and put on trial.
The judge questions his identity, suggesting
he may really be Tengaku, who is still wanted
for breaking out of jail. Confusion erupts and
Kakutayū seizes the opportunity to abscond.

The magistrate Tōyama Kinshirō (Tōyama no
Kinsan) is appointed to investigate the disastrous
trial. He discovers that the judge had assumed
that Kakutayū was the falsely accused priest and
planned to help him. This leads Tōyama to delve
into Tengaku's case. Nobuwaka, a prostitute since
the attempted joint suicide, provides evidence,

as does her former lover, the thief Yūten Kozō.
Tengaku is pardoned for his jailbreak, while
Yūten Kozō and Kakutayū end up in custody.

The print

Shunsen portrays Ichikawa Ennosuke II, an
acknowledged master of the role, as villainous
thief Kakutayū. The character, closely identified
with real Tokyo underworld figure Kiyomizu
Sadakichi, is shown wielding the dagger with
which he commits murder. The same actor often
plays both Tōyama and Kakutayū.

Ichikawa Ennosuke II (1886–1963)

Ichikawa Ennosuke II was born into an
established kabuki family, but had a great
interest in modernising the art form. As a young
man he participated in progressive modern
theatrical movements and was one of the few
early-twentieth century actors who travelled
outside of Japan. The experience led him to
establish the New Dance movement, produce
a number of modern plays and stage Western
dramas. Ennosuke II was the doyen of Japanese
theatre after the Second World War.

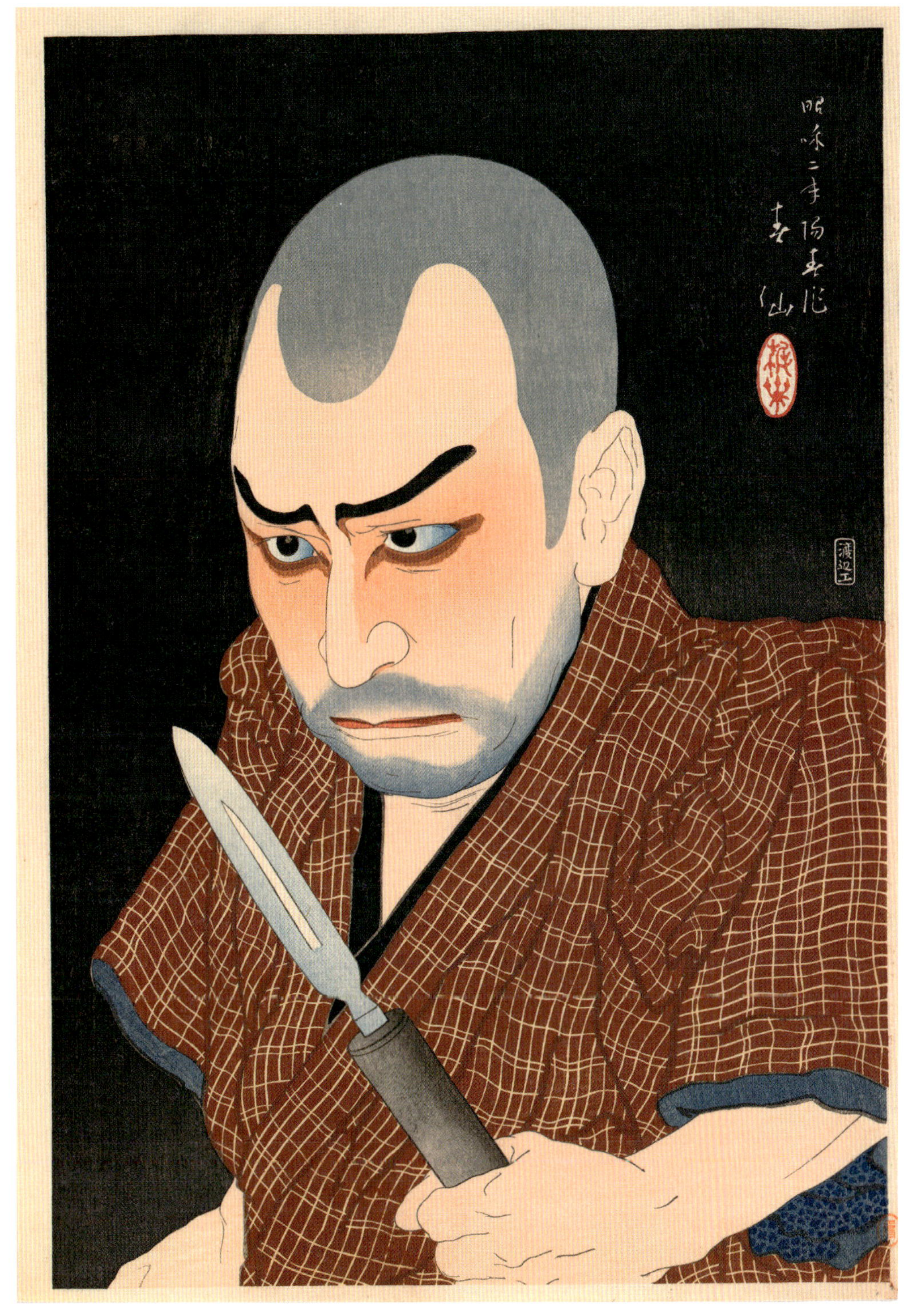

Ichikawa Kigan V as Otomi in 'Sympathetic chatter and the scandalous haircomb' 1927 from the series *Collection of creative portraits by Shunsen* [Ichikawa Kigan V Genjidana no Otomi] woodblock print; ink and colour on paper sheet: 40.2 x 27.4 cm, image: 38.0 x 25.6 cm National Gallery of Australia, Canberra, gift of Jennifer Gordon, 1998

Sympathetic chatter and the scandalous haircomb (Yowa nasake ukina no yokogushi)

written by Segawa Jokō III, first kabuki performance in 1853

The popular play, also known as *Scar-face Yosa* (Kirare Yosa), was inspired by a Tokyo gang leader's brutal assault on an early-nineteenth century musician, Yoshimura Ichisaburō IV, after he discovered Ichisaburō's affair with his mistress Osato. Ichisaburō and Osato later married and had a daughter named Otomi.

The drama opens at Kisarazu Beach near Tokyo. The handsome young wastrel Yosaburō falls instantly in love with Otomi, the geisha mistress of gangster Akama Genzaemon. Tragically, Genzaemon hears of the clandestine affair and catches the lovers together. Yosaburō is captured and tortured. He survives, but is left with hideous scars. Otomi escapes and is pursued to the beach by Genzaemon's servant, who tells her that Yosaburō has been killed. She leaps into the water but is rescued by her estranged brother Tazaemon. Each lover now believes the other to be dead.

Years later, Otomi is living peacefully under Tazaemon's guardianship unaware that he is her brother. One night she returns from the local *onsen* (bathhouse) and shelters a shopkeeper, Tōhachi, from the evening's storm. Tōhachi amuses Otomi with a dance and she avoids his amorous advances. Meanwhile, Yosaburō, now a criminal and swindler, approaches Otomi's house with the thief Yasu. Yosaburō keeps watch while Yasu enters to extort money. Listening outside, Yosaburō hears his former lover's voice. He rushes in to greet her, but his passion instantly cools when she does not recognise him. Assuming Otomi is with another man, Yosaburō delivers a cynical speech about love and fate, suggesting that Otomi owes him a great deal for causing his suffering and misfortune. Tazaemon enters and explains that Otomi is not his lover, but under his care. He gives Yosaburō money to turn his life around so that he can look after Otomi. The crooks depart, counting their money.

The play's final scenes are rarely staged. After many difficulties Yosaburō drinks a potion that cures his scars, making him unrecognisable to the police. Otomi, by then married to a crime lord, is still in love with Yosaburō and kills her husband so that she can reunite with her lover.

The print

Shunsen's image of Ichikawa Kigan V in the role of Otomi depicts the scene in which she returns from the bathhouse and meets Tōhachi, the comical character of the play. Otomi holds a cloth in her hands and a red bag of rice husks, used for washing, between her teeth.

Ichikawa Kigan V (1887–1978)

Ichikawa Kigan V was the name held by Onoe Taganojō III between 1911 and 1927. The actor was born in Tokyo and was a pupil of Ichikawa Sadanji II. He was an *onnagata* star, specialising in wife roles. In 1968 he was designated an Important Intangible Cultural Property.

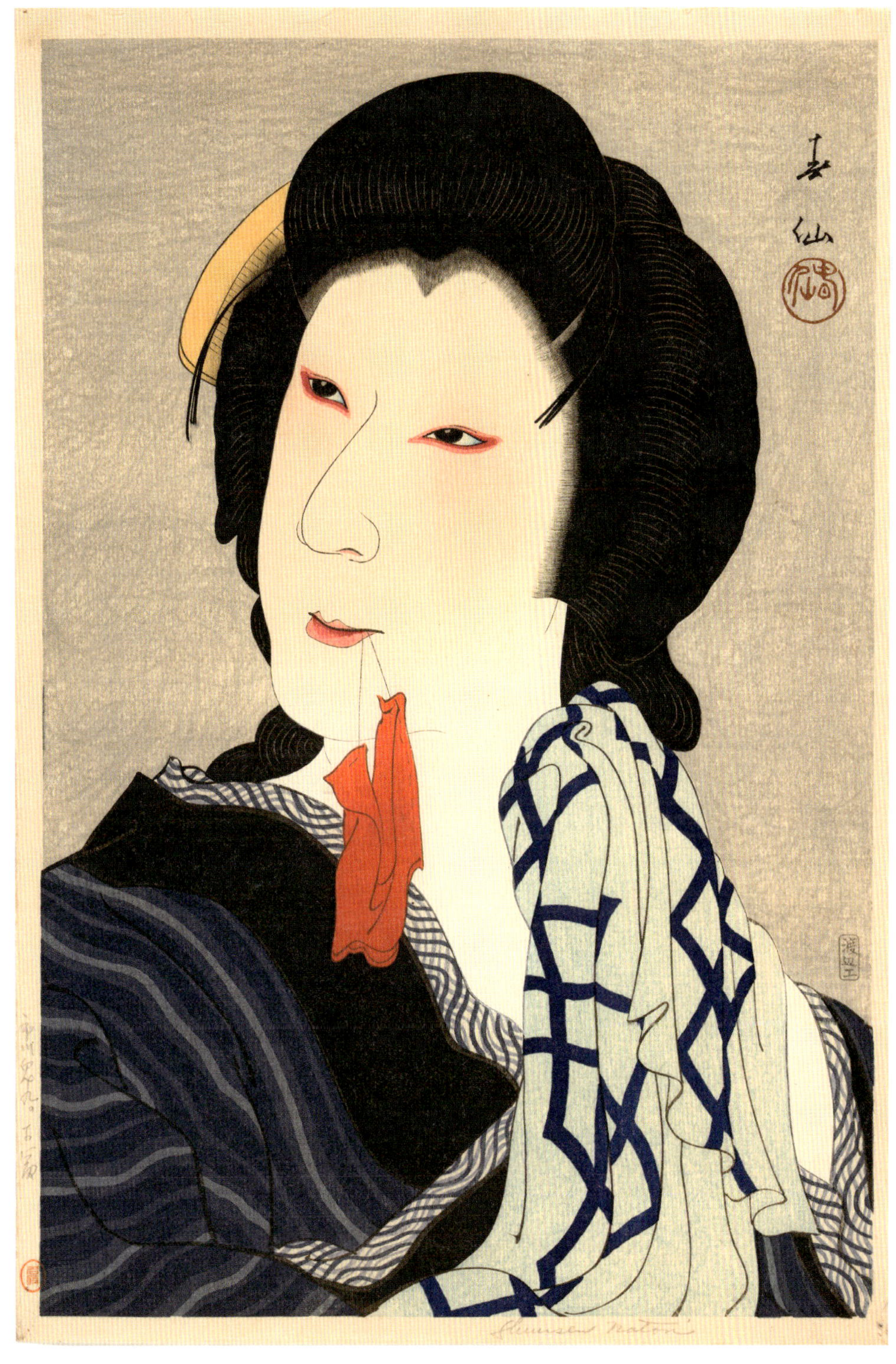

Ichikawa Shōchō II as Umegawa and Kataoka Gadō IV as Chūbei in 'A message of love from Yamato' 1927 from the series Collection of creative portraits by Shunsen
[Ichikawa Shōchō II Kataoka Gadō IV Umegawa Chūbei]
woodblock print; ink and colour on paper
sheet: 40.2 x 27.6 cm, image 38.4 x 25.6 cm
National Gallery of Australia, Canberra,
gift of Jennifer Gordon, 1998

A message of love from Yamato (Koi no tayori Yamato ōrai)

written by Namiki Shōzō II, Tatsuoka Mansaku, Suga Sensuke and Wakatake Fuemi, first kabuki performance in 1796

The play retells the popular love story of Umegawa and Chūbei. It is derived in part from *A courier from hell* (Meido no hikyaku), an early eighteenth century puppet drama by Chikamatsu Monzaemon (1653–1725).

Chūbei, the disowned son of a farmer, works as an Osaka money courier. He has spent his fortune on Umegawa, the young prostitute he loves. He embezzles, and later repays, a deposit for Umegawa's bond from Hachiemon, a wealthy and malicious client who knows of Chūbei's love for the beautiful prostitute. When Hachiemon finds out that his money had been misappropriated, he plans to foil Chūbei by paying for Umegawa himself. Meanwhile Chūbei tells the anxious Umegawa that he is unable to come up with the money.

Chūbei is still in the establishment when brothel manager Jiemon urges Umegawa to go with Hachiemon, who arrives and demands Umegawa. The faithful Umegawa stalls, hoping her lover will save her. A principled man, Jiemon opts to gamble on Chūbei's return. Hachiemon scathingly insults Chūbei, who is eavesdropping nearby. Chūbei confronts Hachiemon and breaks the seal of a packet of government funds he is carrying, sending gold coins clattering to the floor. (This was a serious offence, and productions vary on its deliberateness.) Chūbei pays for Umegawa and hurries her away, terrified that his crime will be discovered. Meanwhile, Hachiemon finds the packet's official seal and reports the theft. A manhunt is launched.

Chūbei tells Umegawa of the situation and she begs for three days together before they commit suicide. The lovers travel to Chūbei's home village. Umegawa pleads with Chūbei's father to see his son one last time, but he refuses. Umegawa persists, blindfolding him so that he can bid his son farewell without setting eyes on him. The lovers are eventually apprehended.

The print

Shunsen portrays Chūbei—played in the gentle romantic *wagoto* style—and his lover, the beautiful prostitute Umegawa, in a single print.

Ichikawa Shōchō II (1886–1940)

Born in Tokyo, Shōchō II was the son of a brothel owner. He took up acting with the support of Ichikawa Sadanji I, and developed into a leading *onnagata* (female-role) actor, specialising in romantic characters. Shōchō II's wife was also a stage performer.

Kataoka Gadō IV (1882–1946)

Tokyo actor Gadō IV, the son of Kataoka Nizaemon X, eventually took the stage name Kataoka Nizaemon XII. Known for his coldly ethereal beauty, he was most famous as an *onnogata* but also performed male roles. In 1946 the actor was murdered by a destitute neighbour jealous of his wealth and lifestyle at a time of great scarcity.

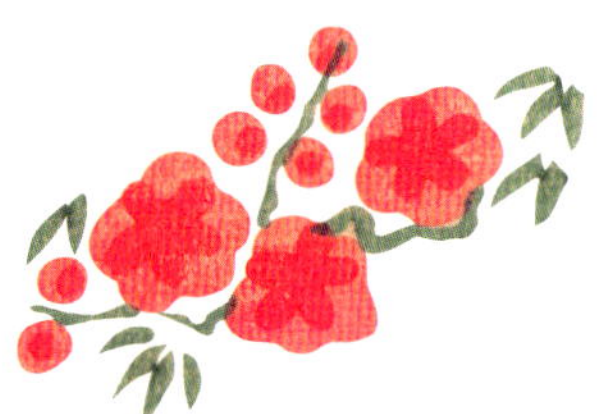

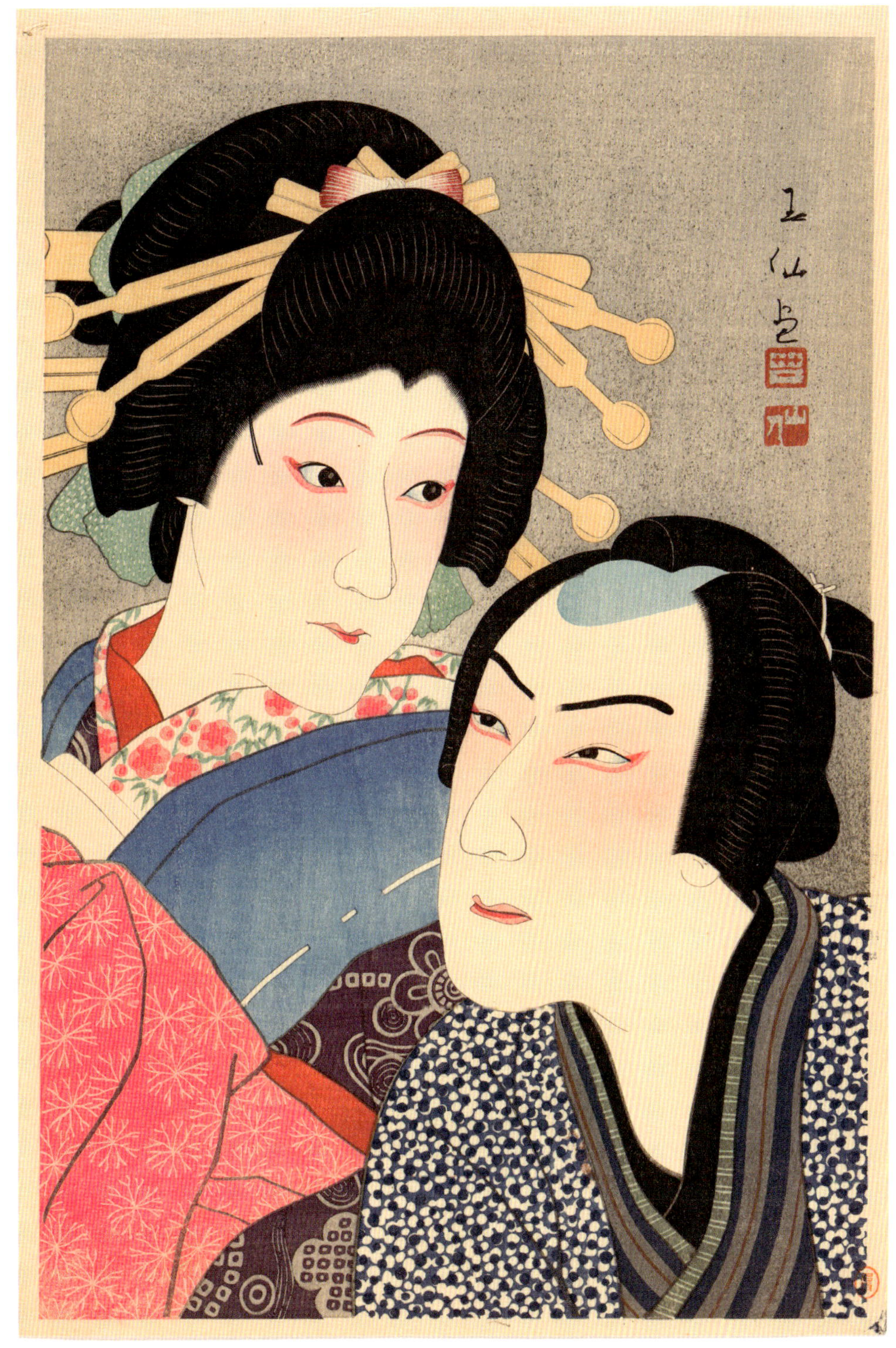

Sawada Shōjirō as the swordsman Hayashi Buhei 1927 from the series *Collection of creative portraits by Shunsen*
[Sawada Shōjirō Hayashi Buhei]
woodblock print; ink and colour on paper
sheet: 40.0 x 27.2 cm, image 38.1 x 25.6 cm
National Gallery of Australia, Canberra,
gift of Jennifer Gordon, 1998

The print

The twenty-seventh print of Shunsen's seminal series was issued in 1927. Instead of a kabuki actor it depicted Sawada Shōjirō, founder and star of the New National Theatre (Shinkokugeki), a company that staged plays by contemporary playwrights without the elaborate stylisation of kabuki or *nō* theatre. The company's more realistic approach was particularly successful for enacting sword fights. Shunsen has portrayed Shōjirō as the enormously popular swordsman Hayashi Buhei, a character in a number of modern dramas from the early-twentieth century.

Sawada Shōjirō (1892–1929)

Sawada Shōjirō was an extremely idealistic actor committed to modernising Japanese theatre. He studied at Waseda University where he joined a modern theatre group led by maverick playwright and Shakespeare translator Tsubouchi Shōyō. The group produced Western and modern Japanese plays. Shōjirō later became the star of another modern troupe, although artistic differences eventually caused him to pursue other options.

As a young man Shōjirō was opposed to the dominance of commercialism over high art and in 1917 eventually set up his own company, New National Theatre (Shinkokugeki). At the time successful modern theatre companies relied on the popularity of female stars and without one Shōjirō faced significant financial difficulties. His only hope to buoy his flagging company was popularising his productions, which he did by featuring realistic sword fights. Audiences familiar with the slow stylised struggles of kabuki were understandably enthralled by convincing action involving real weapons. The violent scenes proved to be sensational hits and the actor developed a theory of compromise, known as the half-step principle, through which he aspired to gradually introduce audiences to modern acting concepts.

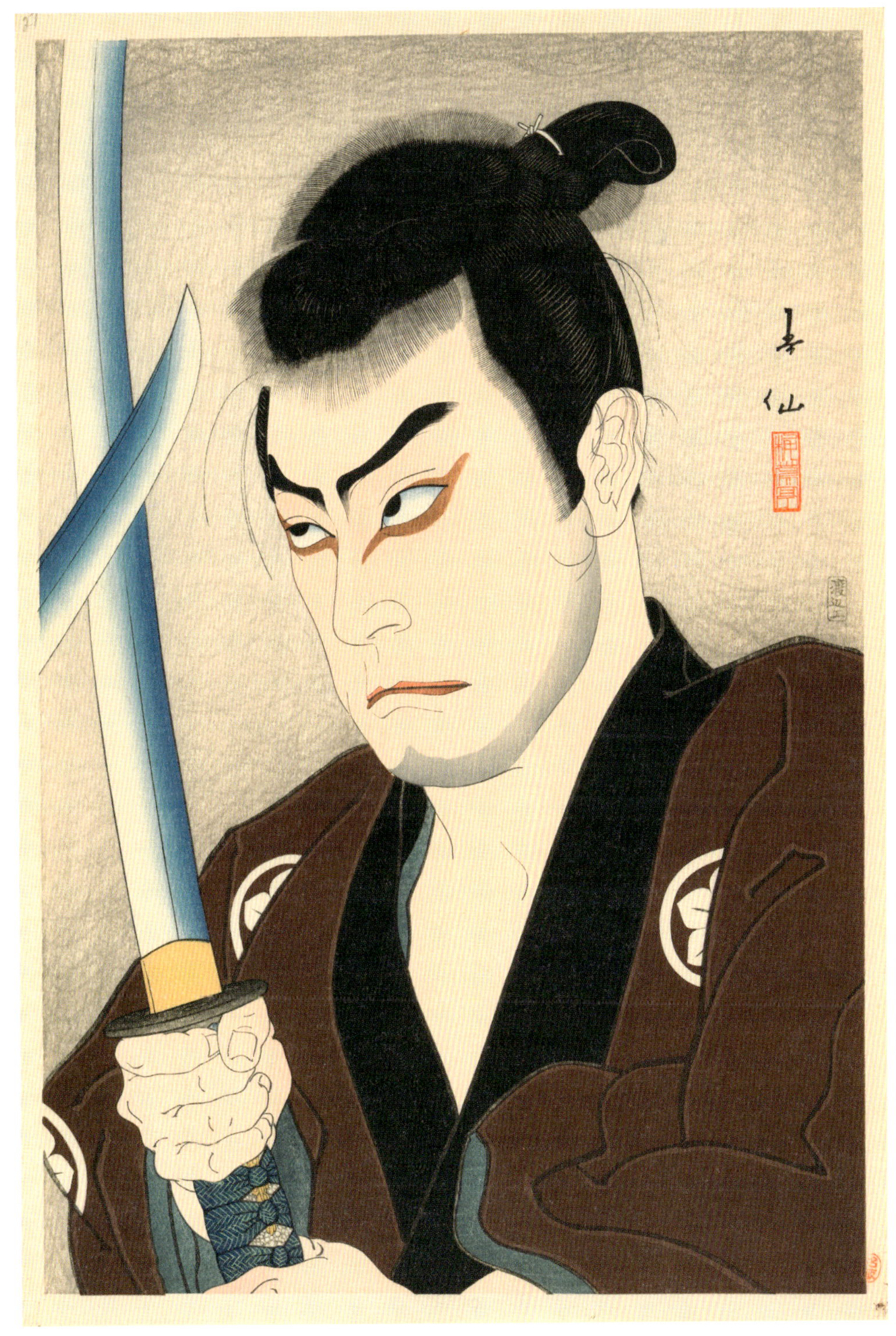

The adventures of the Hakata damsel (Hakata Kojorō nami makura)

written by Chikamatsu Monzaemon, first kabuki
performance in 1776

The grisly and humiliating public punishment
imposed on a group of convicted smugglers
in the early-eighteenth century inspired the
renowned playwright Chikamatsu Monzaemon
(1653–1725) to create *The adventures of the
Hakata damsel* for the puppet theatre. The play
was later adapted for the kabuki stage.

The main protagonists are a pirate, Kezori
Kuemon, and a reputable trader from Kyoto,
Komachiya Soshichi, travelling on business
aboard Kuemon's ship. The pirate brags about
his strength and fighting skills to Soshichi, who
reveals his father's strictness and his love for
the prostitute Kojorō. Soshichi is teased for his
sentimentality and retires to his cabin. Kuemon
takes on board contraband and Soshichi, who
has seen the illegal cargo, is thrown overboard
but manages to survive.

The drama continues at a brothel in Hakata.
Soshichi arrives, penniless and in disarray, in
search of Kojorō. Reciprocating his love, she
invites him in. Soon Kuemon arrives. Generously
dispensing gifts, Kuemon is fawned over by the
brothel's managers. Kojorō then approaches
Kuemon, who is her friend, asking him for the
money to pay her bond so that she can leave
with her lover. Kuemon is amazed to see Soshichi
alive. Sensing that Soshichi must be a lucky
man, he promises to give Kojorō the money
on the condition that Soshichi joins his illegal
enterprise. Soshichi reluctantly agrees.

Over the years Soshichi prospers as a smuggler.
Soshichi's father, Sozaemon, visits his luxurious
house and immediately grasps that his son's
wealth must have been acquired dishonestly. He
organises to sell Soshichi's possessions, including
a sign belonging to Kezori Kuemon. This causes a
swordfight between Soshichi and the pirate that
only ends when Sozaemon manages to return
the sign to Kuemon. Sozaemon then disinherits
Soshichi. Kojorō and Soshichi decide to run away
together but leave separately. The authorities
catch up with Soshichi on the road and he kills
himself. Kuemon and his gang of pirates are
eventually brought to justice and exiled.

The print

In this evocative portrait, Shunsen illustrates
Nakamura Fukusuke IV with a solemn expression
in the role of Soshichi, a man forced by
circumstance to become an outlaw. He wears a
cloak to protect his identity when engaging in
criminal activity.

Nakamura Fukusuke IV (1875–1948)

The adopted son of Nakamura Baigyoku II,
Fukusuke IV was born in Osaka where he first
appeared in kabuki in 1880. The actor was
a member of the Osaka troupe headed by
Nakamura Ganjirō I and performed in both
male and female roles. Rising to become one
of kabuki's leading stars, he took the name
Nakamura Baigyoku III in 1935.

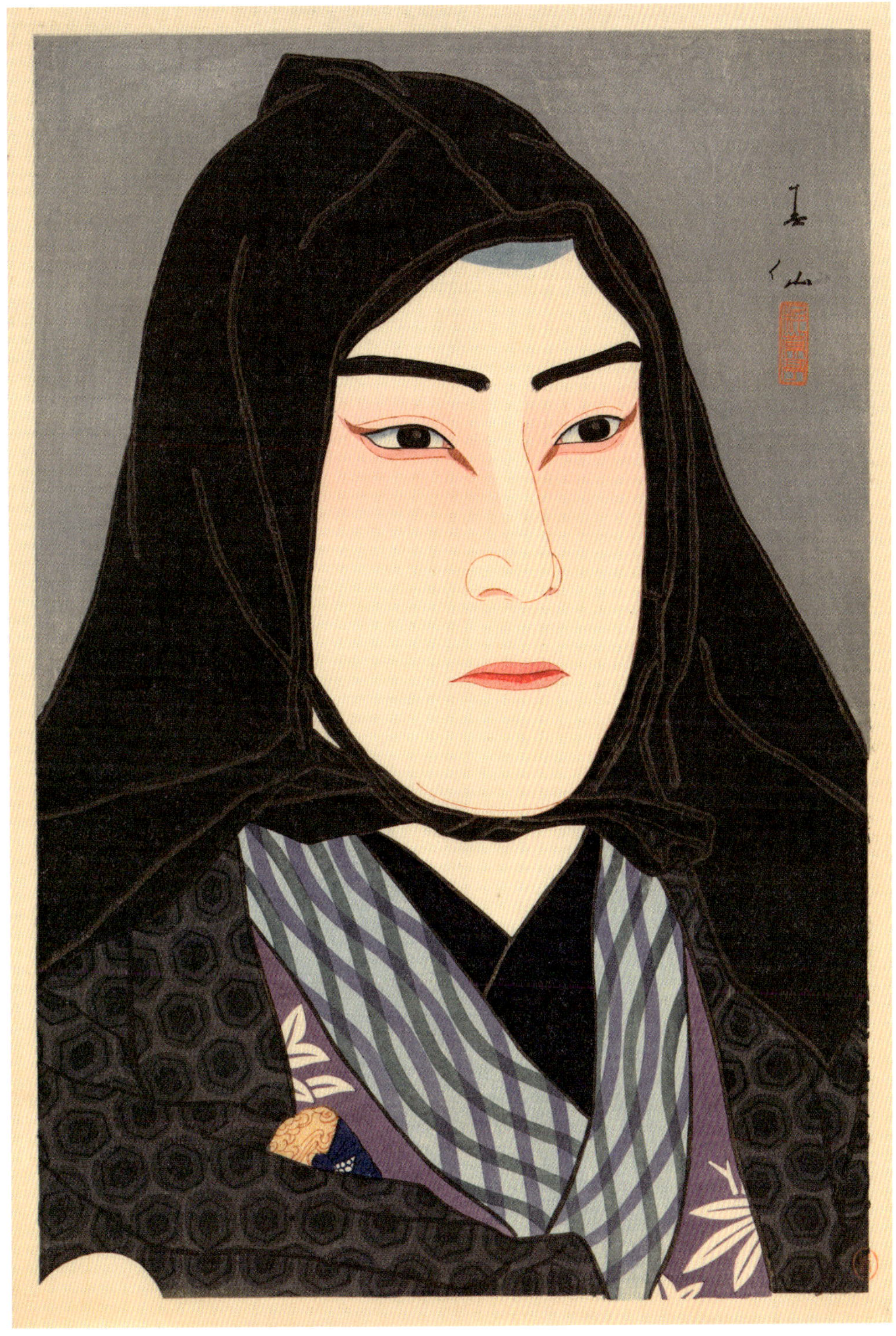

*Ichimura Uzaemon XV as Kataoka Naojirō in
'The faithful samurai'* 1925 from the series
Collection of creative portraits by Shunsen
[Ichimura Uzaemon XV Iriya Naoji]
woodblock print; ink, colour and mica on paper
sheet: 40.1 x 27.5 cm, image: 38.1 x 26.2 cm
National Gallery of Australia, Canberra,
gift of Jennifer Gordon, 1998

The faithful samurai (Naozamurai)

written by Kawatake Mokuami, first kabuki
performance in 1881

The faithful samurai, like many of Mokuami's
popular bandit plays, was inspired by characters
and events from Tokyo's seamy underworld.
Originally a part of *The first flowers of Ueno* (Kumo
ni magō Ueno no hatsuhana) introduced in 1881,
it has been performed as an independent play
since 1910.

The faithful samurai recounts the tragic love story
of Michitose, a beautiful prostitute, and Naojirō,
a charming and dashingly handsome ex-samurai
who has turned to a life of crime. Naojirō,
ironically nicknamed Naozamurai or 'the faithful
samurai', is undoubtedly a criminal, but often has
honourable motives.

At the play's outset, Naojirō has been outlawed.
The action begins at a noodle shop near
Yoshiwara, Tokyo's red-light district. Police spies
question the owners about a nearby house
associated with Michitose's brothel. After they
leave, the fugitive Naojirō enters. He wishes
to see his lover one last time. A fellow gang
member, Ushimatsu, warns Naojirō of impending
danger and he swiftly exits.

After wading through the night snow (mimed in
performance), Naojirō is reunited with Michitose.
Meanwhile, Ushimatsu has betrayed Naojirō to
the police. Having led Michitose to believe he is a
wealthy samurai, Naojirō reveals his true identity.
She has always known, however, and pleads
to go with him. Haunting music accompanies
a dance expressing the pair's tormented love.
Before the lovers escape, the police surround
them. Naojirō flees, with Michitose calling after
him in anguish. Naojirō is later captured and
Michitose kills herself.

The print

The beloved Ichimura Uzaemon XV appears
in this evocative print as honourable criminal
Naojirō, hurrying to meet his lover Michitose.
The delicate background of the image illustrates
the snowy night, achieved on stage with
backdrops and pieces of cotton and paper.
The details of Naojirō's simple costume are
faithfully represented.

Ichimura Uzaemon XV (1874–1945)

Ichimura Uzaemon XV is believed to have been
the son of Charles Le Gendre, a French-born
American general and diplomat who served as
a foreign affairs advisor in Japan from 1872 to
1875, and Ito Ikeda, daughter of Meiji-period
politician Matsudaira Yoshinaga. Uzaemon
XV was adopted as a young child by theatre
manager and actor Uzaemon XIV, and debuted
in 1881. He had exceptional stage presence
and became one of kabuki's foremost *nimaime*
(romantic young male) actors, even continuing
to play these characters as an old man.
Supremely popular, Uzaemon's stage partnership
with Onoe Baikō VI was considered a golden
combination. Uzaemon was evacuated from
Tokyo in 1945, but died soon after of a heart
attack. He is buried beside Onoe Baikō VI.

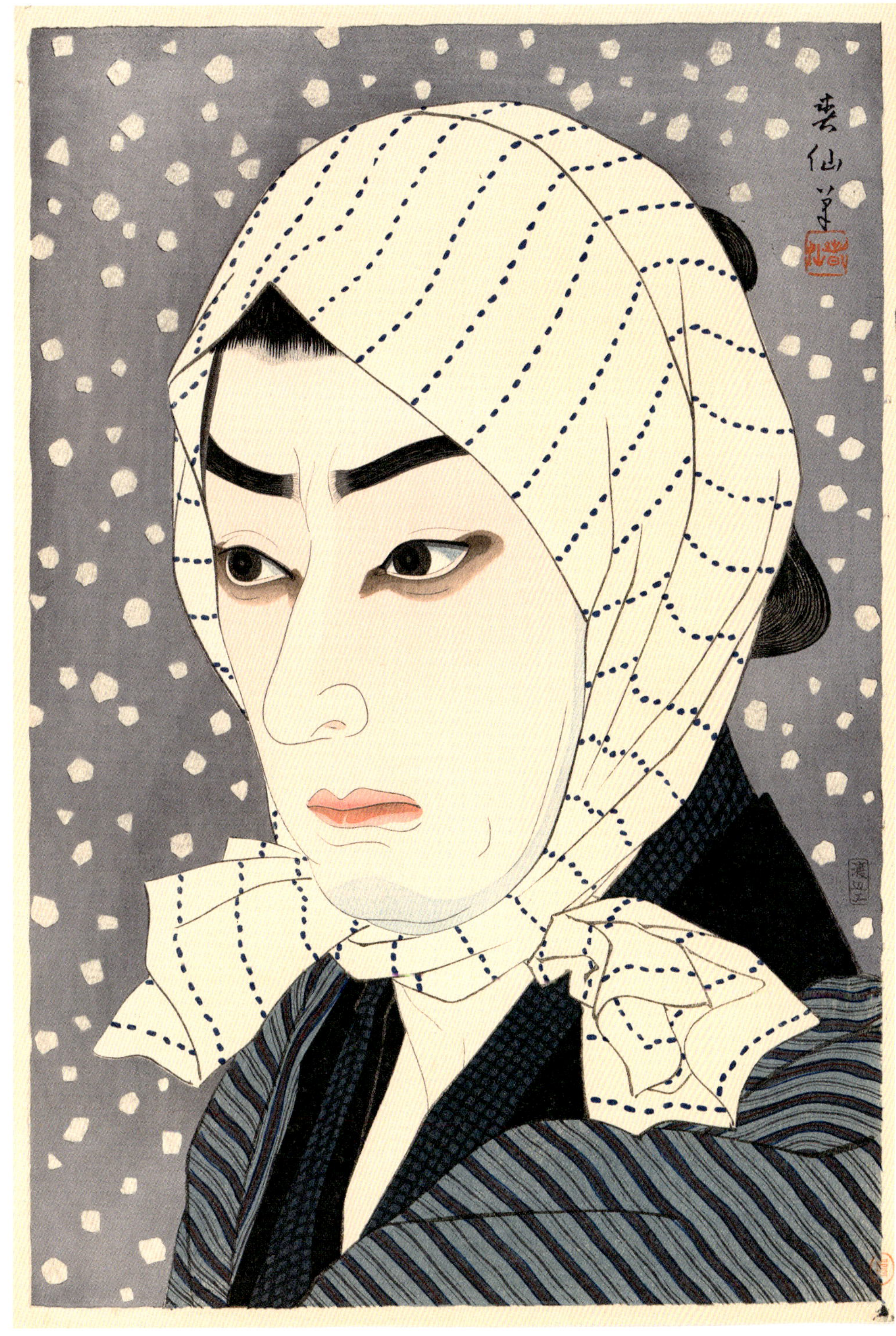

Morita Kanya XIII as Kajiwara Genta Kagesue in 'A beginner's version of the rise and fall of the Heike and Genji clans' 1928 from the series Collection of creative portraits by Shunsen
[Morita Kanya XIII Genta Kagesue]
woodblock print; ink and colour on paper
sheet: 40.1 x 27.6 cm, image: 38.0 x 25.6 cm
National Gallery of Australia, Canberra,
gift of Jennifer Gordon, 1998

A beginner's version of the rise and fall of the Heike and Genji clans (Hiragana Seisuiki)

written by Matsuda Bunkodō, Miyoshi Shōraku, Sen Zensuke et al, first kabuki performance in 1740

A beginner's version of the rise and fall of the Heike and Genji clans is set against the power struggles within the Minamoto (or Genji) faction during their twelfth-century war with the Taira (or Heike). Only one of the drama's storylines is outlined here—the fate of the sons of Minamoto general Kajiwara Kagetoki.

Kajiwara Kagetoki and his son Kajiwara Genta Kagesue are away fighting at the battle of Uji River. At Kagetoki's stronghold, the servants admire a suit of armour that has arrived for Genta from the shogun. They praise the cultured young lord and denounce his degenerate brother Heiji Kagetaka, who tries to seduce Chidori, a beautiful maid in love with Genta. Later, the household is disturbed by the announcement that Genta has failed to lead the armies across the river and been orded to commit suicide by his father.

Genta returns and Chidori lovingly greets her master. Heiji enters, demanding to know of the battle. Genta explains that he forded the perilous Uji with warrior Takatsuna. Heiji sneeringly surmises that Takatsuna was the first to reach the bank. Later, Genta tells his mother Enju that Takatsuna mediated to pardon Kagetoki for a major violation. As repayment, Genta relinquished the honour of first crossing. Genta would rather die than tell his father, so Enju cleverly inflicts the penalty of disinheritance, thus eliminating the option of honourable samurai suicide. Genta departs with Chidori.

Much later, Chidori is working as a prostitute while Genta struggles to regain his title. Genta's mother, disguised as a samurai, goes to the brothel to buy Chidori's freedom. Genta arrives to collect his armour and is dismayed to find it has been pawned to pay for his visits to Chidori, who indicates her willingness to die for her lover. Enju, in a room above, is moved and pours money down to Chidori. Genta recovers his armour and displays great courage in battle. The play ends with the samurai resuming his place as Kajiwara heir.

The print

The print depicts Morita Kanya XIII as Kajiwara Genta Kagesue. Genta wears elegant court costume and white makeup, symbolising his nobility. The arrow-feather motif on his robe is the Kajiwara family crest, while the patterning of the fabric echoes the crest of the Morita Kanya actors. The headdress evokes legendary tales in which Genta shot branches of plum blossoms from his bow during battle.

Morita Kanya XIII (1885–1932)

The son of Morita Kanya XII, Kanya XIII was from a long line of actors and theatre producers. Known for his attractiveness and delicate frame, he became a respected *wagoto* (romantic male) actor. Kanya XIII was an intellectual who thoroughly researched roles and participated in the Literary Theatre (Bungei-za) group, established in 1915 to modernise kabuki.

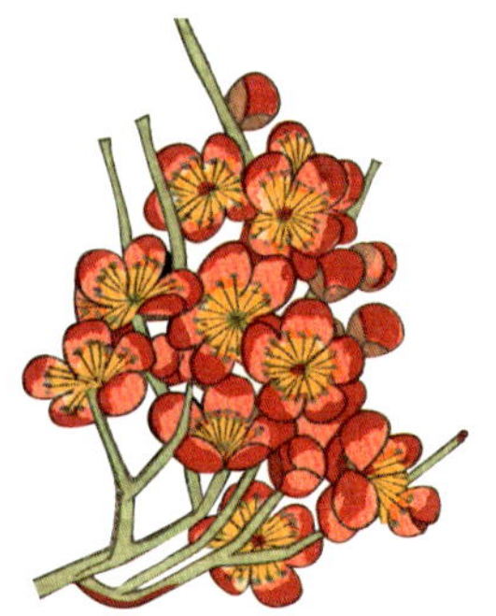

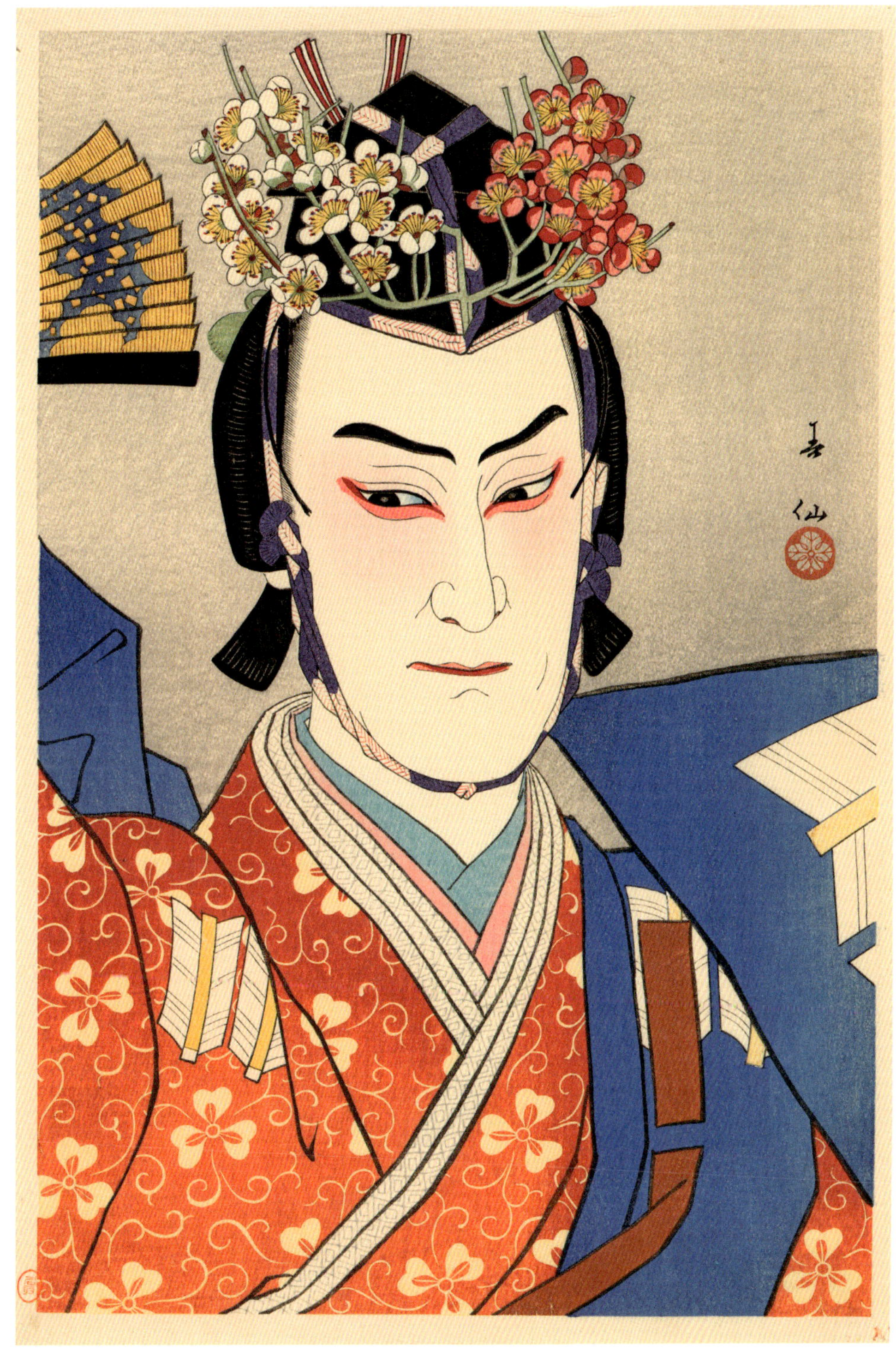

*Sawamura Sōjūrō VII as Narihira Reizaburō in
'A flower in a snowstorm: Oshizu and Reiza'* 1927
from the series *Collection of creative portraits
by Shunsen*
[Sawamura Sōjūrō VII Koisogahara Narihira Reiza]
woodblock print; ink and colour on paper
sheet: 40.0 x 27.0 cm, image: 38.2 x 25.8 cm
National Gallery of Australia, Canberra,
gift of Jennifer Gordon, 1998

A flower in a snowstorm: Oshizu and Reiza (Fubuki no hana Oshizu Reiza)

written by Kawatake Mokuami, first kabuki performance in 1867

A tragedy of forbidden love, *A flower in a snowstorm* is set in Tokyo during the Edo period (1615–1868). The main characters are the lovers Reizaburō (or Reiza), the devastatingly handsome adopted son of a shopkeeper, and Oshizu, a beautiful entertainer who was raised by an outcast. The couple are so much in love that people know them as Narihira Reiza and Komachi Oshizu after great lovers of Japanese legend. They have a child, Chiyomatsu, but their relationship remains illegitimate because of Oshizu's lowly upbringing. Reiza's adoptive father, Soemon, wishes Reiza to marry his daughter, Ohaya.

The lovers are together when an important sword entrusted to Reiza is stolen. Reiza attempts to kill himself, but Oshizu's father saves him and takes him and Oshizu back to his home. Soemon's wife, Omin, comes to find Reiza. He departs and later, out of filial piety, marries Ohaya.

The play resumes a month later. Oshizu's constant tears have blinded her, and she is guided through the snow by her son. Suddenly, Oshizu suffers a fit and falls before a large statue of the Buddhist saint Jizō. Reiza and Soemon find her lying in the snow. Reiza cannot acknowledge to his father his feelings for Oshizu, or his relationship to the child Chiyomatsu, but he tells the audience that only duty prevents him from marrying her. Soemon hurries away to find medicine, leaving Reiza, Oshizu and their child to lament the cruelty of fate. Soemon returns with a remedy and urges Reiza away. The lovers part for the last time, as the beautiful Oshizu tenderly embraces their son in the falling snow.

The print

Sawamura Sōjūrō VII appears in this print as Narihira Reiza, the romantic male lead character. Shunsen captures the sorrow inherent in the play's wintry final scene, when the lovers part for the last time.

Sawamura Sōjūrō VII (1875–1949)

Thought to be the natural son of a temple priest, Sōjūrō VII was adopted by the Tokyo actor Sawamura Takasuke IV and began his stage career in 1881. He trained in Tokyo and Osaka, and was a founding member of the Imperial Theatre Company. He later joined the Shōchiku Company. Sōjūrō VII's mastery of traditional kabuki acting was only truly recognised after the Second World War. He was renowned as a *wagoto* (gentle, romantic) actor and dancer and also performed *onnagata* (female) roles. Sawamura Sōjūrō VII died on stage performing in *The treasury of the loyal retainers* in 1949.

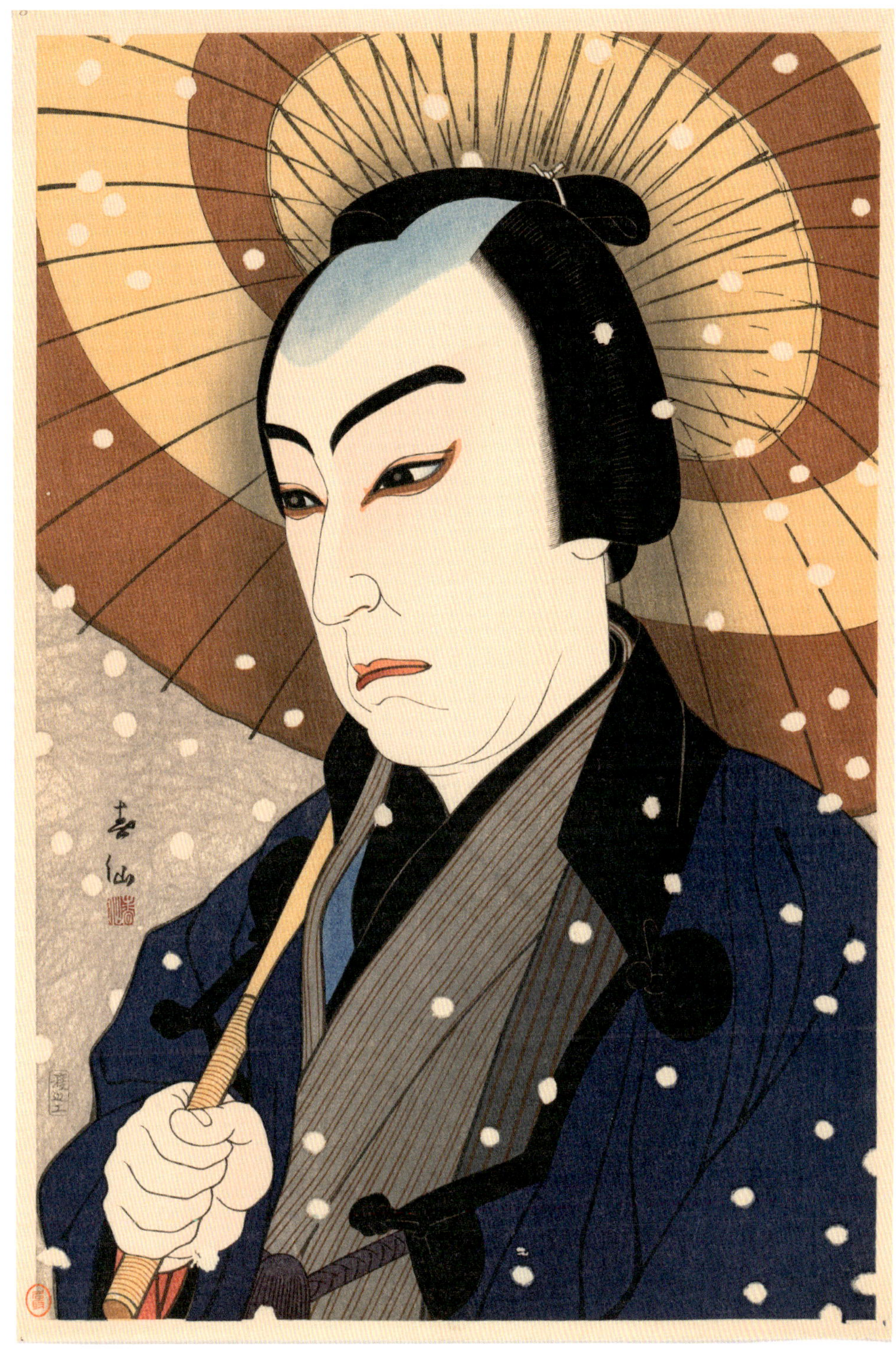

Nakamura Fukusuke V as Ohan in 'The Katsura River and the eternal bonds of love' 1928 from the series *Collection of creative portraits by Shunsen*
[Nakamura Fukusuke V Ohan]
woodblock print, embossing; ink and colour on paper
sheet: 40.8 x 27.3 cm, image: 38.2 x 25.4 cm
National Gallery of Australia, Canberra, gift of Jennifer Gordon, 1998

The Katsura River and the eternal bonds of love (Katsuragawa renri no shigarami)

written by Suga Sensuke, first kabuki performance in 1777

The Katsura River and the eternal bonds of love is a double-suicide play based on earlier kabuki and puppet-theatre dramas. The original story is said to have been inspired by an early-eighteenth century love-suicide involving a teenage girl and her middle-aged lover at Kyoto's Katsura River, although specific details vary.

On a business trip, the merchant Chōemon encounters the beautiful young Ohan, the daughter of his neighbour and fiancée of his wife's brother. She has been on a pilgrimage with her father's apprentice Chōkichi. Ohan asks Chōemon—her father's friend and contemporary—to allow her into his room in order to escape the romantic advances of Chōkichi. Chōemon and Ohan fall immediately and deeply in love and sleep together.

At the Rokkaku Temple, Chōkichi tells Chōemon's wife, Okinu, about the affair. Fearing her husband and brother will be disgraced, Okinu bribes Chōkichi not to publicise the scandal. Meanwhile, at the family shop, Chōemon's stepmother and her son Gihei plot to improve their standing in the family by stealing some money and accusing Chōemon of the crime. The household is divided, as Chōemon is supported by Okinu and his father. Earlier, Gihei had discovered the affair of Chōemon and Ohan. He presents a love letter from Ohan, addressed to her lover 'Chō', as further evidence of Chōemon's untrustworthiness. Okinu defends her husband and coerces Chōkichi to claim that he is Ohan's lover.

Alone with her husband, Okinu reveals that she knows about the scandalous affair. Chōemon begs her to pardon him and she agrees. When Okinu leaves, Chōemon expresses his deep depression and resolves to commit suicide. Ohan suddenly enters, apparently to end their entanglement, but drops a letter as she leaves. The note tells Chōemon that she is pregnant and plans to drown herself in the Katsura River. Chōemon follows Ohan, lifting her onto his back to carry her to the river where they kill themselves.

The print

Shunsen depicts Nakamura Fukusuke V as Ohan in *The Katsura River and the eternal bonds of love*. She is dressed in a beautiful kimono and shown sorrowfully clutching a letter to her lover Chōemon.

Nakamura Fukusuke V (1900–33)

Fukusuke V was born in Tokyo, the adopted son of Nakamura Utaemon V. His first public performance was in 1904 at the Tokyo Theatre. He was best known for his dancing skills and helped pioneer kabuki's New Dance movement. He played romantic female roles and was revered for his beauty and femininity. Tragically, the actor died at a young age.

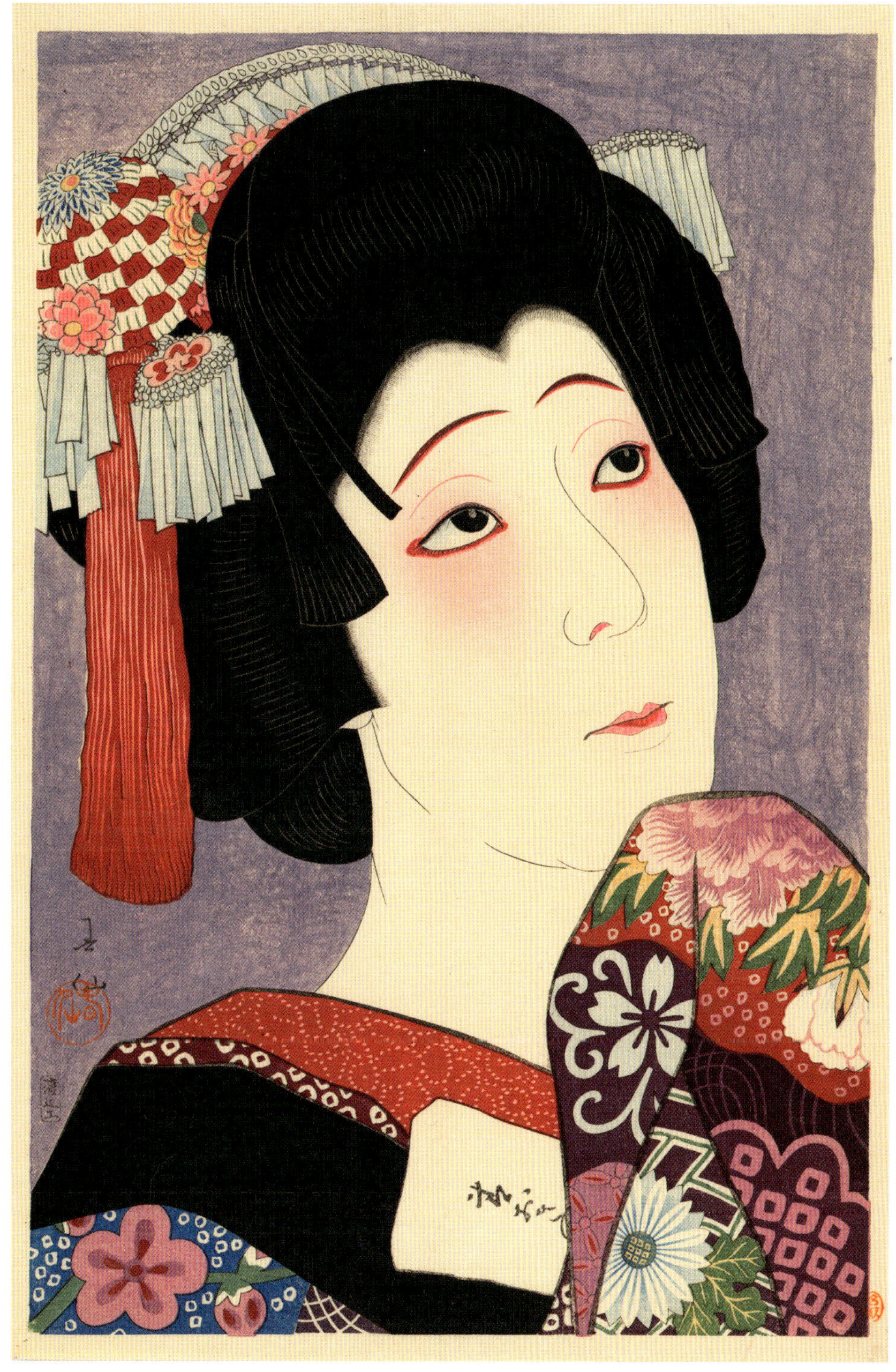

*Bandō Jusaburō III as Mizuhiki Seigorō in
'Fight of Megumi'* 1928 from the series *Collection
of creative portraits by Shunsen*
[Bandō Jusaburō III Mizuhiki Seigorō]
woodblock print, embossing; ink and colour
on paper
sheet: 40.2 x 28.0 cm, image: 37.8 x 27.8 cm
National Gallery of Australia, Canberra,
gift of Jennifer Gordon, 1998

Fight of Megumi (Megumi no kenka)

versions written by Takeshiba Kisui, Segawa Jokō
II and Kawatake Mokuami, kabuki performances
from the early-nineteenth century

In 1805, at Tokyo's Shiba Shinmei Shrine, a band
of firefighters clashed with a group of sumo
wrestlers, resulting in one death. Sumo wrestlers
and firemen were popular with kabuki audiences
and the incident was dramatised in a number of
plays including *Fight of Megumi*, also known as
The match in harmony (Kami no Megumi wagō
no torikumi).

In a pleasure district of Tokyo, a boisterous
sake-fuelled party is held for the sumo wrestler
Yotsuguruma Daihachi. In the adjoining room
Tokyo firemen enjoy a more sedate celebration.
As the revelry continues, one of the sumo
wrestlers knocks the room partition onto one of
the firemen. His companion, Tatsugorō, prevents
the situation from turning into a brawl but is
abused as a coward by a wrestler. Later that
night, Tatsugorō attacks the insolent wrestler
and is beaten. A *danmari* (silent chase and fight
scene set in the dark) ensues.

Later some of the firemen, having first consumed
plenty of sake, heckle the wrestlers at the sumo
arena in the grounds of the Shiba Shinmei
Shrine. Tatsugorō and Daihachi face off, but
interference prevents their clash. Tatsugorō
then goes to his chief, asking him to protect his
family while he embarks on a mission. Fire chief
Kisaburō understands what he is planning and
gives Tatsugorō a drink of sake to encourage him
to settle the score. Tatsugorō braces himself to
take on Daihachi that night, preparing to fight
to the death.

At the arena, the firemen gather and attack the
wrestlers in an energetic fight scene. Kisaburō
then steps into the fray, with a magistrate and
the powerful head of the shrine. He settles the
dispute, reminding both groups of their shared
status as heroes of Tokyo.

The print

This image presents Bandō Jusaburō III as the
sumo wrestler Mizuhiki Seigorō. To achieve the
illusion of great size, actors wore heavily padded
costumes and high shoes. To enact a sumo
bout, kabuki performers removed their robes to
wrestle, exposing padded flesh-coloured body
stockings.

Bandō Jusaburō III (1886–1954)

Jusaburō III was born into an Osaka kabuki
family. He began performing at the age of five
to great acclaim, especially in his hometown.
He was one of the most famous actors on stage
during the American occupation of Japan,
helping to foster a renewed interest in kabuki
at that time.

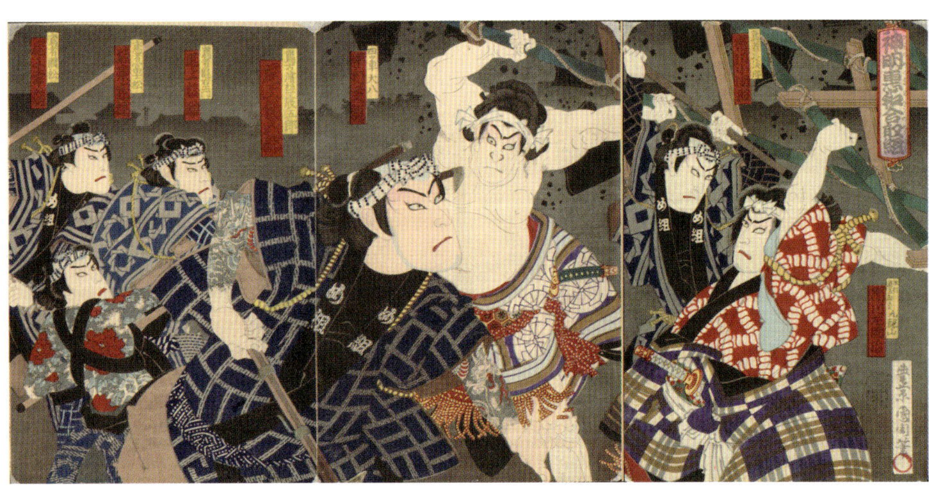

Toyohara Kunichika (1835–1900) *The match in harmony*
1887
woodblock print; ink and colour on paper, 34.0 x 72.0 cm
National Library of Australia, Canberra

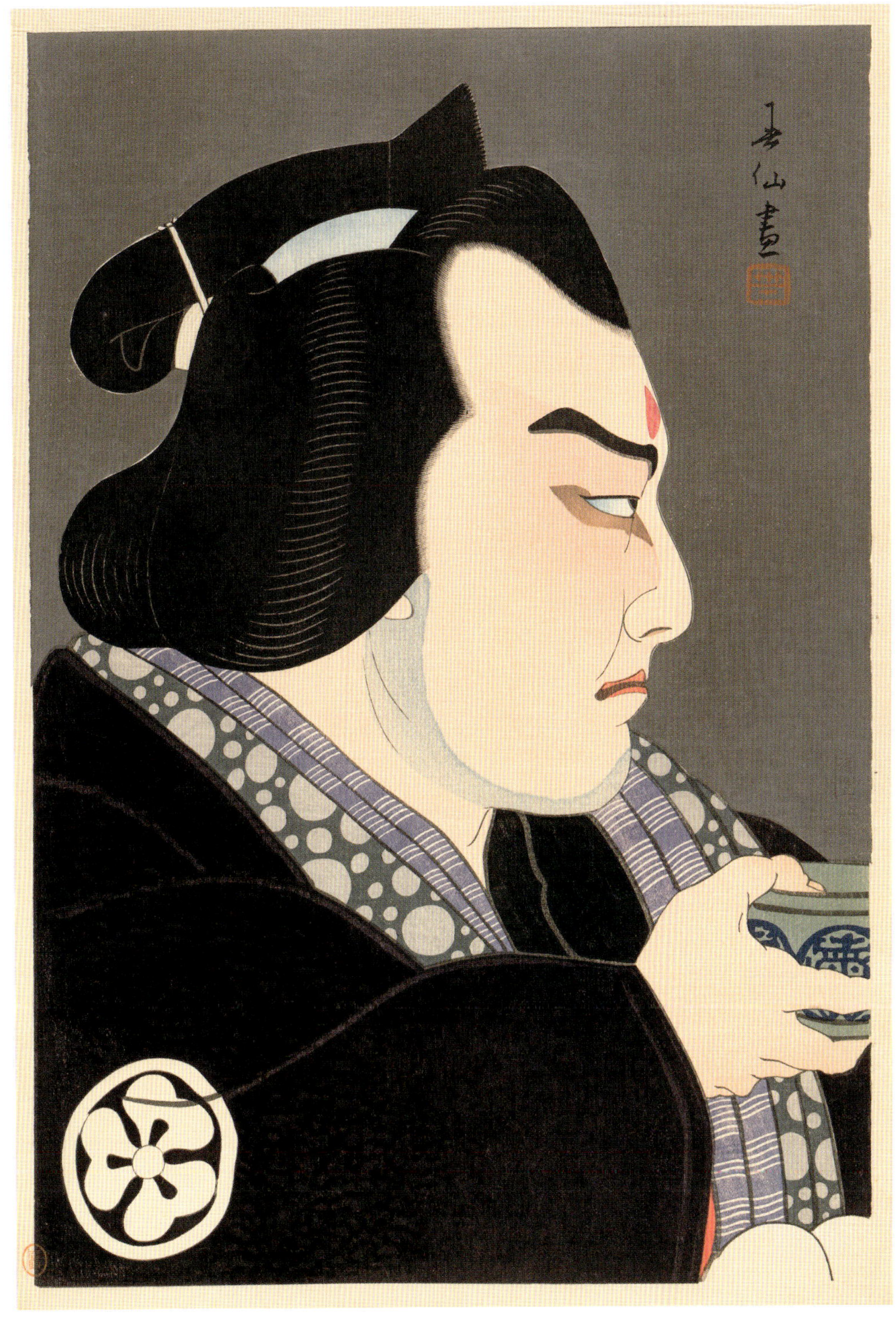

Soganoya Gorō and Choroku as Tochimen Yajirobei and Kitahachi in 'Shank's mare' 1928 from the series *Collection of creative portraits by Shunsen* [Soganoya Gorō Choroku Hiza kurige] woodblock print; ink and colour on paper
sheet: 40.2 x 27.4 cm, image: 38.0 x 25.5 cm
National Gallery of Australia, Canberra,
gift of Jennifer Gordon, 1998

Shank's mare (Hiza kurige)

based on a novel written by Jippensha Ikku in 1802–22, adapted by Tsuruya Nanboku IV in 1827, and by Kimura Kinka in 1928, first kabuki performances from 1827

Shank's mare was a novel by Jippensha Ikku, released in instalments between 1802 and 1822. It traces the absurd and entertainingly ribald exploits of two men, Tochiemon Yajirobei (Yaji) and Kitahachi (Kita), on a tour of the famous stations of the Tōkaidō highway between Kyoto and Tokyo. Numerous episodes from the novel were dramatised for kabuki. From the late 1920s companies regularly produced new comedies for the summer season featuring the clown-like characters, on the lookout for beautiful women and adventure, in scenes enthusiastically appreciated for their slapstick humour.

One incident sees Yaji dressing up as a fox to startle the sleeping Kita. After the joke, the buffoons walk past a graveyard and Yaji collapses in terror because he thinks he has seen a ghost. Intimidated by the eerie atmosphere, Yaji and Kita attack a young boy, who they mistakenly think is a fox in human form. The boy and his father thrash Kita and knock Yaji unconscious. The attackers assume they have killed Yaji and dress him in death robes. When he awakes, he momentarily believes he is a ghost, before rushing after Kita.

The print

In Shunsen's print, Yaji and Kita are depicted in travelling garb. One of the characters glares at the other, probably angered by a prank. Mount Fuji, a famous landmark visible from the Tōkaidō highway, appears in the background.

Soganoya Gorō (1877–1948) and Choroku (dates unkown)

Soganoya Gorō was a supporting actor in an Osaka-based travelling kabuki company. In 1903 he formed the Soganoya Brothers Troupe (Soganoya Ichiza) with his fellow kabuki actor Soganoya Jūrō. The company was dedicated to comedy and many of its productions poke fun at kabuki. The name of the company and its leading stars are also satirical, based on the popular twelfth-century figures Soga Gorō and Soga Jūrō who feature in many kabuki plays. The first Tokyo performances, held from 1905, were unsuccessful, mainly because the audience was unfamiliar with the humour and had difficulty understanding the actors' Osaka accents. The troupe later gained widespread popularity.

Choroku, known for his distinctive round face, was an actor in the troupe.

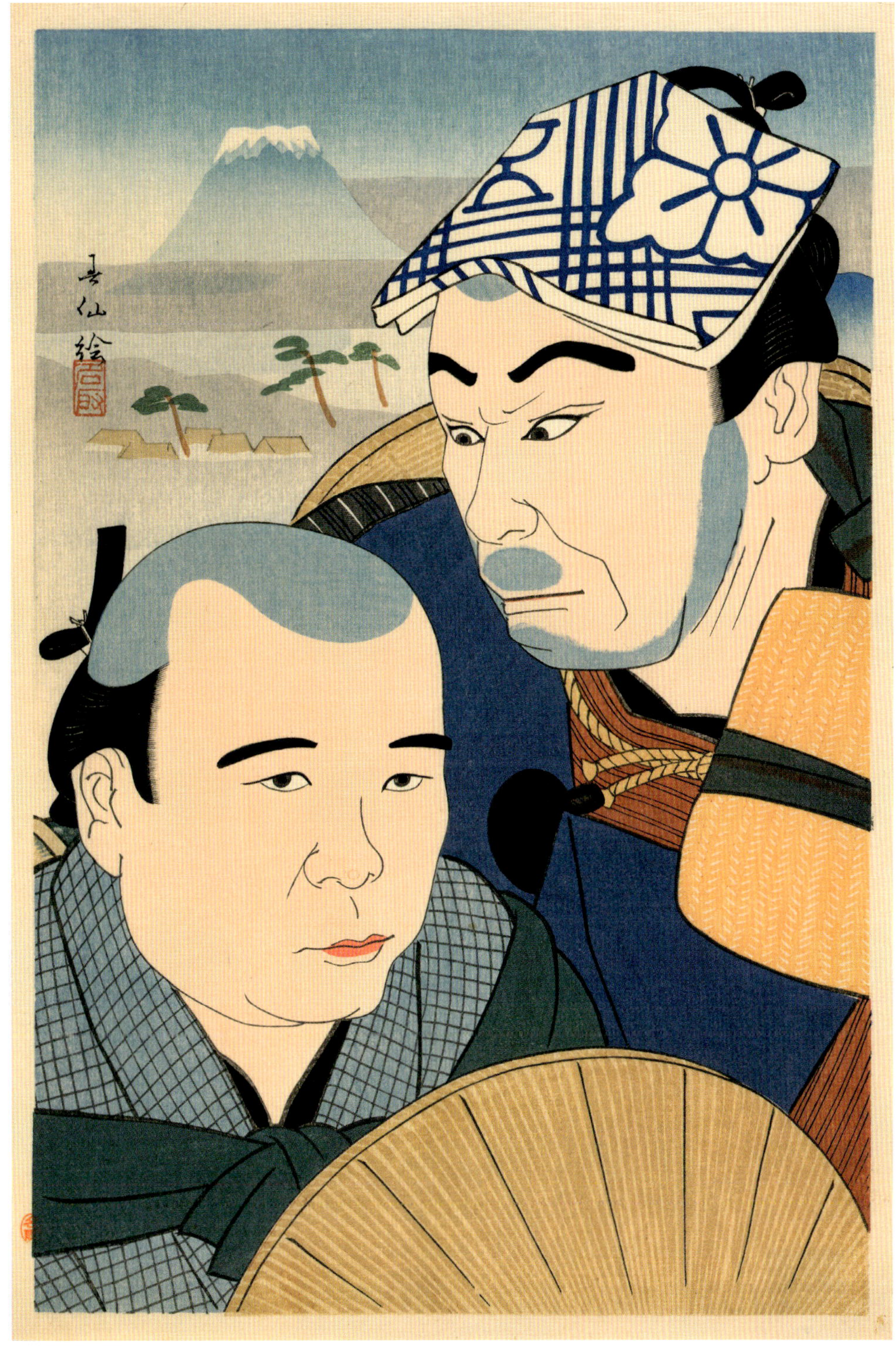

*Bandō Mitsugorō VII as farmer Manbei in
'The sword thief'* 1927 from the series
Collection of creative portraits by Shunsen
[Bandō Mitsugorō VII Tachi nusubito hyakushō
Manbei]
woodblock print; ink and colour on paper
sheet 40.0 x 27.4 cm, image 38.0 x 25.6 cm
National Gallery of Australia, Canberra,
gift of Jennifer Gordon, 1998

The sword thief (Tachi nusubito)

written by Okamura Shikō, first kabuki
performance in 1917

The sword thief is a kabuki dance-drama adapted
from a comedy of the *nō* theatre, Japan's classical
dramatic form. Typical of kabuki adaptations,
its staging mimics the characteristic pine-tree
scenery of *nō* theatre.

Kurobei, a thief and a drunkard, covets a
magnificent sword belonging to the farmer
Manbei. After Manbei has had a few drinks,
Kurobei is able to steal the sword from him.
The farmer later accosts Kurobei and demands
the sword's return. Kurobei insists that the
blade belongs to him. The magistrate Saemon
overhears their argument and tries to settle
the dispute. He takes the sword, resolving to
question both men and have each perform a
dance that expresses the nature of the sword.

Saemon begins by first asking Manbei to
describe the sword and its origin. Kurobei is
able to repeat Manbei's response. This continues
for some time—Saemon questions, Manbei
answers, Kurobei parrots. Saemon is equally
convinced by both men. During the dance,
however, Manbei lowers his voice and moves
away so that Kurobei cannot follow his steps.
Saemon is then able to identify the flummoxed
Kurobei as the thief, and Manbei as the rightful
owner of the sword. The play ends with Saemon
and his men in pursuit of Kurobei.

The print

The print depicts Manbei, dressed in farmer's
clothing, holding the contested sword. Fronds
of the pine-tree scenery can be seen behind the
actor's head.

Bandō Mitsugorō VII (1882–1961)

Mitsugorō VII, the son of actor Morita Kanya
XII, received training from Nakamura Shikan
IV and the kabuki luminary Ichikawa Danjūrō
IX. He began his stage career in 1889 and was
troupe leader at the Ichimura Theatre by 1908.
He was best known as a male-role (*tachiyaku*)
actor and was considered one of the best
dancers of his generation, his talent garnering
him the nickname Odori no Kamisama (God of
Dance). He was often passed over for leading
roles, however, because he was quite short and
lacked a strong masculine voice. Mitsugorō VII
collapsed on the Kabuki Theatre stage during
a performance in 1957 and never acted again.
He wrote a number of acting commentaries
including *Talks on the art of dance* (Buyō geiwa)
published in 1937.

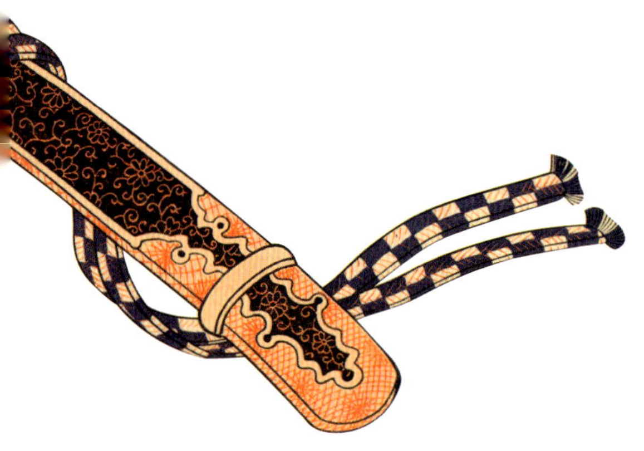

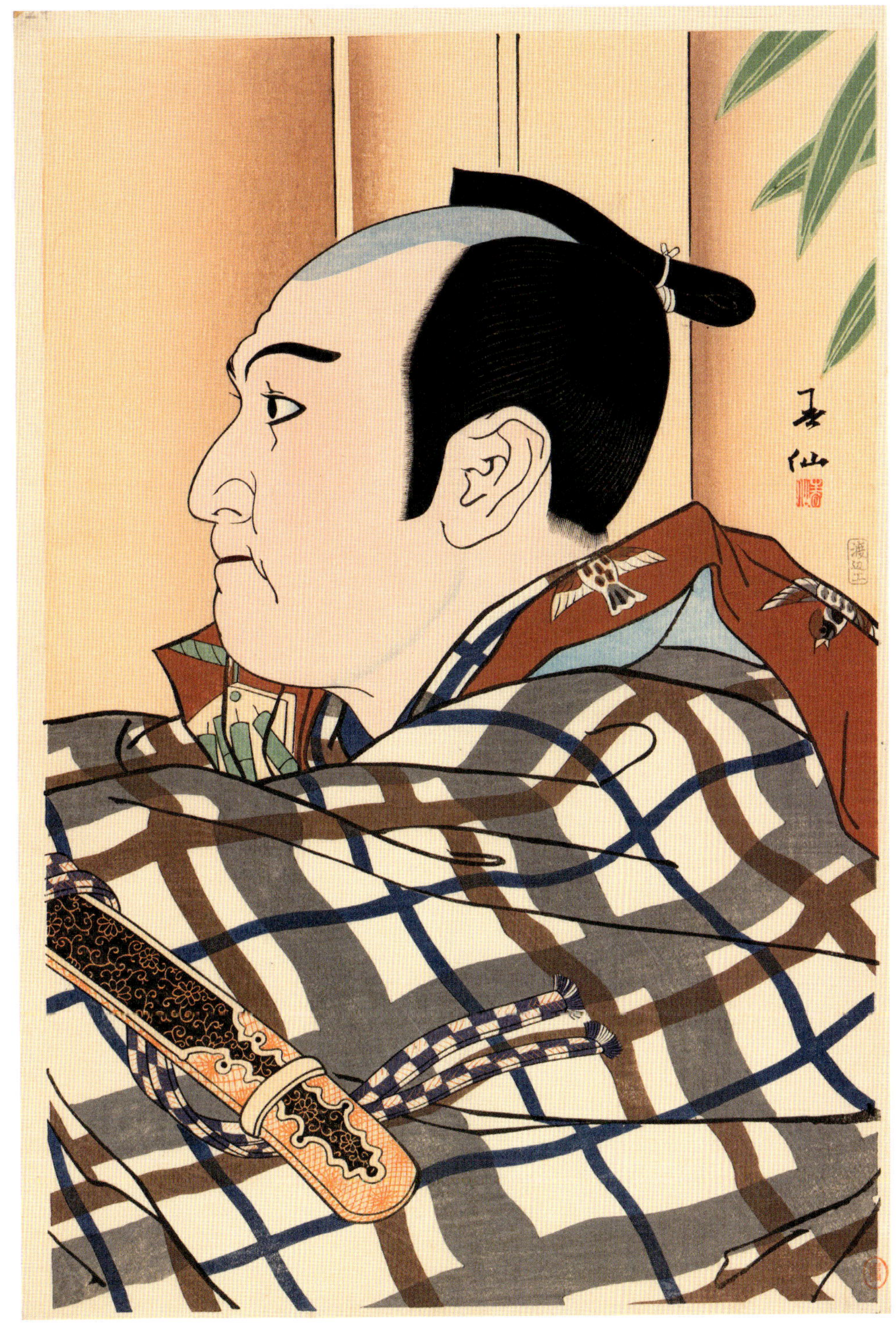

Nakamura Kaisha I as Okaru in 'Love suicides on the eve of the Kōshin Festival' 1928 from the series *Collection of creative portraits by Shunsen* [Nakamura Kaisha yoi Gōshin Okaru] woodblock print; ink and colour on paper sheet: 40.0 x 27.8 cm, image: 38.4 x 25.8 cm National Gallery of Australia, Canberra, gift of Jennifer Gordon, 1998

Love suicides on the eve of the Kōshin Festival (Shinjū yoi Gōshin)

written by Chikamatsu Monzaemon, first kabuki performance in 1775

This play is based on the double suicide of Hanbei and his wife Ochiyo at an Osaka temple on the evening of the 1721 Kōshin Festival. The trigger for their deaths was reputedly Hanbei's father, who tried to seduce Ochiyo. In the play, however, Hanbei's mother is the cause of the tragedy.

Hanbei's severe and diligent mother Okuma loathes his beautiful wife Ochiyo. While her son is visiting his father's grave, she tells the pregnant Ochiyo that Hanbei wants a divorce. Ochiyo is sent to the farm of her father Heiemon, who is being cared for by Okaru, Ochiyo's sister. Okaru is upset to hear of Ochiya's failed marriage— her third. She softens, however, as Ochiyo describes her mother-in-law's cruelty. Heiemon comforts Ochiyo and bitterly disparages Hanbei. Unheralded, Hanbei arrives and is greeted coolly by Okaru. He is shocked to find his wife, who also shuns him. When he understands the situation he is angered that Ochiyo doubted his marriage oath. Hanbei prepares to show his loyalty by killing himself, but Heiemon reminds him that this will cast shame on his mother. Reunited, Hanbei and Ochiyo depart.

Back in Osaka, the couple live apart although Hanbei often visits Ochiya. Okuma sees through the ruse when a messenger brings Hanbei news of his wife. Hanbei is torn between filial piety and marital love. He promises his mother he will divorce Ochiya but asks her first to welcome Ochiya back, to dispel the rumour that she, the mother-in-law, instigated the divorce. Ochiya is overjoyed to return, but soon finds out about Hanbei's vow. He then tells her that the divorce is simply to protect Okuma from being blamed when they commit a love-suicide together. Ochiya is glad to die with her lover if they cannot be together in life. Hanbei divorces and evicts Ochiya, rejoining her outside the house. The play closes with a touching *michiyuki* (literally, travel-going), the name for scenes in which lovers dance to their deaths.

The print

Shunsen's image from *Love suicides on the eve of the Kōshin Festival* shows Nakamura Kaisha I as Okaru. Okaru treats Hanbei with hostility, believing him to have divorced her sister Ochiya. While Okaru is not one of the drama's main characters, she embodies the unwarranted doubt cast on Hanbei's samurai morality.

Nakamura Kaisha I (1875–1945)

A pupil of Nakamura Ganjirō I, Kaisha I was born in Osaka. He played both male and female kabuki roles. In 1899 he relocated to Tokyo where he achieved stage success before returning to Osaka in 1914 and continuing his rise to fame. Kaisha I died in the Second World War bombing of the city.

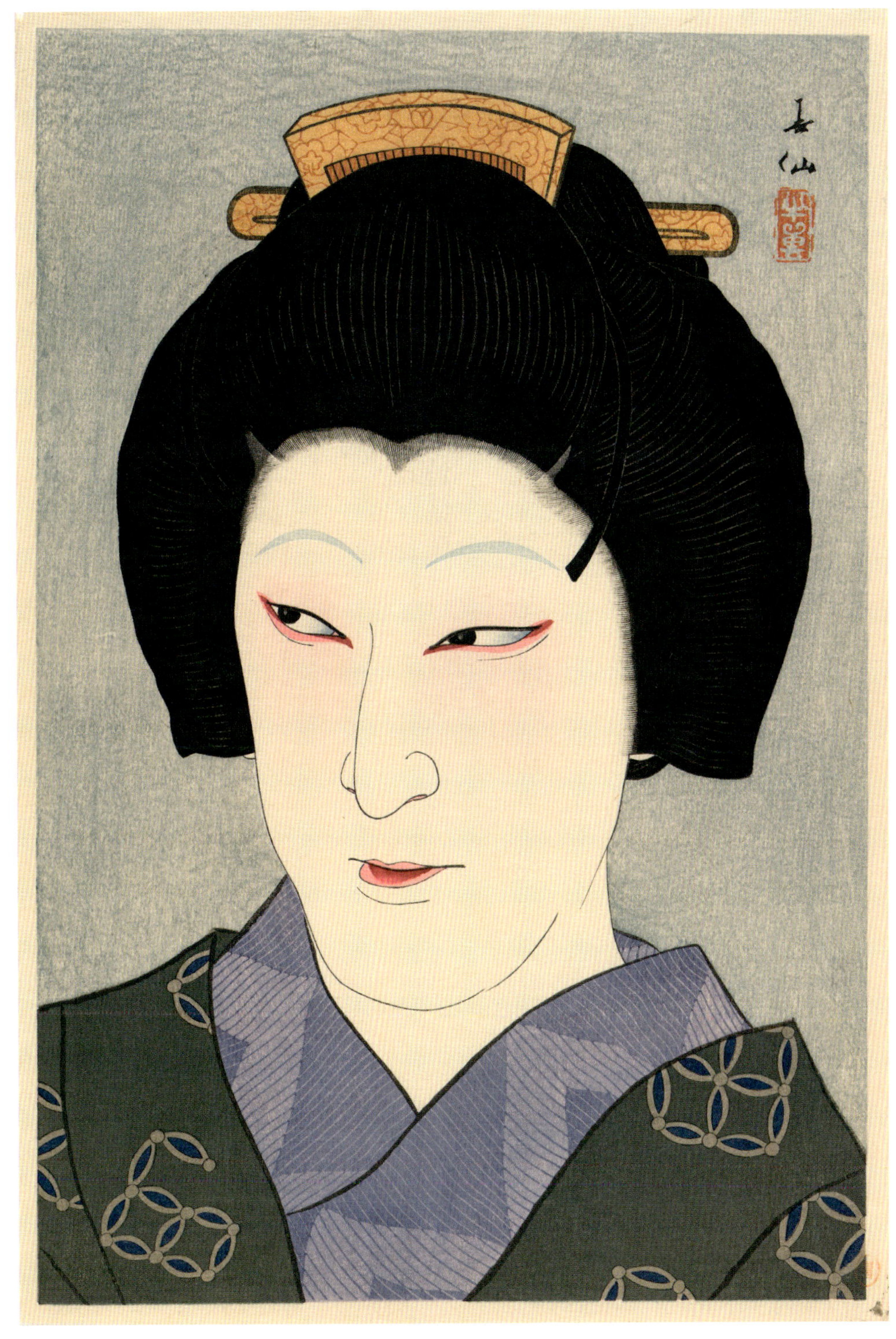

Nakamura Jakuemon III as Yaoya Oshichi in 'The stylish maid and love's dappled cloth' 1927 from the series *Collection of creative portraits by Shunsen*
[Nakamura Jakuemon III Yaoya Oshichi]
woodblock print; ink and colour on paper
sheet: 40.2 x 27.5 cm, image 37.2 x 25.7 cm
National Gallery of Australia, Canberra,
The Poynton Bequest, 2004

The stylish maid and love's dappled cloth (Date musume koi no higanoko)

written by Suga Sensuke, Matsuda Wakichi and Wakatake Fuemi, first kabuki performance in 1773

Oshichi was a real woman, recorded in history because she was burned alive in 1682 as punishment for the crime of arson. Oshichi took shelter with her family at Tokyo's Shosen Temple after her house was burnt down in a terrible fire in 1681. There she fell passionately in love with a young temple attendant, but was parted from him when her house was rebuilt. She set a fire to be able to return to him. Oshichi inspired a number of Japanese novels as well as plays for the kabuki and puppet theatres. In *The stylish maid and love's dappled cloth*, colloquially known as *Greengrocer Oshichi* (Yaoya Oshichi), she is transformed from arsonist to heroine.

Kichisaburō serves at the Kissho Temple in Tokyo (government regulations prohibited the use of actual locations in kabuki). He falls in love with Oshichi, a greengrocer, when she and her family are forced to live at the temple after losing their house in a fire. Tragedy looms, however, as Kichisaburō's father has lost an important heirloom sword. If the sword is not found, Kichisaburō has promised to commit suicide alongside his father.

Kichisaburō goes to Oshichi's house where he hears her father talking of his plans to pay his debts by marrying Oshichi to his creditor, Kamaya Buhei. Kichisaburō departs, leaving a letter telling Oshichi that he will kill himself at sunrise. Oshichi learns from a servant that Kamaya Buhei is known to possess the missing sword. The servant is sent to recover it. Night falls and the locked district gates prevent the distressed Oshichi from reaching Kichisaburō. Oshichi braves a snowstorm to climb the neighbourhood watchtower and beat the drum signifying a fire, knowing the punishment for a false alarm is to be burned alive. The gates open just as the precious sword is brought to Oshichi, who rushes away to find Kichisaburō.

The print

The image captures the moment before Oshichi ascends the watchtower to sound the fire alarm in order to prevent her lover's suicide. In homage to the magic of the puppet theatre—the first dramatic form to realise this scene—kabuki actors developed a mode of portraying Oshichi as though she were a puppet. Shunsen depicts the actor, Nakamura Jakuemon III, in a stylised marionette's pose. The figures behind Oshichi are the puppet handlers.

Nakamura Jakuemon III (1875–1927)

The son of actor Arashi Rishō, Jakuemon III was adopted by Jakuemon II. He began acting in Kyoto as a young boy. Jakuemon III became a leading *onnagata* (female-role) actor, sometimes also playing male characters, and was well-loved on the stages of Tokyo and the Kyoto-Osaka area.

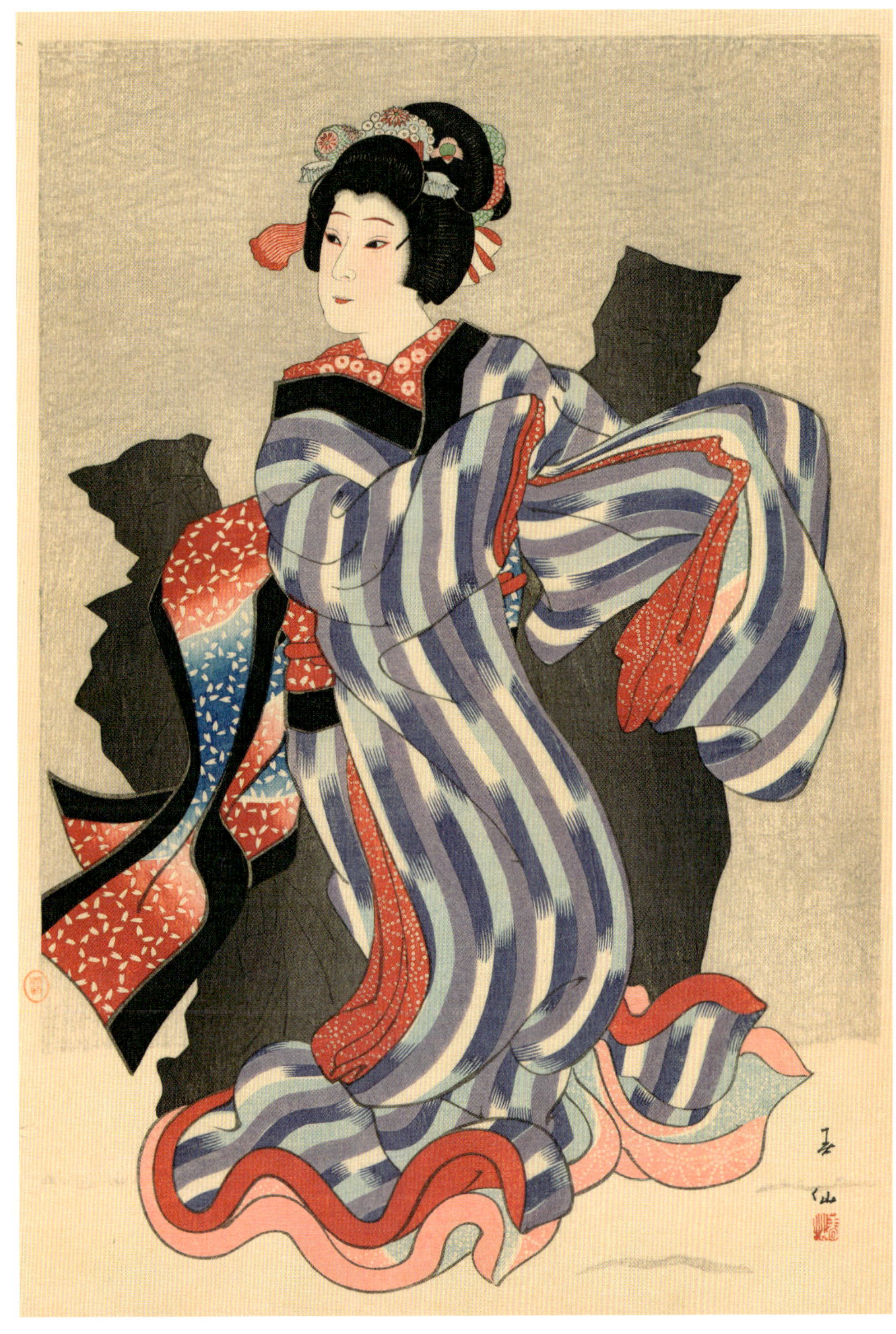

Nakamura Tokizō III and Ichikawa Omezō IV as Tsuru and Kame in 'The crane and the tortoise' 1928 from the series *Collection of creative portraits by Shunsen*
[Nakamura Tokizō III Ichikawa Omezō IV Tsuru kame]
woodblock print; ink and colour on paper
sheet: 40.2 x 27.4 cm, image 38.0 x 25.7 cm
National Gallery of Australia, Canberra,
gift of Orde Poynton Esq, AO, CMG, 2001

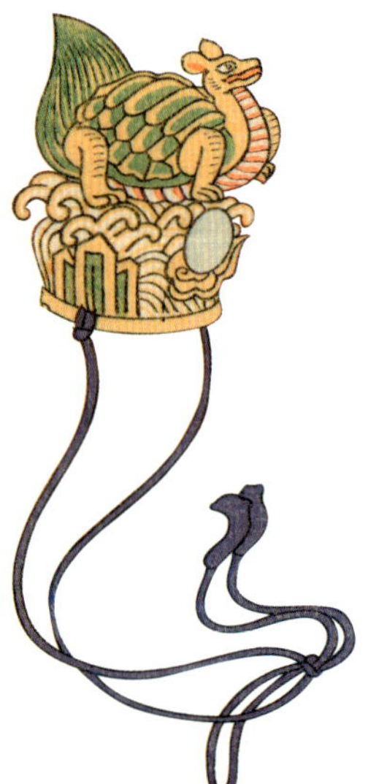

The crane and the tortoise (Tsuru kame)

Set in ancient China at the New Year, *The crane and the tortoise* is a lyrical kabuki dance-drama derived from a short play in the *nō* repertoire. *Nō* is considered to be Japan's classical dramatic form. Dating from the fourteenth century, it is characterised by codified movements rich in symbolic meaning, chanted speech accompanied by drum and flute music, opulent costumes and expressive wooden masks. *Nō* stage settings are minimal, with a distinctive pine-tree backdrop for all plays. As with kabuki, all *nō* roles are performed by men.

The crane and the tortoise is meant to bring good luck and is often performed by child actors. In the kabuki adaptation, the Empress visits the palace's Moon Pavilion. There, two of her noble attendants perform an evocative dance expressing the essence of the crane and the tortoise. In Chinese and Japanese legend, both animals are thought to live for thousands of years and have become prominent symbols of longevity. Haunting *nagauta* complements the dancers' movements. Translated as 'long song', *nagauta* originally referred to monastic music but is now the term for kabuki's vocal, stringed lute (*shamisen*), flute and drum music. *Nagauta* may be performed by a single artist, a small chorus or a full orchestra.

The print

In this delicate image, Shunsen captures the gentle refinement of the dance-drama. The actors Nakamura Tokizō III and Ichikawa Omezō IV—artistic rivals—are presented dancing as the spirits of the two animals that symbolise luck and long life. Particular attention is paid to the details of the actors' costumes; the folds of fabric suggest flowing movements. A crane is discernible in the crown of the female character, while the male courtier holds a similar headdress featuring a tortoise.

Nakamura Tokizō III (1895–1959)

Tokizō III was born in Osaka, the son of kabuki actor Nakamura Karoku III. He debuted as a child and became an important *onnagata* (female role) actor. His brother was Nakamura Kichiemon I and the siblings often played opposite each other. Known for his convincing femininity and lovely voice, the actor starred on stage and in film. Tokizō III had ten children, with many of his sons becoming kabuki, film and television stars.

Ichikawa Omezō IV (1898–1964)

The Tokyo actor Omezō IV was the son of Ichikawa Monnosuke VI and trained with Ichikawa Danjūrō IX. He first appeared on stage at the Kabuki Theatre as a young child. His specialities were *onnagata* (female) and *nimaime* (young, handsome and romantic male) roles, although he also excelled at portraying old men. Having joined the theatre company of Onoe Kikugorō VI in 1917, he inherited the leadership of the troupe in 1949. Three years later, the highly respected Omezō IV became Ichikawa Sadanji III.

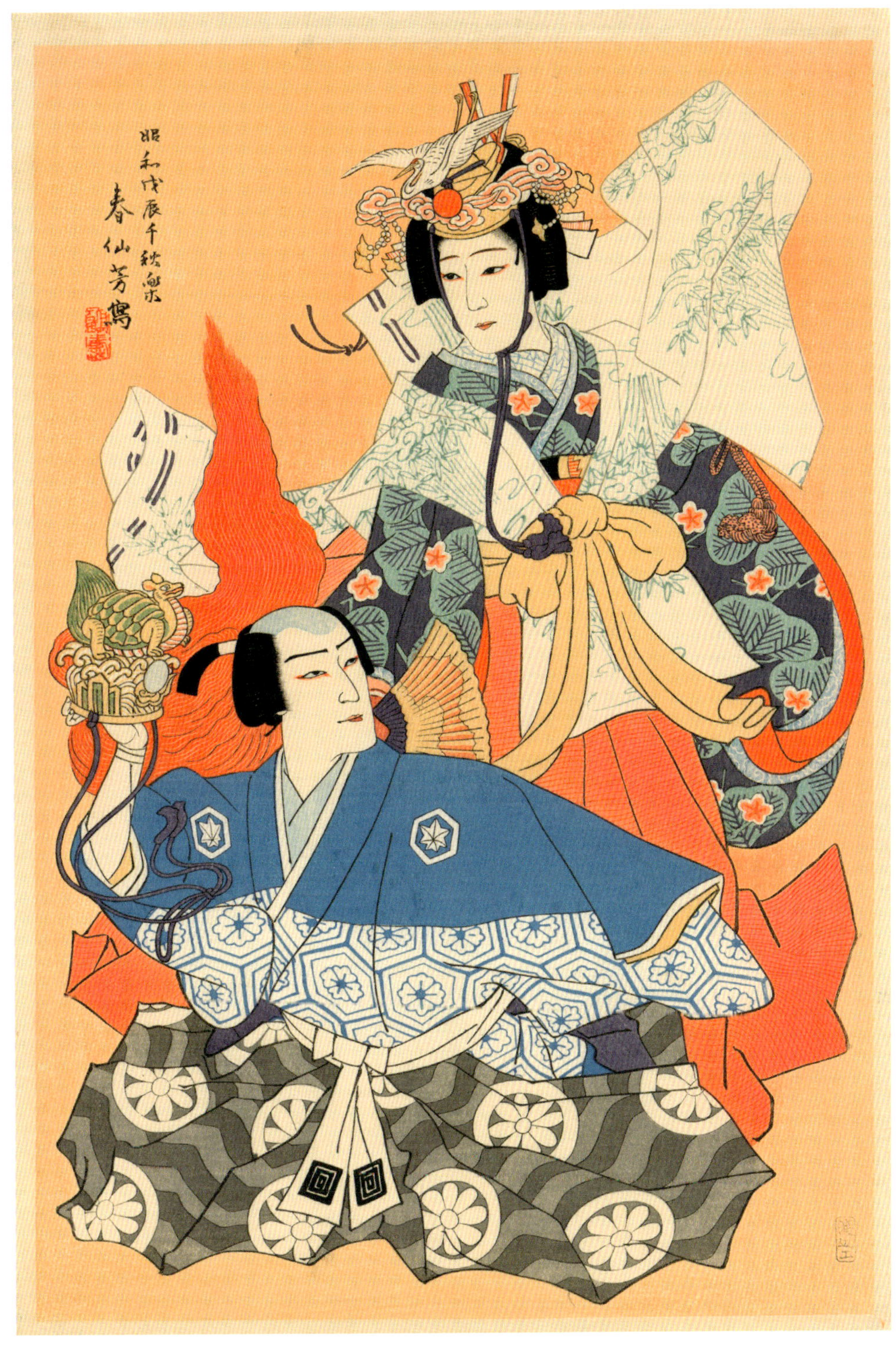

昭和戊辰千秋楽
春仙芳寫

Ichikawa Sumizō VI as Shirai Gonpachi in
'The floating world's pattern and matching
lightning bolts' 1926 from the series *Collection*
of creative portraits by Shunsen
[Ichikawa Sumizō VI Gonpachi]
woodblock print; ink and colour on paper
sheet: 39.4 x 27.0 cm, image: 38.2 x 26.0 cm
National Gallery of Australia, Canberra,
gift of Orde Poynton Esq, AO, CMG, 2001

The Floating world's pattern and matching lightning bolts (Ukiyozuka hiyoku no inazuma)

written by Tsuruya Nanboku IV, first kabuki performance in 1823

Based on an early-nineteenth century novel, the play is one of the most famous and regularly performed dramas by Tsuruya Nanboku IV (1755–1829). It comprises two contrasting stories, often staged independently. The first story demonstrates betrayal and rivalry within the high-ranking samurai class. The second illustrates the beginning of a friendship between a young outlaw, who murdered his uncle to protect his father's good name, and an *otokodate* or 'chivalrous commoner'. *Otokodate* are men glorified as heroes for operating outside the law to protect ordinary people from unscrupulous samurai. More commonly known as 'The well-known Suzugamori' (Gozonji Suzugamori), the second story is a fictitious tale about Shirai Gonpachi and Banzuin Chōbei, real people from different periods in Japanese history.

The action begins at night at Suzugamori, an eerie location where executions take place on the main highway to Tokyo. Thieves are discussing potential targets when a messenger arrives on the scene. They rob the man and read out the bounty notice he is carrying. It offers a reward for the young samurai Shirai Gonpachi, wanted for the murder of his uncle Honjō Suketayū. While they are talking, Gonpachi steps out of his palanquin, expecting to be at Tokyo's busy Kannon Temple. He immediately realises that his palanquin bearers have cheated him.

The thieves attack. Gonpachi triumphs by blinding some of his attackers and impaling, beheading or dismembering others. Innovative stage tricks produce a particularly gory and famous acrobatic struggle. (A man's face appears to have been sliced off, for instance, when a special hinged mask drops to reveal a featureless red mask beneath.)

Banzuin Chōbei has witnessed the fight and is deeply impressed by Gonpachi's superb swordsmanship. Gonpachi tells Chōbei that he has been unfairly forced from his home, but Chōbei sees the letter announcing Gonpachi's crime. Sensing some injustice, however, Chōbei burns the notice and promises to help Gonpachi.

The print

Shunsen's portrait of the handsome young actor Ichikawa Sumizō VI as Gonpachi emphasises the character's noble birth, signified by his white face makeup, and his youth, manifest by the actor's forelock wig (*maegami katsura*). In samurai culture, a boy's forelock is not cut off until he reaches manhood.

Ichikawa Sumizō VI (1886–1971)

Sumizō VI was adopted by Ichikawa Sumizō V after his kabuki debut. The actor followed the progressive star Ichikawa Sadanji II and helped fashion modern kabuki. His youthful face was well suited to young male roles, which he continued to perform as an older man. In 1949 he became Ichikawa Jukai III.

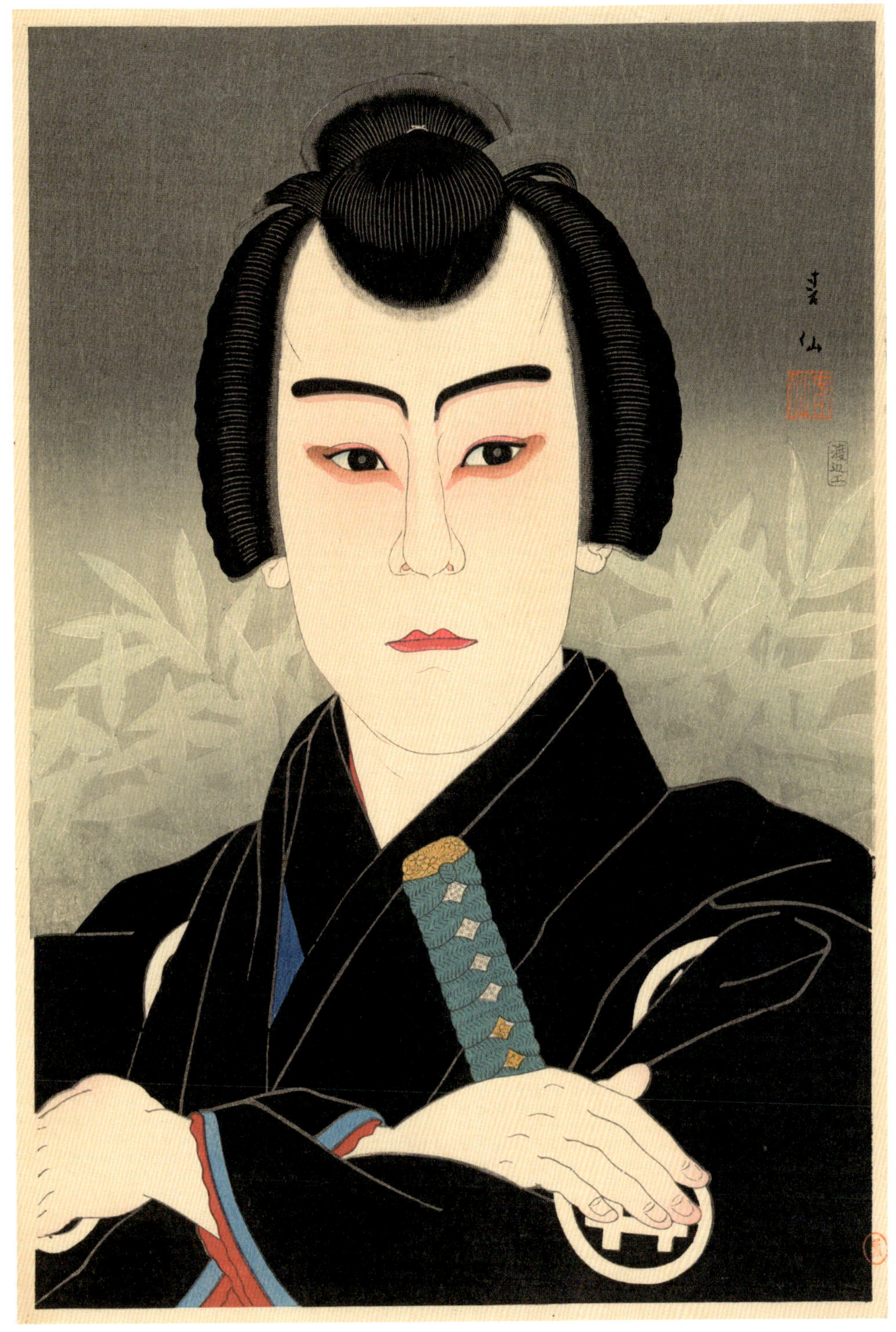

Ichikawa Sadanji II as Narukami in 'Narukami'
1926 from the series *Collection of creative
portraits by Shunsen*
[Ichikawa Sadanji II Narukami]
woodblock print, embossing; ink, colour and
mica on paper
sheet: 40.0 x 27.6 cm, image: 38.0 x 25.8 cm
National Gallery of Australia, Canberra,
purchased 2006

Narukami

written by Tsuuchi Hanjūrō, Yasuda Abun and
Nakada Mansuke, 1742 (earlier versions existed)

Narukami is an independently staged section
of *Narukami and Lord Fudo* (Narukami Fudō
kitayama zakura). The play's eroticism together
with rumours of a curse—after several
mysterious incidents culminated with Ichikawa
Danjuro VIII slashing his wrists while on tour in
the title role in 1851—led to an almost 50-year
break between performances. Since its revival in
1900, the play has delighted audiences with its
blend of history, ancient mythology, comedy and
supernatural elements.

The action occurs in the Heian period (794–1185)
at the mountain retreat of Narukami, a powerful
and pious magical priest. In retribution for
the Emperor's refusal to build him a temple,
Narukami has captured the Dragon God, source
of rain. The beautiful Princess Taema resolves
to break the drought. After bamboozling the
guards, she tells Narukami that she wishes
to wash the clothes of her dead husband at
his waterfall, the only one in the land. She
sensuously describes her tragic love story. The
priest is unsteadied by her words and beauty.

Princess Taema feigns pain and Narukami
puts his hands inside her kimono to heal her.
Suggesting that they marry, the princess
gives him his first drink of sake. Narukami,
overwhelmed by desire and alcohol, is tricked
into telling her how to free the Dragon God.

Once the priest has fallen into a drunken
sleep, Taema cuts the magic cord securing the
dragon. Thunder and lightning are immediately
unleashed. Narukami changes into the flame-
covered Thunder God and pursues Princess
Taema, violently tearing at sacred texts.
(Narukami's transformation is effected by a
costume quick-change. The actor wears two
layers of clothing and pulls threads so that the
top half of the costume falls inside-out, revealing
a top decorated with lightning motifs while
covering the lower half of the costume in the
decorative lining of the outer garment.)

The print

Shunsen's print of Ichikawa Sadanji II is an
arresting big-head portrait (*ōkubi-e*) of the brash
sorcerer-priest Narukami as the furious Thunder
God. The blue lines of makeup and flames visible
behind the huge wig indicate the supernatural.

Ichikawa Sadanji II (1880–1940)

Sadanji II, son of the great Ichikawa Sadanji I,
was born in Tokyo and began acting at an early
age. When his father died he inherited the
management of the Meiji Theatre, but gave it
up and joined the Shōchiku Theatre. In 1906
he went to Europe to study acting, one of the
first kabuki actors to do so. On his return he
pioneered Japan's modern theatre. Fans of the
actor referred to him as *daitōryō* (president).

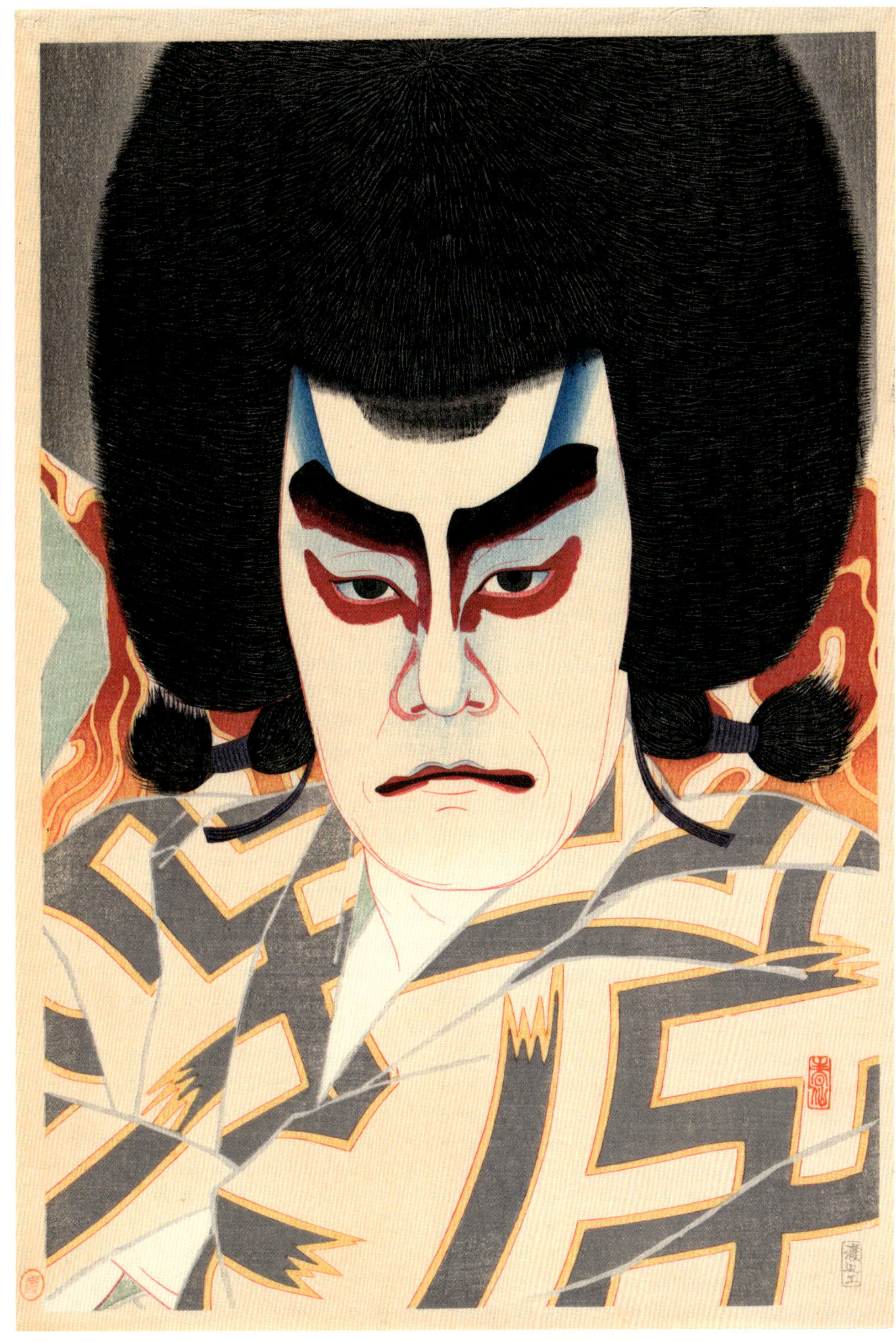

*Matsumoto Kōshirō VII as Benkei in
'The subscription list'* 1935
[Matsumoto Kōshirō VII Kanjinchō]
woodblock print, embossing; ink and colour
on paper
sheet: 39.0 x 53.0 cm, image: 37.2 x 51.7 cm
National Gallery of Australia, Canberra,
Pauline and John Gandel Fund, 2011

The subscription list (Kanjinchō)

written by Namiki Gohei III, first kabuki
performance in 1840

One of kabuki's most famous dance-dramas,
The subscription list was adapted from a *nō*
play. The kabuki version has featured *nō*-
inspired costumes and scenery since its first
staging, when it was unusual to blur the line
between *nō* and kabuki. The play dramatises
events surrounding the twelfth-century schism
between Minamoto Yoritomo and his brother
Yoshitsune. The main character is Yoshitsune's
famously loyal retainer, Benkei. Many plays
portray Benkei as recklessly aggressive, but
The subscription list emphasises his samurai spirit,
valour and intelligence.

The play is set when Yoritomo's distrust has
forced Yoshitsune to flee, disguised as a humble
porter. His four closest retainers are dressed as
yamabushi (mountain-dwelling) warrior-priests.
The journey is dangerous, with Yoritomo's
men stationed at various roadblocks. Togashi
no Sagaemon is in command at the Ataka
barrier. He has been told that Yoshitsune will
try to escape in the guise of a mountain priest.
Yoshitsune and his retainers enter. Benkei tells
Sagaemon that his group are priests on their way
to Nara, raising money for a temple dedication.
Sagaemon tells him that no *yamabushi* may pass.
Benkei prepares his men to fight, loudly warning
of the grave sin of killing a priest. Sagaemon
tests Benkei's authenticity—challenging him
to recite the names of the donors to his cause.
Benkei holds up a blank scroll and invents a list of
names. Sagaemon signals the party to continue
their journey. Suddenly, one of Sagaemon's
guards catches a glimpse of Yoshitsune and
announces that the porter may be the fugitive.
Benkei again uses his wits. He abuses Yoshitsune
and strikes him with a stick—a shockingly brave
act for a samurai, as harming one's lord was

punishable by death. Sagaemon, never fooled
by Benkei's act, is deeply impressed by the
retainer's ingenuity, audacity and devotion to his
master. He is also confused about his loyalties in
relation to Yoshitsune, a high-ranking Minamoto
general. A courageous Sagaemon acts in support
of samurai honour, allowing Yoshitsune and his
men through the gate.

Beyond the blockade, Yoshitsune pardons the
grovelling Benkei for beating him. Sagaemon
approaches and in conciliation presents Benkei
with a drink of sake, which he guzzles greedily.
The play ends with Benkei, despite his inebriated
state, fearing a trap and directing his men to flee
the gathering.

The print

Shunsen depicts one of kabuki's most celebrated
(*mie*) poses—when Benkei, dressed as a
warrior-priest and holding a blank scroll, readies
himself to convince Yoritomo's men that he is
not harbouring the renegade Yoshitsune. The
artist captures the tension of the moment and
accurately illustrates the details of Benkei's
mountain-priest disguise.

Matsumoto Kōshirō VII (1870–1949)

Kōshirō VII was legendary for performing the role
of Benkei in *The subscription list* over 1600 times.

See page 67 for actor's biography.

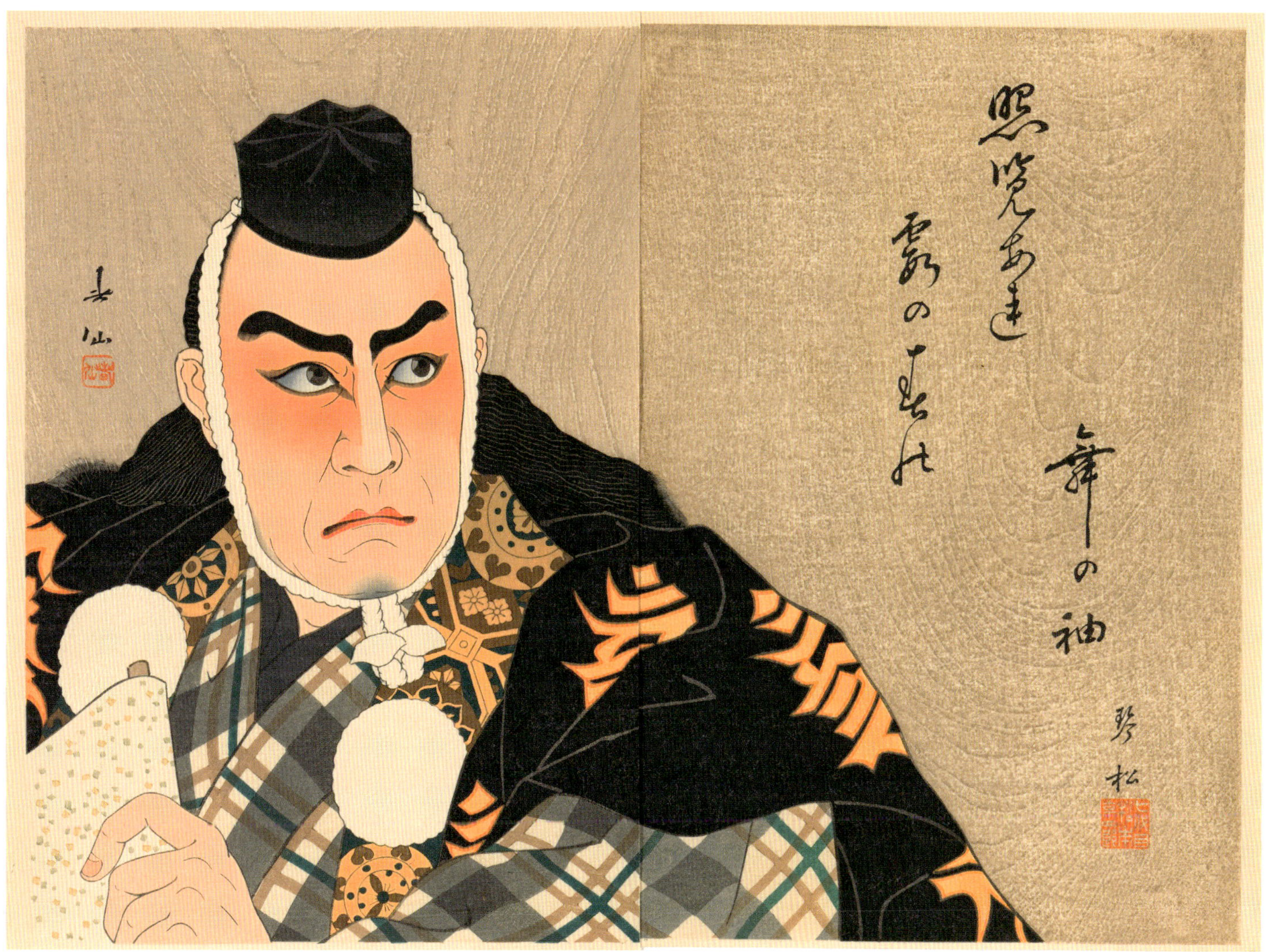

舞の袖
雲のなこり
琴松

Ōkōchi Denjirō as Tange Sazen 1931 from the series *Supplement to collection of portraits by Shunsen*
[Ōkōchi Denjirō Tange Sazen]
woodblock print; ink and colour on paper
sheet: 40.0 x 27.3 cm, image: 37.5 x 26.0 cm
National Gallery of Australia, Canberra,
Pauline and John Gandel Fund, 2011

Tange Sazen

original story written by Fubō Hayashi, the first Tange Sazen films were made in 1928

A fictional character, Tange Sazen is a loyal samurai who is betrayed and ambushed in an attack during which he loses his right eye and right arm. His superb swordsmanship intact, Tange Sazen becomes a *rōnin* (masterless samurai).

Fubō Hayashi's stories featuring Tange Sazen first appeared as a serial novel published between October 1927 and May 1928 in Osaka's *Daily News* (Mainichi Shinbun). Instantly popular, the sensational tales and extraordinary character of Tange Sazen appealed to film companies. Three studios released Tange Sazen films in 1928, two of which starred Ōkōchi Denjirō. The many film adventures of the essentially good-hearted hero include a 1935 satire on earlier Tange Sazen movies, *The million ryō pot* (Tange sazen yowa: hyakuman ryō no tsubo), which was remade in 2004.

The print

Shunsen's portrait depicts film star Ōkōchi Denjirō as his most famous character, Tange Sazen, in the same style the artist used to portray leading kabuki actors of the period. The image encapsulates the raw strength and distinctive appearance of the one-armed, one-eyed *rōnin*, emphasising the long scar across his missing eye. A grimacing Tange Sazen is shown in the act of pulling out his sword, dressed in his familiar calligraphy-embellished robe. The work is one of a group of 15 supplementary prints to *Collection of creative portraits by Shunsen* released between 1931 and 1934.

Ōkōchi Denjirō (1898–1962)

Born Masuo Ōbe in Fukuoka, Ōkōchi Denjirō starred primarily in historical drama films (*jidaigeki*). He studied with the innovative actor Sawada Shōjirō, founder of the popular New National Theatre (Shinkokugeki), which was famous for presenting plays featuring convincing sword fights. In 1925 he joined Japan's oldest film studio, Nikkatsu (established 1912). Denjirō appeared in over 100 films between 1926 and 1962, at least eight of which were Tange Sazen pictures. A small museum dedicated to the actor is located in the grounds of one of his former residences in Kyoto.

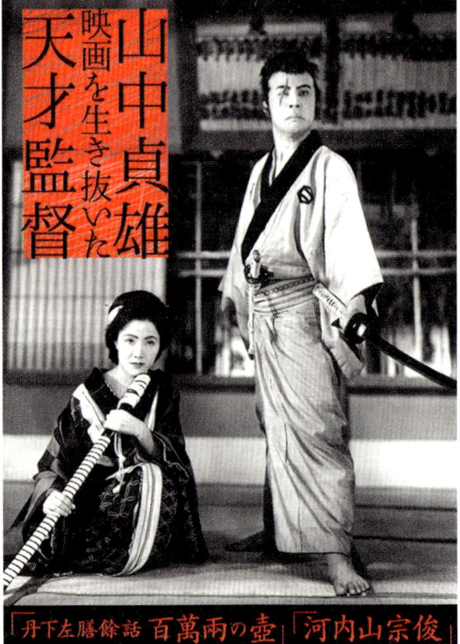

(right) **Nikkatsu** Poster for the film *The million ryō pot* (Tange sazen yowa: hyakuman ryō no tsubo) 1935

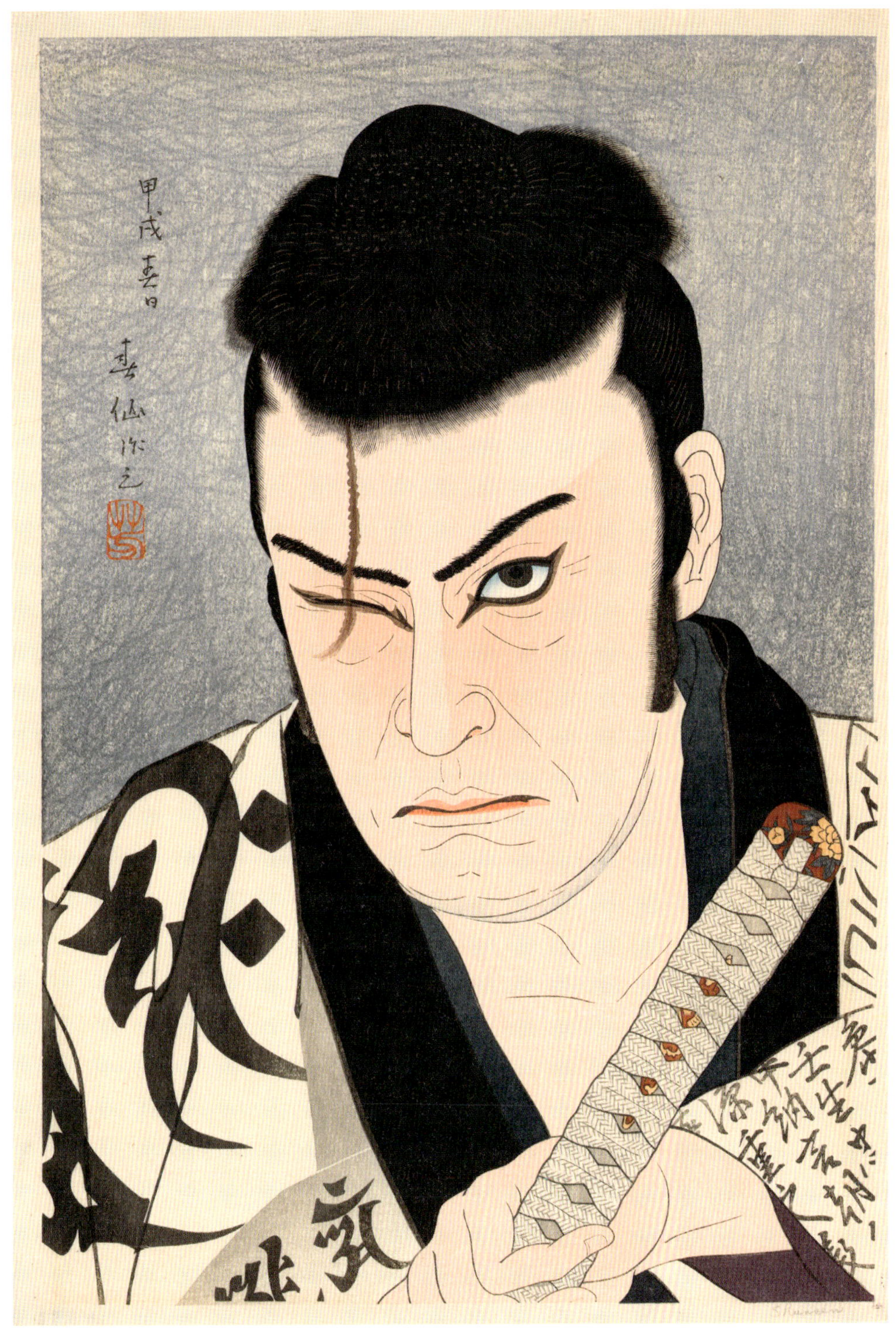

Matsumoto Kōshirō VII as Ikyū in 'Sukeroku: flower of Edo' 1929 from the series *Supplement to collection of portraits by Shunsen*
[Higi no Ikyū]
woodblock print, embossing; ink, colour and mica on paper
sheet: 38.1 x 25.4 cm, image: 36.4 x 24.5 cm
National Gallery of Australia, Canberra, Pauline and John Gandel Fund, 2011

Sukeroku: flower of Edo (Sukeroku: yukari no Edo zakura)

written by Tsuuchi Jihei II, Tsuuchi Hanemon, first kabuki performance in 1713

Sukeroku: flower of Edo conveys the lively atmosphere of Tokyo's Yoshiwara red-light district during the early-eighteenth century. The play's main characters are drawn from Japanese history and legend—Sukeroku and Shinbei are based on Soga no Gorō and Soga no Jūrō, samurai brothers who succeeded in an audacious twelfth-century vendetta. The play opens outside the Miuraya bordello, the building's dramatic red facade set against blossoming cherry trees. Splendidly dressed, the prostitute Agemaki sweeps onto the stage with her entourage. She encounters Mankō, the mother of her fiancé, the charming playboy Sukeroku. Mankō grumbles that Sukeroku, once a good man, now only brawls instead of dutifully trying to recover the precious heirloom sword stolen from his father. Agemaki expresses her concern. Mankō then gives permission for their marriage and exits. The beautiful Agemaki preens herself as an important samurai client, Ikyū, arrives. His infatuation with Agemaki is clear, as is her disdain for him. Sukeroku makes a stylish entrance, posing with an umbrella decorated with a bullseye. He rudely insults Ikyū, then pours a bowl of noodles over the old samurai's friend and takes on a pack of thugs in a boisterous scuffle. Finally Sukeroku challenges Ikyū, who stalks away.

Shinbei, Sukeroku's younger brother, pesters Sukeroku to concentrate on their quest. Sukeroku reveals the aim of his hooliganism— to force men to expose their weapons in the hope of finding the sword. Sukeroku believes that Ikyū is the thief. The brothers practice their insults on hapless bystanders, until Mankō walks past and is deeply upset by their vulgarity. Sukeroku explains and Mankō presents her son with a magical jacket that will protect him, but kill her, if he loses his temper.

Later, Ikyū and his retinue emerge from the brothel. Sukeroku pinches him, inciting an argument. Ikyū forgets to conceal his blade and Sukeroku sees that he is holding the lost sword. Ikyū departs. That night Sukeroku dresses in white, signifying his intent to fight to the death, and prepares to ambush Ikyū. The white-bearded samurai soon appears and Sukeroku demands the sword. Ikyū drops his outer garments to reveal a white robe. The pair duel and Sukeroku kills Ikyū. Injured, he collects the sword and takes cover (jumping into a huge barrel of water in some productions). In the chaos of the discovery of Ikyū's body, Amegaki hides Sukeroku beneath her extravagant costume and arranges his escape, promising to join him soon.

The print

This powerful portrait of the kabuki star Matsumoto Kōshirō VII as Ikyū conveys the character's wickedness. Ikyū is depicted in one of the elaborate robes for which the play is renowned, his hand upon the stolen sword. The superb print is embellished with flecks of glittering mica and the waves of the villain's beard are embossed.

Matsumoto Kōshirō VII (1870–1949)

See page 67 for actor's biography.

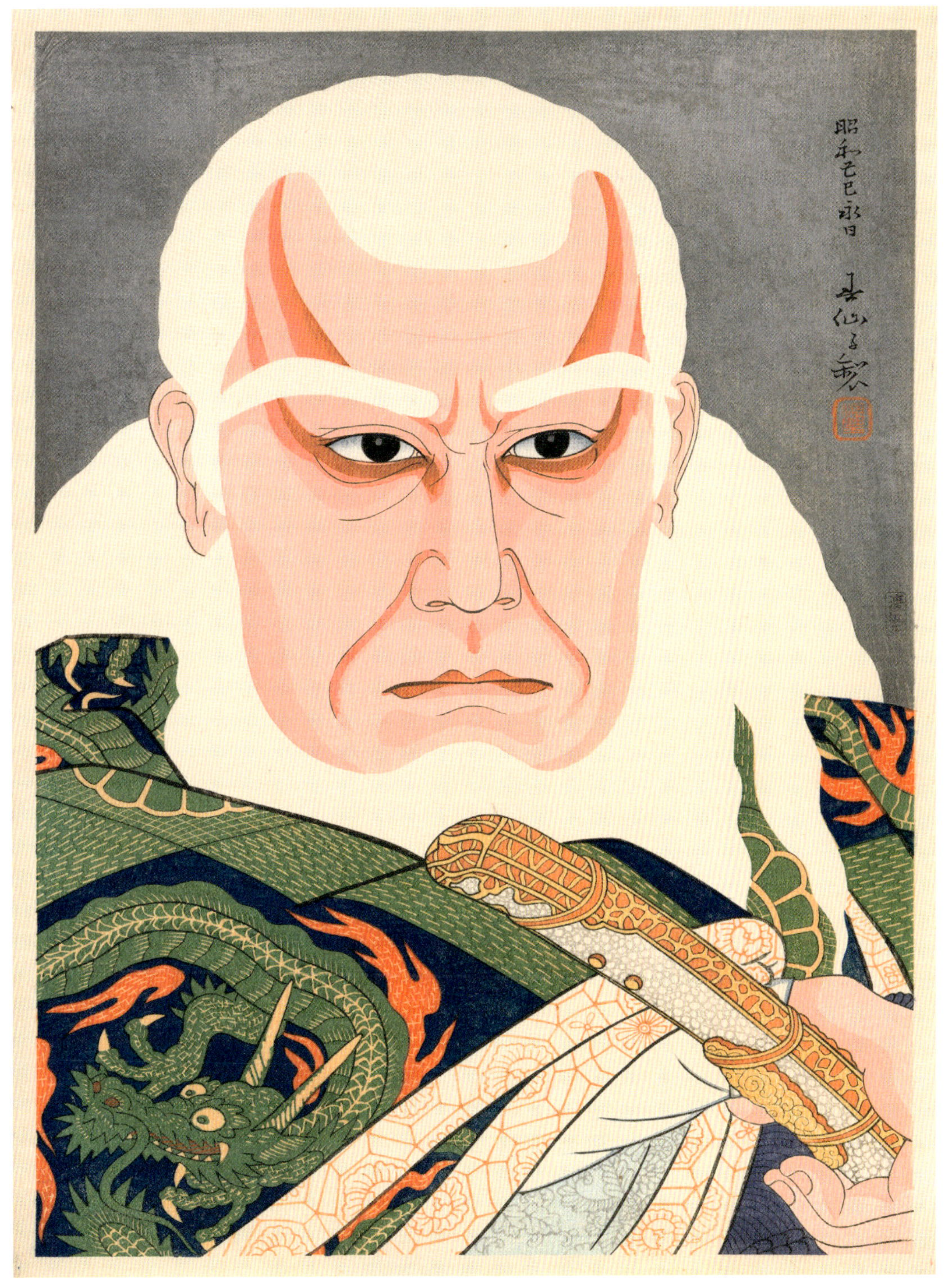

*Ichimura Uzaemon XVI as Benten Kozō in
'The glorious picture book of Aoto's exploits'* 1950
watercolour on paper
sheet: 36.2 x 25.4 cm, image: 31.0 x 21.8
National Gallery of Australia, Canberra,
Pauline and John Gandel Fund, 2011

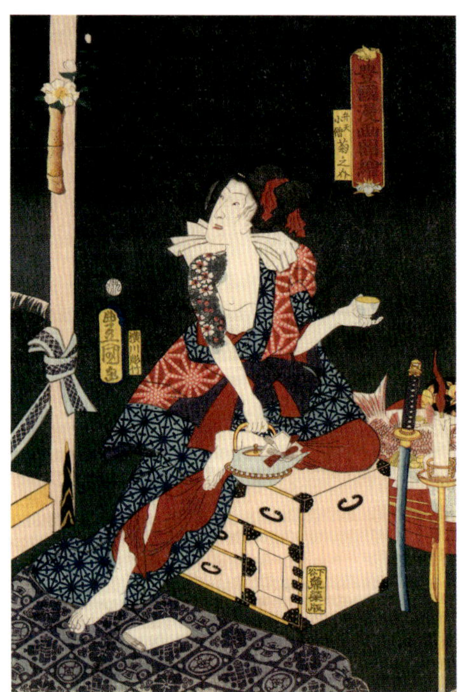

(below) **Utagawa Kunisada** (1786–1865) *Iwai Kumesaburō III as Benten Kozō Kikunosuke* from the series *'Toyokuni's caricature pictures'* 1864
woodblock print; ink and colour on paper, 38.7 x 25.5 cm
Museum of Fine Arts, Boston, William Sturgis Bigelow Collection

The glorious picture book of Aoto's exploits (Aotozōshi hana no nishiki-e)

written by Kawatake Mokuami, first kabuki performance in 1862

Commonly known as *Benten the thief* (Benten Kozō) or *Five men of the white waves* (Shiranami gonin otoko), the play is an action drama about a gang of daring thieves. The actor Onoe Kikugorō V reputedly asked Mokuami to write the play after seeing woodblock prints by Utagawa Kunisada (1786–1865) depicting famous nineteenth-century actors as the criminal folk heroes in earlier kabuki plays.

The glorious picture book of Aoto's exploits opens with the beautiful Princess Senjū making offerings for her recently deceased father and fiancé Kotarō, who she never had the chance to meet. Benten Kozō tricks Senjū into believing that he is Kotarō and she gives him a precious incense burner. The action shifts to a nearby commotion. Akaboshi Jūzaburō, retainer of the real Kotarō, is caught stealing temple donations to buy medicine for Senjū's mother. Two samurai recover the money and are confronted by Tadanobu Rihei, a bandit posing as a *rōnin* (masterless samurai). Rihei blackmails them but is then robbed by Nangō Rikimaru, a member of Nippon Daemon's band of thieves.

At a mountain shrine, Benten confesses his true name and falsely tells Senjū that he had tried to save Kotarō. Senjū throws herself off the cliff. Nippon Daemon steals the burner from Benten, who is persuaded to enlist in the gang. Meanwhile, Rihei and Jūzaburō also decide to join Daemon. The newly formed gang goes on a crime spree.

One of their scams sees Benten, dressed as a samurai woman, entering a shop with Rikimaru. Feigning furtiveness, he steals an item and the clerk hits him on the forehead. Rikimaru demands compensation for the injury. A man, introducing himself as Tamashima Ittō, accuses Benten of deception. In a scene famous for its eroticism, Benten drops his kimono and exposes his tattoos. When the shopkeeper, Kōbei, pays Benten and Rikimaru to leave quietly, Ittō's expression abruptly changes—he is Daemon in disguise. The thieves tie up Kōbei, who announces that he is Benten's father, fired from the service of Senjū's father due to suspicion over a stolen incense burner.

Later, police chase the bandits who use their umbrellas as weapons. They go their separate ways at the Inase River, promising to meet in Kyoto. After a number of skirmishes and a murder, the police are in hot pursuit of Benten. The play ends with Benten, cornered on the roof of a temple, commiting *seppuku* (suicide by disembowelment). The other thieves are later captured or turn themselves in.

The image

Shunsen's watercolour, a study for an unpublished actor portrait, presents the dashing young criminal Benten Kozō in the scene in which the robbers gather at the Inase River and battle the police with their umbrellas. Benten is depicted wearing his distinctive purple robe, decorated with chrysanthemums and a snake coiled around a lute (*biwa*).

Ichimura Uzaemon XVI (1905–52)

Uzaemon XVI was the son of Ichimura Uzaemon XV. The talented Tokyo actor performed female roles and romantic male heroes.

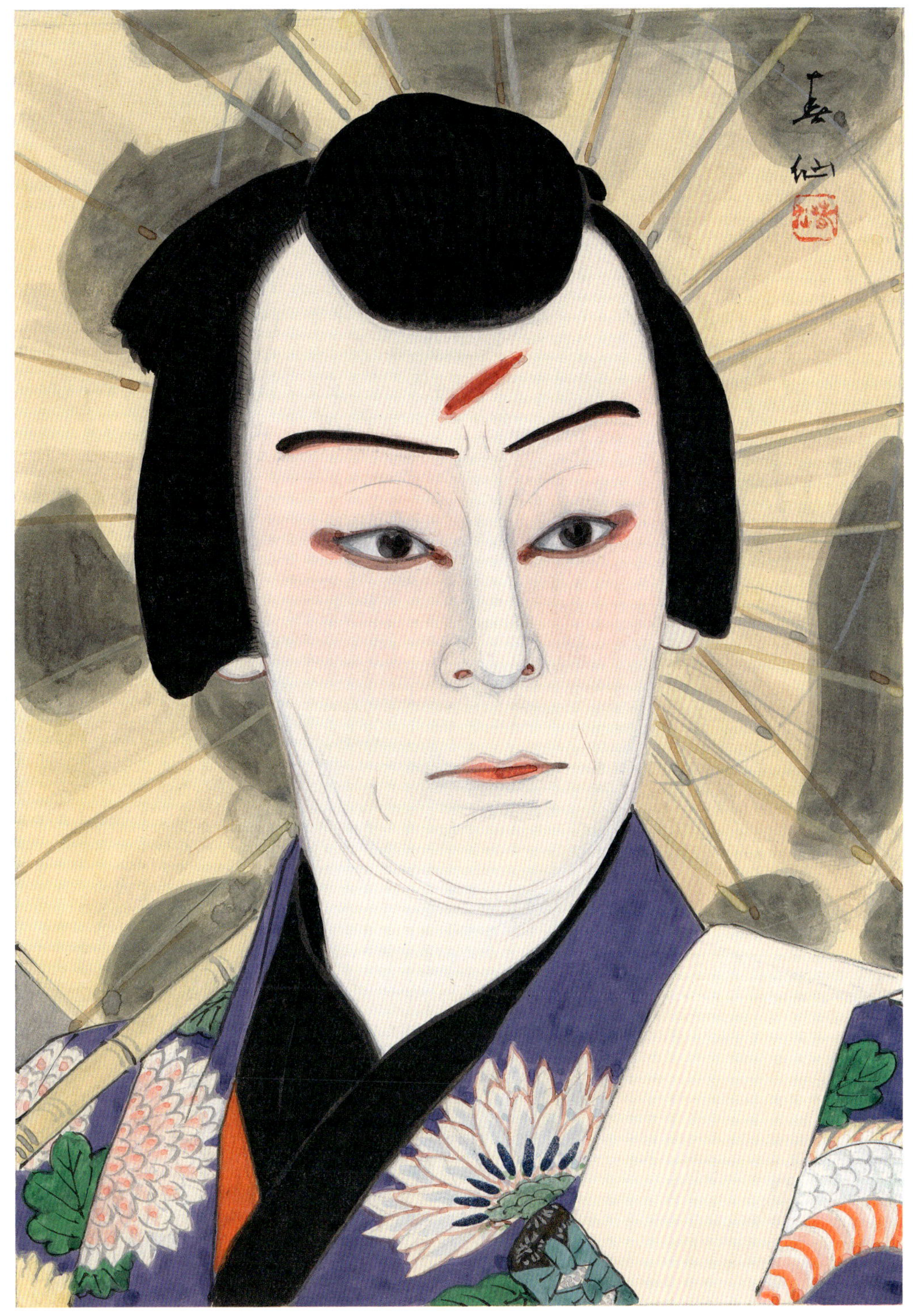

BIBLIOGRAPHY

Banham, Martin (ed), *The Cambridge guide to theatre*, Cambridge University Press, Cambridge, 1995.

Blair, Dorothy, *Modern Japanese prints: printed from a photographic reproduction of two exhibition catalogues of modern Japanese prints published by the Toledo Museum of Art in 1930 and 1936*, Toledo Museum of Art, Toledo, 1997.

Bowers, Faubion, *Japanese theatre*, C E Tuttle Co, Tokyo, 1974.

Brandon, James (ed), *Chūshingura: studies in kabuki and the puppet theatre*, University Press of Hawaii, Honolulu, 1982.

Brandon, James (ed), *Kabuki: five classic plays*, University of Hawaii Press, Honolulu, 1992.

Brandon, James (ed), *The Cambridge guide to Asian theatre*, Cambridge University Press, Cambridge, 1993.

Brandon, James & Leiter, Samuel, *Kabuki plays on stage: brilliance and bravado*, University of Hawaii Press, Honolulu, 2002–03.

Brandon, James & Leiter, Samuel, *Kabuki plays on stage: darkness and desire*, University of Hawaii Press, Honolulu, 2002–03.

Brandon, James & Leiter, Samuel, *Kabuki plays on stage: restoration and reform*, University of Hawaii Press, Honolulu, 2002–03.

Brandon, James & Leiter, Samuel, *Kabuki plays on stage: villainy and vengeance*, University of Hawaii Press, Honolulu, 2002–03.

Brazell, Karen (ed), *Traditional Japanese theater: an anthology of plays*, Columbia University Press, New York, 1998.

Brown, Kendall, *Taishō chic: Japanese modernity, nostalgia, and deco*, University of Hawaii Press, Honolulu, 2001.

Brown, Kendall & Goodall-Cristante, Hollis, *Shin-hanga: new prints in modern Japan*, Los Angeles County Museum of Art, Los Angeles, 1996.

Dower, John, *Embracing defeat: Japan in the wake of World War II*, W W Norton and Co, New York, 1999.

Gerstle, C Andrew, *Chikamatsu: five late plays*, Columbia Univeristy Press, New York, 2001.

Gerstle, C Andrew, *Kabuki heroes on the Osaka stage 1780–1830*, British Museum Press, London, 2005.

Halford, Aubrey S & Halford, Giovanna M, *The kabuki handbook: a guide to understanding and appreciation with summaries of favourite plays, explanatory notes, and illustrations*, C E Tuttle Co, Tokyo, 1956.

Henshū Iinkai, *Kabushiki Kaisha Mitsukoshi 85-nen no kiroku (Records of the 85 years of Mitsukoshi Co)*, Mitsukoshi Co, Tokyo, 1990.

Herwig, Arendie & Herwig, Henk, *Heroes of the kabuki stage: an introduction to kabuki with retellings of famous plays*, Hotei Publishing, Amsterdam, 2004.

Hironaga Shūzaburō, *Bunraku: Japan's unique puppet theatre*, Tokyo News Service, Tokyo, 1964.

Ikeda Tamio, *Regards d'acteurs Natori Shunsen: Estampes de Natori Shunsen (1886–1960) de la série des 36 portraits d'acteurs de kabuki 'Shunsen nigao-e shu' éditée de 1925 à 1929*, Tanakaya, Paris, 2001.

Japanese National Commission for UNESCO, *Theatre in Japan*, Ministry of Finance, Tokyo, 1963.

Jippensha Ikku, *Shank's mare*, Thomas Satchell (trans), C E Tuttle Co, Tokyo, 1960.

Jones, Stanleigh H, *Sugawara and the secrets of calligraphy*, Columbia University Press, New York, 1985.

Jortner, David, McDonald, Keiko & Wetmore, Kevin (eds), *Modern Japanese theatre and performance*, Lexington Books, Lanham, 2006.

Kabuki yonhyakunenten zuroku, Kyōdō Tsūshinsha, Tokyo, 2003.

Keene, Donald (trans), *Major plays of Chikamatsu*, Columbia University Press, New York, 1961.

Keene, Donald (trans), *Chūshingura (The treasury of loyal retainers): a puppet play by Takeda Izumo, Miyoshi Shoraku, and Namiki Senryu*, Columbia University Press, New York, 1971.

Kerr, Alex, *Lost Japan*, Lonely Planet Publications, Melbourne, 1996.

Kimura Rieko, *Dance in Japanese modern art*, Tochigi Prefectural Museum of Fine Arts, Tochigi, 2003.

Kincaid, Zoë, *Kabuki: the popular stage of Japan*, Macmillan, London, 1925.

Kincaid, Zoë, *Tokyo vignettes*, Sanseido Co Ltd, Tokyo-Osaka, 1933.

Kushigata Shunsen Museum of Art, *Natori Shunsen: Kushigata Chōritsu Shunsen Bijutsukan shozō Natori Shunsen sakuhin mokuroku (Natori Shunsen: collection of Kushigata Shunsen Museum of Art)*, Kushigata Shunsen Museum of Art, Kushigata, 2002.

Leiter, Samuel L, *The art of kabuki: famous plays in performance*, University of California Press, Berkeley, 1979.

Leiter, Samuel L, *New kabuki encyclopedia: a revised adaptation of kabuki jiten*, Greenwood Press, Westport, 1997.

Leiter, Samuel L, *The art of kabuki: five famous plays*, Dover Publications, Mineola, 1999.

Leiter, Samuel L (ed), *A kabuki reader: history and performance*, M E Sharpe, New York, 2002.

Leiter, Samuel L, *Historical dictionary of Japanese traditional theatre*, Scarecrow Press, Lanham, 2006.

Leiter, Samuel L, *Rising from the flames: the rebirth of theater in occupied Japan, 1945–1952*, Lexington Books, Lanham, 2009.

Malm, William P, *Nagauta: the heart of kabuki music*, C E Tuttle Co, Rutland, 1963.

Menzies, Jackie (ed), *Modern boy, modern girl: modernity in Japanese art 1910–1935*, Art Gallery of New South Wales, Sydney, 1998.

Merritt, Helen, *Modern Japanese woodblock prints: the early years*, University of Hawaii Press, Honolulu, 1990.

Merritt, Helen, *Guide to modern Japanese woodblock prints: 1900–1975*, University of Hawaii Press, Honolulu, 1992.

Minnich, Helen Benton, *Japanese costume and the makers of its elegant tradition*, C E Tuttle Co, Rutland, 1963.

Miyamori Asataro (trans), *Masterpieces of Chikamatsu: the Japanese Shakespeare*, E P Dutton, New York, 1926.

Newland, Amy Reigle & Uhlenbeck, Chris, *Ukiyo-e to shin hanga: the art of Japanese woodblock prints*, Mallard Press, New York, 1990.

Newland, Amy Reigle (ed), *Printed to perfection: twentieth century Japanese prints from the Robert O Mueller collection*, Hotei Publishing, Amsterdam, in association with Arthur M Sackler Gallery, Smithsonian Institution, Washington DC, 2004.

Newland, Amy Reigle (ed), *The Hotei encyclopedia of Japanese woodblock prints*, Hotei Publishing, Amsterdam, 2005.

Noma Seiji, *Watashi no hansei* (My life until now), Dai Nihon Yūbenkai Kōdansha, Tokyo, 1939.

Okamoto Shirō, *The man who saved kabuki: Faubion Bowers and theatre censorship in occupied Japan*, University of Hawaii Press, Honolulu, 2001.

Powell, Brian, *Kabuki in modern Japan: Mayama Seika and his plays*, St Martin's Press, New York, 1990.

Powell, Brian, *Japan's modern theatre: a century of change and continuity*, Japan Library, London, 2002.

Richie, Donald & Watanabe, Miyoko (trans), *Six kabuki plays*, Hokuseido Press, Tokyo, 1963.

Richie, Donald, *A hundred years of Japanese film: a concise history*, Kodansha, Tokyo, 2005.

Satō Takumi, *Kingu no jidai: kokumin taishu zasshi no ko kyo sei* (The era of King: the public nature of the magazine for the masses), Iwanami Shoten, Tokyo, 2002.

Scott, Adolphe C (trans), *Kanjincho: a Japanese kabuki play*, Hokuseido Press, Tokyo, 1953.

Scott, Adolphe C, *Genyadana: a Japanese kabuki play*, Hokuseido Press, Tokyo, 1953.

Scott, Adolphe C, *The kabuki theatre of Japan*, George Allen and Unwin, London, 1955.

Sekikawa Natsuo, *Shirakaba-tachi no Taishō* (The Taishō period for the Shirakaba group), Bungei Shunjū, Tokyo, 2005.

Shaver, Ruth M, *Kabuki costume*, C E Tuttle Co, Rutland, 1966.

Shaw, Glenn W (trans), *Tojuro's love and four other plays by Kikuchi Kan*, Hokuseido Press, Tokyo, 1956.

Shōchiku Theatre Company performance of scenes from *The subscription list*, Tokyo, 2011.

Shōchiku Theatre Company performance of scenes from *Yoshitsune and the thousand cherry trees*, Tokyo, 2011.

Smith, Lawrence, *Modern Japanese prints 1912–1989: woodblocks and stencils*, British Museum Press, London, 1994.

Takemura Tamio, *Taishō Bunka* (The culture of the Taishō period), Kodansha, Tokyo, 1980.

Taylor, Beverley, *Yoshitsune senbon zakura: the visual dimension in a kabuki performance*, PhD Thesis, University of Hawaii at Manoa, 1995.

Watanabe Shōzaburō, *Catalogue of woodcut colour prints of S Watanabe*, S Watanabe, Tokyo, 1936.

Watanabe Shōzaburō, *Mokuhanga mokuroku*, S Watanabe, Tokyo, 1940.

Winegrad, Dilys Pegler (ed), *Dramatic impressions: Japanese theatre prints from the Gilbert Luber collection*, University of Pennsylvania Press, Philadelphia, 2007.

Yoshimoto Mitsuhiro, *Kurosawa: film studies and Japanese cinema*, Duke University Press, Durham, 2000.

Yume-o egaite hanayakani: Takarazuka Kageki 80-nen-shi (Picturing dreams, spectacularly: 80 years of Takarazuka Revue), Takarazuka Kagekidan, Takarazuka, 1994.

CONTRIBUTORS

Chiaki Ajioka

Dr Chiaki Ajioka graduated from Musashino Art University, Tokyo. She has an MA from the University of Melbourne and a PhD in Art History from the Australian National University. Ajioka was Curator of Japanese Art at the Art Gallery of New South Wales from 1996 until 2003. Prior to that she was the senior Japanese subtitler at SBS Television. Ajioka has curated many exhibitions including *Modern boy, modern girl: modernity in Japanese art 1910–1935* (1998), *Hanga: Japanese creative prints* (2000), *Heroes and villains in Japan's floating world* (2001), *Seasons: the beauty of transience in Japanese art* (2003) and *Japan in Sydney: Professor Sadler and modernism 1920–30s* (2011). She contributed to the publication *Since Meiji: perspectives on the Japanese visual arts 1968–2000* (2012).

Melanie Eastburn

Melanie Eastburn is Curator of Asian Art at the National Gallery of Australia. She was curator of the exhibition *Black robe white mist: art of the Japanese Buddhist nun Rengetsu* and co-editor of the accompanying publication (2007). In 2002–04 Eastburn worked at the National Museum of Cambodia in Phnom Penh, through Australian Volunteers International. Prior to that she was Curator of Asian Decorative Arts and Design at the Powerhouse Museum, Sydney, where she curated the Japanese street fashion exhibition *FRUiTS: Tokyo street style— photographs by Shoichi Aoki*. Her book *Papua New Guinea Prints* (2006) was based on her research as the inaugural recipient of the National Gallery of Australia's Gordon Darling Fellowship for the study of Australasian prints.

Lucie Folan

Lucie Folan is Curator of Asian Art at the National Gallery of Australia. She is curator of the exhibition *Stars of the Tokyo stage: Natori Shunsen's kabuki actor prints*. Folan has contributed to many exhibitions and publications including *Sari to sarong: 500 years of Indian and Indonesian textile exchange* (2003) and *Life, death and magic: 2000 years of Southeast Asian ancestral art* (2010). She was co-editor of the exhibition catalogue *Black robe white mist: art of the Japanese Buddhist nun Rengetsu* (2007) and has written for a range of publications in Australia and Asia on aspects of South and Southeast Asian art. In 2006–07 Folan worked at the National Museum of Cambodia in Phnom Penh, through Australian Volunteers International.

C Andrew Gerstle

C Andrew Gerstle is Professor of Japanese Studies at the School of Oriental and African Studies (SOAS), University of London. He has published widely on Japanese drama, literature, *ukiyo-e* art and erotic books (*shunga*). Recent publications include *Edo onna no shungabon* (Shunga books for women) (2011), and translations of two 18th-century erotic parodies, *Onna shimegawa oeshi-bumi* (2007) and *Bidō nichiya johōki* (2010), published by the International Research Center for Japanese Studies. He is the author of *Chikamatsu: five late plays* (2001) and co-author of *Kabuki heroes on the Osaka stage, 1780-1830* (2005) and *Ryūkōsai zuroku: Kamigata yakusha nigao-e no reimei* (2009). Gerstle is co-curator, with Timothy Clark and Akiko Yano, of an exhibition on *shunga* erotic art at the British Museum (2013).

Robyn Maxwell

Robyn Maxwell is Senior Curator of Asian Art at the National Gallery of Australia. A renowned textile specialist, she is the author of *Textiles of Southeast Asia: tradition, trade and transformation* (1990, reprinted 1994 and 2003). Maxwell was previously Senior Lecturer in Art History at the Australian National University, specialising in Asian art, textile history, museum history and curatorship. In 1997-98 she was Visiting Professor at the National Museum of Ethnology, Osaka, Japan. Maxwell has curated numerous exhibitions and published and lectured widely on Asian art. Recent exhibitions and publications include *Life, death and magic: 2000 years of Southeast Asian ancestral art* (2010), *The Bronze Weaver: a masterpiece of 6th century Indonesian sculpture* (2007) and *Sari to sarong: 500 years of Indian and Indonesian textile exchange* (2003).

Amy Reigle Newland

Amy Reigle Newland is an independent scholar of Japanese woodblock prints. As editor and author her publications include *Yoshitoshi: masterpieces from the Ed Freis collection* (2011), *The golden journey: Japanese art in Australian collections* (2009), *Hotei encyclopedia of Japanese woodblock prints* (2006), *Printed to perfection: twentieth century Japanese prints from the Robert O Muller Collection* (2005), *The courtesan's day: hour by hour* (2004), *The commercial and cultural climate of Japanese printmaking* (2004), *Crows, cranes and camellias: the natural world of Ohara Koson, 1877–1945* (2001) and *The female image: 20th century prints of Japanese beauties* (2000).

INDEX

Published in conjunction with the National Gallery of Australia's exhibition *Stars of the Tokyo stage: Natori Shunsen's kabuki actor prints* touring nationally in 2012 and 2013.

Distributed in Australia by

New South Books
54 Beach Street
Coogee NSW 2034
Australia

Distributed in the United States of America by

University of Washington Press
1326 Fifth Avenue, Ste 555
Seattle, WA 98101-2604
United States of America

The National Gallery of Australia is an Australian Government Agency

nga.gov.au

Produced by NGA Publishing
National Gallery of Australia, Canberra

Edit: Melanie Cariss
Design and production: Kirsty Morrison
Rights and permissions: Nick Nicholson
Index: Sherrey Quinn
Printed in China by the Australian Book Connection, Melbourne

National Library of Australia Cataloguing-in-Publication entry

Title: *Stars of the Tokyo stage: Natori Shunsen's kabuki actor prints* / Lucie Folan … [et al.]

ISBN: 9780642334275 (pbk.)

Notes: Includes bibliographical references and index.
Subjects: Shunsen, Natori. Kabuki in art–Exhibitions.
Actors–Portraits. Prints–Exhibitions

Other Authors/Contributors: Folan, Lucie.

Dewey Number: 769.074

(front cover) **Natori Shunsen** *Ōkōchi Denjirō as Tange Sazen* 1931 (detail)

(pp 2–3) **Natori Shunsen** *Nakamura Fukusuke V as Ohan in 'The Katsura River and the eternal bonds of love'* 1928 (detail)

(pp 8–9) **Natori Shunsen** *Nakamura Ganjirō I as Sakata Tōjūrō in 'Tōjūrō's love'* 1925 (detail)

(pp 14–15) **Natori Shunsen** *Onoe Baikō VI as Sayuri in 'Bridge of Return'* 1925 (detail)

(pp 20–1) **Natori Shunsen** *Ichikawa Sadanji II as Narukami in 'Narukami'* 1926 (detail)

(pp 26–7) **Tsukioka Yoshitoshi** (1839–92) *Ichikawa Danjūrō IX as Musashibō Benkei in 'The subscription list'* 1890 (detail)

(pp 34–5) **Natori Shunsen** *Matsumoto Kōshirō VII as Umeōmaru in 'Sugawara's secrets of calligraphy'* 1926 (detail)

(pp 42–3) **Natori Shunsen** *Nakamura Utaemon V as Yodogimi in 'A sinking moon over the lonely castle where the cuckoo cries'* 1926 (detail)

(pp 54–5) **Natori Shunsen** *Nakamura Shikaku II as Shizuka Gozen in 'Yoshitsune and the thousand cherry trees'* 1925 (detail)